I0800796

Doris Lessing

MANCHESTER
1824

Manchester University Press

CONTEMPORARY WORLD WRITERS

SERIES EDITOR JOHN THIEME

ALREADY PUBLISHED IN THE SERIES

Peter Carey BRUCE WOODCOCK
Amitav Ghosh ANSHUMAN MONDAL
Maxine Hong Kingston HELENA GRICE
Kazuo Ishiguro BARRY LEWIS
Hanif Kureishi BART MOORE-GILBERT
David Malouf DON RANDALL
Rohinton Mistry PETER MOREY
Timothy Mo ELAINE YEE LIN HO
Toni Morrison JILL MATUS
Alice Munro CORAL ANN HOWELLS
Les Murray STEVEN MATTHEWS
Michael Ondaatje LEE SPINKS
Caryl Phillips BÉNÉDICTE LEDENT
Amy Tan BELLA ADAMS
Ngugi wa Thiong'o PATRICK WILLIAMS
Derek Walcott JOHN THIEME
Salman Rushdie ANDREW TEVERSON
R. K. Narayan JOHN THIEME

CWW

Doris Lessing

SUSAN WATKINS

Manchester University Press

Published by Manchester University Press
Altrincham Street, Manchester M1 7JA, UK
www.manchesteruniversitypress.co.uk

British Library Cataloguing-in-Publication Data is available

Library of Congress Cataloging-in-Publication Data is available

ISBN 978 0 7190 9734 8 *paperback*

First published by Manchester University Press in hardback 2010

This paperback edition first published 2015

Printed by Lightning Source

Contents

Series editor's foreword

Contemporary World Writers is an innovative series of authoritative introductions to a range of culturally diverse contemporary writers from outside Britain and the United States or from 'minority' backgrounds within Britain or the United States. In addition to providing comprehensive general introductions, books in the series also argue stimulating original theses, often but not always related to contemporary debates in post-colonial studies.

The series locates individual writers within their specific cultural contexts, while recognising that such contexts are themselves invariably a complex mixture of hybridised influences. It aims to counter tendencies to appropriate the writers discussed into the canon of English or American literature or to regard them as 'other'.

Each volume includes a chronology of the writer's life, an introductory section on formative contexts and intertexts, discussion of all the writer's major works, a bibliography of primary and secondary works and an index. Issues of racial, national and cultural identity are explored, as are gender and sexuality. Books in the series also examine writers' use of genre, particularly ways in which Western genres are adapted or subverted and 'traditional' local forms are reworked in a contemporary context.

Contemporary World Writers aims to bring together the theoretical impulse which currently dominates post-colonial studies and closely argued readings of particular authors' works, and by so doing to avoid the danger of appropriating the specifics of particular texts into the hegemony of totalising theories.

Acknowledgements

I read my first Doris Lessing novel, *Martha Quest*, in the third year of my English degree at Liverpool University. It was a set text on a course called 'The Art of the Novel', taught by Simon Dentith. I continued working on Lessing's fiction as part of my PhD thesis and in my first single-authored book, *Twentieth-Century Women Novelists: Feminist Theory into Practice* (2001), included sections on *The Golden Notebook* and the short story 'To Room Nineteen'. I have taught Lessing's work often and continue to think that her writing is ambitious and thought provoking, if often misunderstood. Students' reactions to her work have often endorsed this perception and I would particularly like to thank the students on my MA Contemporary Literatures module – 'Doris Lessing: Narrating Nation and Identity' – for their insights and open-mindedness.

My motivation for writing this book was to try to understand Lessing's writing as part of a continued engagement with colonialism, decolonisation, race, nation and empire; I also wanted to consider how Lessing's work connects these ideas with concepts of gender, class and age.

This book was finished during a period of research leave funded by the School of Cultural Studies at Leeds Metropolitan University in semester 2, 2008–9 and I would like to thank the School for supporting the project. In 2004 I gave a paper at the First International Doris Lessing Conference in New Orleans and met several US Lessing scholars: Judith Kegan Gardiner, Debrah Raschke, Roberta Rubenstein, Phyllis Perrakis, Sandra Singer and Christine Sizemore have all been particularly supportive of my work and I would like to thank them here. I would also like to thank the School for funding my attendance at the Conference.

In 2007 I organised the Second International Conference on

Lessing's work at Leeds Metropolitan University. The School of Cultural Studies hosted this event and supported it financially, as did the Doris Lessing Society. The Conference was a wonderful creative and intellectual spur for this book. I would like to thank several people for their help during the Conference: Pat Cook and Elaine Newsome provided invaluable administrative support. All the members of the steering group of CWWN (Contemporary Women's Writing Network), particularly Professors Lucie Armitt, Mary Eagleton and Clare Hanson and Dr Alice Ridout, gave of their intellectual input, time and moral support during the stressful period of the Conference itself, as did the members of the English Literature team at Leeds Met. I would particularly like to thank Mary and Alice for their friendship and for many interesting discussions about Lessing, and also John Thieme, series editor for Contemporary World Writers, for his enthusiasm for Lessing's work and this book. Lastly, I want to thank Ian Strange for his support and encouragement always.

Earlier versions of particular sections of chapters 2, 4, 5 and 6 previously appeared in the following places: Susan Watkins, 'Going "Home": Exile and Nostalgia in the Writing of Doris Lessing', in *Women's Writing 1945–60: After the Deluge*, ed. Jane Dowson, 2003, Palgrave Macmillan, pp. 191–204, reproduced with permission of Palgrave Macmillan; 'The "Jane Somers" Hoax: Aging, Gender and the Literary Marketplace', in *Doris Lessing: Border Crossings*, eds Alice Ridout and Susan Watkins, London: Continuum, 2009, pp. 75–91, reproduced with permission of Continuum; 'Writing in a Minor Key', *Doris Lessing Studies*, 25, 2, 2006, 6–10; 'Writing in a Minor Key: Doris Lessing's Late Twentieth-Century Fiction', in *Doris Lessing: Interrogating the Times*, eds. Phyllis Perrakis, Debrah Raschke and Sandra Singer, Columbus: Ohio State University Press, 2010, reproduced with permission of Ohio State University Press; '"Grande Dame or New Woman?": Doris Lessing and the Palimpsest", *LIT: Literature, Interpretation, Theory*, 17, 3–4, 2006, 243–62, reproduced with permission of Taylor and Francis; Susan Watkins, 'Remembering Home: Nation and Identity in the Recent Writing of Doris Lessing', 2007, *Feminist Review*, 85, 97–115, reproduced with permission of Palgrave.

Chronology

1919	Doris May Tayler born in Persia (now Iran) where her father is a bank manager
1925	Moves to Southern Rhodesia (now Zimbabwe) where her parents begin farming
1927–31	Attends Dominican Convent school, Salisbury, as a boarder
1931–34	Attends Salisbury High School
1934	At age 14 leaves school
1939	Marries Frank Wisdom, a civil servant
1939	Birth of son, John
1941	Birth of daughter, Jean
1943	Begins publishing poems and stories in *New Rhodesia* and *Rafters* as D. M. Wisdom
	Divorces Frank Wisdom
1945	Marries Gottfried Lessing, a German Jewish communist exile
1946	Birth of son, Peter
1949	Divorces Gottfried Lessing
	Moves to Cape Town, South Africa
	Publishes stories and poems in the South African journals *Standpunte* and *Trek*
1950	Moves to London with her son Peter
	The Grass is Singing
1951	*This Was the Old Chief's Country*
1952	*Martha Quest*
1953	*Five: Short Novels*
1954	*A Proper Marriage*
	Wins the Somerset Maugham Award of the Society of Authors for *Five*
1956	*Retreat to Innocence*

1957 *The Habit of Loving*
Going Home
1958 *Each his own Wilderness* produced at the Royal Court, London
Mr Dollinger produced at the Oxford Playhouse
A Ripple from the Storm
1959 *Fourteen Poems*
1960 *The Truth about Billy Newton* produced at the Salisbury Playhouse
In Pursuit of the English
1962 *Play with a Tiger* first produced at the Royal Theatre, Brighton and then the Comedy Theatre, London
Play With A Tiger
The Golden Notebook
1963 *A Man and Two Women*
1964 *African Stories*
1965 *Landlocked*
1966 *The Black Madonna*
Winter in July
1967 *Particularly Cats*
1969 *The Four-Gated City*
1971 *Briefing for a Descent into Hell*
1972 *The Story of a Non-marrying Man and Other Stories*
1973 *This Was the Old Chief's Country: Collected African Stories Vol. 1*
The Sun Between their Feet: Collected African Stories Vol. 2
The Summer Before the Dark
1974 *The Memoirs of a Survivor*
A Small Personal Voice: Essays, Reviews, Interviews
1976 Wins the French Prix Médici étranger (the Medici prize for non-French authors)
1978 *To Room Nineteen, Collected Stories, Vol. 1*
The Temptation of Jack Orkney, Collected Stories, Vol. 2
1979 *Shikasta*
1980 *The Marriages Between Zones Three, Four, and Five*
1981 *The Sirian Experiments*
Österreichischer Staatspreis für Europäische Literatur (Austrian State Prize for European Literature)
1982 *The Making of the Representative for Planet 8*
Shakespeare-Preis der Alfred Toepfer Stiftung F. V. S. Hamburg (the Hamburg Shakespeare Prize)

1983 *The Sentimental Agents in the Volyen Empire*
(as Jane Somers) *The Diary of a Good Neighbour*
1984 (as Jane Somers) *If the Old Could …*
The Diaries of Jane Somers
1985 *The Good Terrorist*
1986 W. H. Smith Literary Award
1987 *Prisons We Choose to Live Inside*
The Wind Blows Away Our Words
Palermo Prize
Premio Internazionale Mondello (the Mondello Prize)
1988 *The Fifth Child*
1989 *The Doris Lessing Reader*
Particularly Cats and More Cats
Premio Grinzane Cavour Prize
1992 *London Observed*
African Laughter: Four Visits to Zimbabwe
1994 *Shadows on the Wall of the Cave*
Conversations
Under My Skin, Volume One of My Autobiography, to 1949
1995 *Spies I Have Known, and Other Stories*
Playing the Game
James Tait Black Memorial Book Prize
Los Angeles Times Book Prize
1996 *Love, Again*
Play with a Tiger and Other Plays
1997 *Walking in the Shade, Volume Two of My Autobiography, 1949–1962*
1999 *Mara and Dann*
Problems, Myths and Stories
Premio Internacional Catalunya
2000 *Ben, In the World*
The Old Age of El Magnifico
2001 *The Sweetest Dream*
David Cohen British Literary Prize
Companion of Honour from the Royal Society of Literature
Premio Principe de Asturias (Prince of Asturias Prize)
2002 *On Cats*
S.T. Dupont Golden PEN Award
2003 *The Grandmothers*
2004 *Time Bites: Views and Reviews*

2005 *The Story of General Dann and Mara's Daughter, Griot and the Snow Dog*
2007 *The Cleft*
Nobel Laureate in Literature
2008 *Alfred and Emily*

1

Contexts and intertexts

Doris Lessing's *In Pursuit of the English* (1960) provides an excellent point of entry into the extensive body of her work. It also allows us to begin to understand some of the contexts and intertexts that have been important in her writing. Issues of exile and migration are at the centre of this text and her work as a whole, suggesting the importance, but also the instability, of identity. Lessing is interested in ideas about class, nation, 'race' and gender, but, more importantly, in the links between these concepts and in the ways they overlap with and merge into one another. The generic indeterminacy of *In Pursuit* brings to the fore Lessing's critical relation to the constraints of genre and her qualified suspicion of categories like realism and experimentalism, fiction and autobiography. Her constructive and complex use of autobiographical material also creatively interacts with, indeed generates, her interest in the writer or artist both as figure in and producer of the text.

In Pursuit is based on Lessing's experiences on first arriving in England from Southern Rhodesia and trying to find somewhere to live. She also writes about this period of her life in the second volume of her autobiography, *Walking in the Shade* (1997) and in *The Four-Gated City* (1969), the final novel in the five-volume *Children of Violence* sequence (1952–69). However, unlike official autobiography or fiction, *In Pursuit* is generically rather indeterminate. Originally subtitled 'a documentary', the text is part memoir, part autobiographical essay and part fiction. Lessing describes it variously as 'biography in a comic mode'[1] but also as 'more like a novel'.[2] It is written in the first person and on occasion the narrator is referred to as 'Doris'; however, in *Walking in the Shade* Lessing describes the text as '"true" … but not as true as what I would write now … it is too well-shaped for life'.[3] *In Pursuit* is, as Louise Yelin makes clear, rich in intertexts. In its focus on one London house as a microcosm of English society it draws on and also satirises a long-established literary convention whereby the well-to-do country estate encapsulates English values and customs. It also alludes to the tradition (variously philanthropic, documentary and critical) of writing about the working class represented by works as various as Henry Mayhew's *London Labour and the London Poor* (1861), George Orwell's *The Road to Wigan Pier* (1937) and Richard Hoggart's *The Uses of Literacy* (1957).[4]

Events in *In Pursuit* take place in 1949–50, the period of 'austerity Britain',[5] characterised by dependence on food imports (leading to continued rationing), economic hardship and a housing crisis in London as a result of the Blitz. The third Labour government (1945–51) undertook a significant programme of nationalisation of British industry, created the National Health Service and introduced national insurance. The Labour government is unpopular, however, with most of the characters in the text. Doris's landlady, Flo, is equivocal about free-at-point-of-need medical care because it brings with it women from 'the Welfare', who snoop on her parenting skills. The foreman repairing bomb damage to Doris's rooms thinks that things are no different under a Labour government and that '"what the Government gives with one hand … it takes back with the other"'.[6] However, by the end of the text, 'austerity Britain' gradually begins to give way to 1950s culture, which is signalled by the coming of television and the era of the teenager. The communal warmth of the kitchen-dining room, where enormous Italian meals were served and suggestive banter was rife, is replaced by 'food that could be eaten off people's knees as they watched' and ironic teenage backchat 'from the telly' (224) that the older generation doesn't understand.

The title of the text suggests that 'Doris' is looking for 'the

English' and she admits that she also wanted to write a piece called 'In Pursuit of the Working-Class' (6). What Lessing does not pursue explicitly, but is in fact preoccupied with, is the other women renting rooms in the house where she is living. 'Doris' is a single mother who initially needs a job in order to survive: issues of work outside and inside the home are at the forefront of the lives of all the women characters. Mrs Skeffington, for example, is a victim of domestic violence who is exhausted by her daughter's night-time crying and is desperate enough to abort her unwanted pregnancy. She works full time outside the home. The landlady, Flo, neglects her daughter Aurora because she wants to return to restaurant work. Rose, who becomes the narrator's close friend, has an unsatisfactory on–off relationship with Flo's brother-in-law Dickie and is uncertain about the impact of agreeing to pre-marital sex on her chances of marriage. She works outside the home in a shop, does unpaid housework for Flo and teases 'Doris' for her slovenly domestic ways, which are the consequence of her privileged colonial background, where housework was done by servants. Miss Privet, who is befriended by the narrator at the end of the text, is a prostitute who believes that her job is the only one with real security for women (218). The narrator never really finds the English working class that she is in pursuit of; instead she finds a community of women who are all, in their different ways, trying to negotiate different kinds of work: emotional, sexual and domestic. Maybe these women are the 'working class' that Doris seeks? The transition from post-war austerity culture to the 1950s is also marked clearly in terms of gender. Doris's landlady asks 'Welfare' if her daughter could go to a council nursery: 'But the reply was that Flo had a nice home and it was better for small children to be with their mothers. Besides, the council nurseries were closing down. "Women marry to have children," said the official when Flo said she was trained for restaurant work and wanted to go back to it' (125). Changes in attitudes to women working outside the home and the closure of state nurseries that opened during the war suggest that the domesticity of the 1950s is clearly on the horizon.

1949–50 was also a period of changes in the composition of Britain's cities and in what remained of the British empire. These developments also altered ideas about nationality. Shortages in the workforce led to increasing immigration from the Caribbean from 1948 onwards and the idea of 'Commonwealth' replaced that of empire as a consequence of processes of decolonisation after the Second World War. According to Louise Yelin, the 1948 British Nationality Act 'distinguished two classes of British subjects: citizens of the United Kingdom and its colonies – in effect, white colonials – and Commonwealth citizens'; over a decade later, the 1962 Commonwealth Immigrants Act 'restricted immigration on the part of black Africans, West Indians and South Asians but not on the part of white former colonials'.[7] Lessing's essay is set the year after the British Nationality Act took effect and was first published in 1960, just before the Commonwealth Immigrants Bill was passed. It is clear, therefore, that this legislation can provide a framework for *In Pursuit*: in the decade between the year when the essay is set and its date of publication racial violence increased, finally resulting in rioting in Notting Hill, where *In Pursuit* takes place. Yelin suggests that '"ethnic nationalism", in which race, culture and ethnicity play a primary role' began to dominate ideas of Englishness in this period;[8] John McLeod claims that ideas of national identity deriving from place of birth are replaced in the 1950s by those deriving from inherited lineage and bloodlines.[9] However, exactly how the text deals with these changes has been disputed. Yelin claims that the text 'largely ignores' issues of race and immigration from the Caribbean and that this is 'only in part' because it is set prior to the worst episodes of racial violence and organised opposition to immigration. She argues that the text's significant project is to establish Lessing's Englishness and her status as an English writer.[10] In contrast, McLeod prefers to see the text as offering a challenge to 'exclusionary models of English identity', a challenge which Lessing recognises as particularly necessary in the climate of 1960, after a decade when 'race rose to prominence as the key arbiter of identity and belonging'.[11]

It is certainly the case that the narrator's focus in *In Pursuit* is on ideas of Englishness and foreignness defined in terms that avoid an emphasis on skin colour or contemporary definitions of 'race'. This could be seen as a regrettable omission that springs from the privileged perspective of colonial whiteness, or a deliberate refusal of emerging models of national identity defined in terms of 'race'. Undoubtedly, Lessing's concern is to establish the shifting, transient nature of Englishness, but also its enduring mythical power. She begins the essay with a series of comic vignettes about her father that typify the stereotype of the English eccentric, but focuses on what Englishness is *not* more than on what it *is*. She establishes the extent to which Englishness is not commensurate with Britishness by contrasting her father with her mother, who 'would refer to herself as Scottish or Irish according to what mood she was in, but not, as far as I can remember, as English' (2). She lists the variety of meanings 'English' might have in a colony:

> In the colonies or Dominions, people are English when they are sorry they ever emigrated in the first place; when they are glad they emigrated but consider their roots are in England; when they are thoroughly assimilated into the local scene and would hate ever to set foot in England again; and even when they are born colonial but have an English grandparent. This definition is sentimental and touching. When used by people not English, it is accusatory. My parents were English because they yearned for England, but knew they could never live in it again because of its conservatism, narrowness and tradition. They hated Rhodesia because of its newness, lack of tradition, of culture. They were English, also, because they were middle-class in a community working-class. (8)

Englishness is therefore a mirage, a fiction, made up of contradictions and only present via absence. The things the narrator's parents long for about England (tradition, culture) are those things they miss in Southern Rhodesia, but also precisely the things they repudiated in England and that prompted them to leave. The final return to ideas about class and nationality only serves to substitute one lacunae or aporia for another: just before this passage, the narrator summarises her fruitless search for the working class. Communist Party (CP) ideology (with which the narrator has become increasingly involved) rejects a number of her potential contenders for the 'genuine' working class: first of all the native African population, who, she is told, are not working class but 'semi-urbanized peasants'; second, the Londoners she shares a house with during her first year in England (presumably the characters we are later introduced to in the text), who, she is told, are not working class but 'lumpen proletariat, tainted by petty bourgeois ideology' (7); third, those members of the CP who themselves come from working-class backgrounds, who are 'not typical'; fourth, miners, who 'are members of a very specialized, traditionalized trade' and 'nothing whatsoever to do with the working-class as a whole' (7–8). Finally she is told, with much irony, to take a trip back to Africa 'where the black masses are not yet corrupted by industrialism' (8), which returns her to where she started.

This circuitous route through a number of potential definitions of the 'working class' gives the reader an early clue to the result of the narrator's pursuit of 'the English'. 'Doris' describes herself as an 'exile' (2) and an 'alien' (6) and imagines England as a 'grail' (9). She insists that Englishness can only be understood by those on the periphery of the Commonwealth, stating that 'the definitive thesis on Virginia Woolf will come, not from Cambridge, but from Cape Town' (30). Yelin argues that her exile status actually allows the narrator 'a privileged state of being in which she is English even if she has never been to England'.[12] In contrast, I would suggest that the perception of herself as enjoying a privileged outsider perspective actually allows her to recognise the insubstantiality but also the emotive and hegemonic power of most claims to authentic Englishness, *including her own*. This is an important discovery for narrator and reader in the opening chapter of the text.

As we continue reading, 'Doris' finds somewhere to live and begins to get to know better both the people she is sharing a house with and the area of London in which she is living. It becomes clear to her that her understanding of Englishness as flimsy and precarious is shared by Rose, her closest friend, who is unable to successfully define Englishness. She explains and defends Flo's practice of attempting to charge extortionate rents, saying '"It's because she's a foreigner, it's not her fault"' (56). When 'Doris' presses her to explain what 'kind' of a foreigner Flo is, the following exchange ensues:

> 'I'm not saying anything against her; don't think it. She's English really. She was born here. But her grandmother was Italian, see? She comes from a restaurant family. So she behaves different. And then the trouble is, Dan, isn't a good influence – not that I'm saying a word against him.'
>
> 'Isn't he English?'
>
> 'Not really, he's from Newcastle. They're different from us, up in places like that. Oh no, he's not English, not properly speaking.'
>
> 'And you?'
>
> She was confused at once. 'Me dear? But I've lived in London all my life. Oh, I see what you mean – I wouldn't say I was English so much as a Londoner, see? It's different.' (56–7)

Later on, Rose refers back to this conversation:

> 'I'm from London, as I told you. That's what I mean when I say I'm not English. Not really. When I talk of English, what I mean is, my grandad and my grandma. That's English. The country. They were quite different from us – I mean my mother and me. I liked visiting with them, but they didn't really understand, not really, not what living was like. They were shut off, see?' (106)

Although Rose's understanding of national culture is broad enough to include difference, Yelin argues that this perception, along with other minority voices in the text, is subordinated to the 'satirical eye and ironic voice of the narrator and to the authority of the would-be English writer, Doris Lessing'.[13] In contrast, McLeod sees this passage as evidence of an 'untidy inclusiveness' that Lessing 'comes to value'.[14] It is certainly the case that Rose's words have the effect of 'disappearing' Englishness and stripping it down until we have to acknowledge that the Emperor's new clothes consist of nothing. Being born here doesn't make Flo English; those from the Northern regions of the country, like Dan, are not English; being a Londoner fails to guarantee Englishness. The only solid definition of Englishness is consigned to the rural past, but Rose acknowledges the mythical nature of this pastoral vision when she admits that her grandparents were 'shut off' from life, presumably her life in the present and in the city.

The question Yelin raises about the narrator's and indeed the author's attitude towards and involvement in this view of Englishness is clearly an important one, which is connected to the apparent 'omission' of Caribbean immigration and issues of 'race'. McLeod argues that in the text 'new versions of older racist attitudes are seen to be forming, ones which would ultimately influence the violence of the late 1950s as in the Notting Hill riots'. He also suggests that 'Lessing is careful to record racist representations of black newcomers in London'.[15] However, rather than merely mentioning instances of white Londoners' casual racism towards black immigrants from New Commonwealth countries, Lessing also demonstrates that these attitudes impinge on 'Doris' indirectly. Before she settles in Flo and Dan's house, the narrator goes to see some rooms she has heard are to let and is asked where she is from. She is also told that the landlady 'won't take foreigners' (37). When she asks what is meant by a foreigner, the woman showing her the rooms asks her again where she comes from. When 'Doris' says she is from Africa the woman nervously asks '"You're not a black?"' (37). The conversation continues:

> 'Do I look like one?'
> 'One never knows. You'd be surprised what people try to get away with these days. We're not having blacks. Across the road a black took to the bottle on the first floor. Such trouble they had. We don't take Jews either.' (38)

Later, when 'Doris' says she doesn't like the rooms and won't be taking them, the woman concludes:

> 'If I'd known you were a foreigner, it would have saved me so much time, wouldn't it? One must have thought for other people, these times.'
>
> 'What kind of a foreigner do you think I am?'
>
> 'I've known people before, calling it sunburn.' (38–9)

The suggestion is clearly made here that the woman's definition of 'black' is capacious: it can expand to include anyone who, despite appearing to be white, is a 'foreigner'. The fear of black skin is literally extensive. I do not wish to suggest that 'Doris' in any way shares the position of black immigrants struggling against racist attitudes. However, I think we can certainly reject Yelin's view that *In Pursuit*'s deconstructive strategy in relation to others' Englishness actually works to shore up the narrator's (and Lessing's) claims to it.

The narrator's and the author's stance in relation to the people she meets in London is clearly a privileged one. Although she, like the other women in the text, has to get a job initially, a short while after she moves in to Flo and Dan's house, she gets an advance from a publisher and can concentrate on her writing. The narrator does have the attitude of privileged outsider/observer of the mores of those she meets, but this is always presented as something that those she lives with recognise and comment on, even if they name it in different ways. Rose, for example, cannot understand why 'Doris' should wish to carry on meeting up with the con-man variously known as Bobby Brent, Andrew McNamara and Alfred Ponsonby. When the narrator explains that she is interested in him because she has never met anyone like him before, Rose responds with a simple '"Yes?"' (57). The narrator reads this as follows: 'Interested, are you? Well, I can't afford to be *interested* in scoundrels. Fancy yourself, don't you?' (58). A few pages later, the narrator asks Rose to explain why she dislikes this attitude in her. She replies: '"You talk like he's an animal in a zoo"' (66). The narrator tries to justify herself as follows: '"If you went to a new country, you'd like to meet new kinds of people too … Well, wouldn't you?"' (66). Rose picks up on the narrator's detachment from the material consequences of befriending a con-man and also notes the way she is able to view him as the object of her gaze (or as an animal in a zoo). Later in the text, when 'Doris' befriends the prostitute, Rose is deeply hurt by the implied equation between the narrator's friendship with Miss Privet and herself. Partly this is a result of Rose's conventional morality, but it is also a result of her concern that she is not a genuine friend, but nothing more than an object of interest for the narrator.

The narrator connects her 'interested', detached attitude to the people she meets to her own position as someone who has just arrived in a new country; it is clear that the position of exile or alien (as she refers to herself earlier) provides her with the ability to dissect and analyse what she sees. However, this position is also equally a consequence of (and linked in the narrator's and Lessing's mind) to the 'writer's-eye' view, which inevitably sees people and situations as potential creative material. The people she lives with, however, refuse to recognise the validity of this approach to life and, on occasion, seem to answer back to the possibility of their own construction as 'characters' in the narrator's writing. Flo interrupts the narrator constantly when she is writing and is 'incapable of understanding that ordinary people, whom she might know, could write something which would in due course become a book' (127). Flo is faced with mounting evidence of the fact that 'Doris' is a published writer (a typescript and a published book with identical text, for example). She responds to this realisation as she does to other proof of her cultural capital, such as her trips to the theatre and the public library and shelves full of books, with the same comment: '"I don't hold it against you"' (127). The narrator at first mistakenly thinks this phrase to be equivalent to 'the middle-class "not at all", or "very well"' (127), but realises that she was wrong: she had 'failed to understand the depths of her disapproval and disappointment in me' (127).

Quite what this disapproval consists of is unclear, but what is clear is that the work of *writing* is not seen as 'work' by anyone else in the house. Flo tells 'Doris' that she was glad to hear she was stopping working because she needs the company during the day. She adds that '"everybody works in this house, except that

Miss Powell, if you can call that work"' (126). Her definition of work is work outside the home, with a confused, humorous and grudging allusion to the 'work' involved in Miss Powell's sexual relationship with the con-man Bobby Brent. In interrupting and refusing the narrator's definition of writing as work (she tells Flo '"Now I really do have to work"' to which she replies '"Who's to make you?"' (127)) Flo enacts a disruptive gesture which has the effect of negating 'Doris's' identity as a writer and effectively answers back to her privileged outsider status. Both 'Doris' and Lessing herself do, I think, recognise the precariousness of the identity of writer: 'Doris' is quite aware of the challenges to the privilege that allows her to hold on to that self-definition. Before she gets the advance, she tells the reader that she 'believed she might not write again … could not even imagine myself writing. The personality "writer" was so far removed from me, it was like thinking about another person, not myself' (92).

The incorporation of challenges to the narrator's privileges – to her understanding of herself as a writer and as uncomplicatedly white for example – does suggest that her deconstruction of Englishness constitutes a refusal of the concept's application to herself as well as to others. Her 'pursuit' of Englishness leads back to herself, but also to the women she meets. As was mentioned earlier, the 'pursuit' that Lessing does not name as such in this text is the pursuit of women. It may seem as if this 'missing' pursuit implies that women are fully present and therefore not in need of definition. (After all, we have seen that those ideas that prove illusory or absent, such as Englishness or the working class are, as a consequence, subject to analysis, explication and deconstruction.) In actual fact, what *In Pursuit* suggests is that in attempting to define Englishness and the working class we have to spend time thinking about women's lives and women's work of all sorts. We can return to Rose, who is, in many ways, at the centre of this text. The narrator spends time on an image of her at night:

> Rose at night, was so different from how she was in the day that I never tired of watching her. As she sat, dark hair loose around her face, eyes dark and brooding, her

> face soft, fluid and shapeless in her loose white dressing-gown, she was a dozen women. With each turn of her head, each movement of her hands, she changed, and races and peoples flowed through her. (105)

As Rose talks about her mother, her grandmother and Flo, all, in their different ways working-class English women, she unconsciously adopts the physical gestures and appearance of each as if to suggest that her own body bears the traces, histories and stories of those women. McLeod notes Lessing's attraction to images of the city in *In Pursuit* as 'insubstantial and disassembled, flimsy and precarious' and links this with her uncertain constructions of 'racial' and national identity.[16] What is apparent in the depiction of Rose here is the similar mutability in Lessing's imaging of femininity and the connections she makes between this and ideas of nation and class.

Lessing's understanding of identity as mutable and uncertain can be partly explained by her personal history. She was born in Kermanshah, Persia (now Iran) on 22 October 1919. Her parents met when her mother nursed her father after he was wounded in the First World War. In 1925 they left England and began farming in the British colony of Southern Rhodesia, where Lessing lived until the age of 30. She came to London after the Second World War with the manuscript of her first novel, *The Grass is Singing* (1950), in her suitcase. Southern Africa has continued to be a preoccupation in her fiction. Her first novel, her early African stories, the first four volumes of the *Children of Violence* series, the 'Mashopi' sections of *The Golden Notebook* (1962) and the last third of her 2001 novel, *The Sweetest Dream* are all set in fictionalised Southern African countries closely based on Southern Rhodesia/Zimbabwe. Even when her work seems to move far from this context, as in her speculative fiction, for example, critics have argued that her writing is still about 'empire and power'.[17]

In non-fiction work Southern Africa figures similarly prominently. The autobiographical essays *Going Home* (1957) and *African Laughter* (1992) cover return visits Lessing made; the gap between these visits and the texts that resulted from them can be explained by the fact that as a consequence of her political views Lessing was a prohibited immigrant in both the Union of South Africa (from 1956 until 1995) and in Southern Rhodesia (from 1956 to 1980). The first volume of Lessing's autobiography is also dominated by her experiences in Southern Rhodesia. The essay 'The Jewel of Africa', which discusses the worsening situation in Zimbabwe under Robert Mugabe's policy of land reapportionment, was published in 2003 in *The New York Review of Books*.[18] Her Nobel acceptance speech, 'A Hunger for Books', contrasts the experiences of writing and reading in the UK and Zimbabwe.[19]

As the child of white settler parents in a British colony who herself relocated from Southern Africa to England, but never quite knew where to think of as 'home', Lessing's personal history provides a very particular, if by no means unique, context and writing perspective, although this was noted by very few commentators when Lessing was awarded the Nobel prize for literature. One of the more thoughtful pieces published at the time did, however, comment as follows:

> Interestingly, many powerful women writers of that generation, such as Ms. Lessing, Isak Dinesen, Marguerite Duras, the Venezuelan Teresa de la Parra, and Christina Stead, all shifted continents relatively early in life. In some cases, they switched languages. I've thought about this aspect of their writing a lot. Had there been no Southern Rhodesia in Ms. Lessing's life, I'm not sure she would have hit upon the technique of the simultaneous notebooks, for instance. But such geographic displacements can also, inadvertently, release in a woman writer a generic power – the power of an exile's soul. Exile, self-induced or not, knows no gender. With an exile, the complaint against women writers – that they housekeep, that they tidy up in their writing, that their themes are too contained – is erased. The moment they are gazing, like James Joyce, at home, from the distance of another continent, to which they don't truly belong, facing, as artists, an intractable geography, at that moment, even a woman writer at mid-century became unburdened by gender.[20]

There are undoubtedly a number of controversial remarks here. Is the experience of exile really as gender neutral as Probst Solomon claims? Can gender be shed like an overcoat and can the experience of exile allow the writer to achieve universality? Are the complaints against women writers mentioned here accurate or, if they are plausible statements about a feminine fictional mode, necessarily negative in the first place? What is certainly true is that this piece is one of the few commentaries on the award of the Nobel prize to link issues of gender and migration in Lessing's writing; it is even more unusual in that it makes connections between these experiences and her formal and structural choices.

Experiences of dislocation and displacement, of 'shifting continents', are undoubtedly formative for writers, but they can operate in a number of different ways. Lessing's story is a privileged one compared to many: it was her parents' choice to leave England and despite their own relative lack of success as farmers, as white British first-generation emigrants they were at the apex of a racially segregated and socially complex society. They lived in Southern Rhodesia as colonial invader-settlers. Throughout her childhood and young adulthood Lessing undoubtedly benefited from her place in this elite social group and yet from an early age her discomfort in this environment and her tendency to dissect and critically analyse it were prominent. As she states in *Under My Skin*, an important but difficult-to-answer question is 'how to account for the fact that all my life I've been the child who says the Emperor is naked, while my brother never, not once, doubted or criticized authority'.[21]

The ambivalences and tensions that appear in what Stephen Slemon refers to as the 'neither/nor territory of white settler-colonial writing' have usefully been defined (by Slemon himself, drawing on the work of Alan Lawson) as 'Second-World' writing. As Slemon summarises it, 'we might profitably think of the category of the settler cultures of Australia, Canada, southern Africa, and New Zealand as inhabiting a "Second World" of discursive polemics – of inhabiting, that is, the space of dynamic *relation* between … binaries such as colonizer and colonized, foreign and native, settler and indigene, home and away'.[22] In fact, it is extremely important that we position Lessing's writing in its 'second world' context and that we acknowledge, as Slemon suggests, that 'second world' is a writing and reading position just as much as a description of particular social and economic arrangements and histories.

An episode from Lessing's 1952 novel, *Martha Quest*, the first in the *Children of Violence* series, is instructive here. Martha has taken a trip to the station in the nearest village and watches the different people there. Martha is thinking about the statement she has just made, rather casually, to a Left-leaning Jewish friend that she '"naturally"' repudiates race prejudice.[23] We are told it is 'not so easy to put flesh and blood on the bones of an intellectual conviction' when in fact 'she could not remember a time when she had not thought of people in terms of groups, nations, or colour of skin first, and as people afterwards'.[24] She watches the different social, ethnic and racial groups at the station and uses the terms available to her to describe them. The Afrikaans's 'very name held the racy poetic quality of their vigorous origins'; the British, 'with their innumerable subgroupings', are 'held together only because they could say "this is a British country" – held together by the knowledge of ownership'. Her only comment about 'the natives' is that they are 'nameless and swarming'.[25] Her use of clichés here (the vigorous, racy Dutch Afrikaans and the swarming natives) is in tension with her ability to recognise these clichés as such and also with her ability to analyse the British in terms of power, social class and assumed racial supremacy. The passage concludes:

> [I]t was as if the principle of separateness was bred from the very soil, the sky, the driving sun; as if the inchoate vastness of the universe, always insistent in the enormous unshrouded skies, the enormous mountain-girt horizons, so that one might never, not for a moment, forget the inhuman, relentless struggle of soil and water and light, bred a fever of self-assertion in its children like a band of explorers lost in a desert, quarrelling in a ecstasy of

> fear over their direction, when nothing but a sober mutual trust could save them. Martha could feel the striving forces in her own substance: the effort of imagination needed to destroy the words *black, white, nation, race*, exhausted her, her flesh ached and her head was heavy on her bones.[26]

The implication that racial, ethnic and social differences are inevitable, deriving directly from the natural world (the soil, the sky, the sun) but particularly from the land, is typical of the white settler, second-world ideology of Southern Rhodesia. Yet at the same time Martha is able to recognise that wherever such perceptions of 'difference' originate, they fail to form a harmonious social and racial hierarchy (with the white British at the top) but are in fact destructive and infantilising. Martha's experience of the physical strain caused by her attempts to critique her own assumptions is generated by her own second-world reading position (as she 'reads' the people and the landscape around her but also her own response to them). Both she and we are, as Slemon puts it, engaged in 'a critical manoeuvre, a reading and writing action'. He continues:

> [I]n the white literatures of Australia, or New Zealand, or Canada, or Southern Africa, anti-colonialist resistance has never been directed at an object as a discursive structure which can be clearly seen as purely external to the self. The Second-World writer, the Second-World text, that is, has always been complicit in colonialism's territorial appropriation of land, and voice, and agency, and this has been their inescapable condition even at those moments when they have promulgated their most strident and spectacular figures of post-colonial resistance.[27]

Martha's sense of herself as caught between acknowledgement of and resistance to the imperial and patriarchal discourses that form her subjectivity creates a curious mixture of feelings. Helen Tiffin describes this well when she suggests that settler-invader colony writers (especially if they are women), are 'hampered – or perhaps energized – by their ambivalent positions within their own systems of colonialist oppression [and] have found-difficulty in constructing a stable – or even unstable – identity'.[28]

The focus on the land and on the dominant (yet at the same time provisional) identities it produces for white settler-invaders is undoubtedly a characteristic that Lessing's writing shares with much second-world literature. Lessing found in Olive Schreiner's *The Story of an African Farm* (1883) a kindred sense of 'Africa the magnificent – mine, and everyone's who knows Africa ... one of the few rare books ... on a frontier of the human mind ... the first "real" book I'd met with that had Africa as a setting'.[29] However, it is also important, as Anthony Chennells argues, to recognise that 'Lessing's experiences were not with Africa – a word which so often operates as a synecdoche, blurring inconvenient distinctions – but with Southern Rhodesia, and the colonial experience in Southern Rhodesia had no counterpart anywhere else in Africa'.[30] Chennells points out the fear that white Southern Rhodesians in the early decades of the twentieth century felt at the prospect of being 'absorbed into South Africa' and the antagonism to Afrikaanerdom which made them keen to remain a British colony. At the same time he also emphasises the ambivalence about Britain that white settlers in Southern Rhodesia felt, particularly with respect to the UK's insistence on retaining a right to veto legislation affecting the native black population (see chapter 2). Chennells summarises the myths that Lessing shares with other Rhodesian writers, although he demonstrates the ways in which she uses them 'selectively', intensifying some while alluding to others ironically. These myths were all intended to 'justify the settlers' presence on the land' and create 'a flattering depiction of the Rhodesian identity'.[31] They included the following:

> (a) The only important human developments on the plateau had been accomplished by a non-African people ... (b) The Ndebele were the whites' natural allies on the plateau ... (c) Before the arrival of the whites, the plateau was an empty wilderness which they were at liberty to shape as they pleased ... (d) Rhodesians were a new nation ... (e) A cultural and biological gap yawned between blacks and whites which was impossible to bridge.[32]

Chennells demonstrates the various ways in which Lessing challenges each of these myths, through, for example, her attention to the precise social gradations that structure a white society which is, in theory, equal; her interest in miscegenation and myths of 'black peril' (see chapter 2) and her attempts to show how the land fails to provide the kind of mythical wholeness that the white settlers seek.

Other Zimbabwean writing draws on ideas about the land and identity in different but also surprisingly similar ways. Writing eight years after Independence, Chennells begins an essay, significantly entitled 'Reading Doris Lessing's Rhodesian Stories in Zimbabwe', by suggesting that Lessing is generally regarded as a peripheral writer in the Zimbabwean national literary tradition because she is white and because of her distance from black nationalism.[33] He notes that the 1987 *Tabex Encyclopedia Zimbabwe* accorded Lessing a brief mention alongside Arthur Shearly Cripps because their liberal narratives 'subverted the dominant discourse of settler novelists',[34] partly through a critical perspective on stereotypes of Africa as the place of adventure and of the primitive. When it comes to Lessing's treatment of the land and identity in her short stories, however, Chennells is equivocal about the links between her writing and post-Independence literature. He notes her tendency to work with a functional opposition between 'a romantic response to the African bush and the capitalism of the settlers which sought to transform it'.[35] He acknowledges that 'no black can read Zimbabwe as the settlers read the Rhodesian bush' and points out that Romantic anti-capitalism is an 'alien', 'European' discourse 'which has not taken root in Zimbabwe'.[36] However, he concludes by suggesting that '[t]he debate between town and country, between capitalist and peasant modes of production still continues. Peasants and veld may be written differently in Zimbabwe to the way in which Lessing wrote them, but her art recognizes equivalent tensions to those which are familiar today and her discourse around those tensions refuses closure'.[37] This last point suggests more areas of continuity between Lessing's writing and post-Independence literature than Chennells seems at first willing to suggest. It is possible that writing eight years into the Mugabe regime Zimbabwean critics may have had more investment in ideas about national identity and literature than is likely in the current political climate.

Robin Visel argues that 'Lessing's work now seems relevant to the neo-colonial turn that Zimbabwe has taken since 1990'.[38] Her 2008 essay on '*The Grass is Singing* as a Zimbabwean Novel' notes many points of connection between the lush imagery of the storm that concludes the novel and Zimbabwean literature of *chimurenga* or resistance 'in which violence is interpreted through ritual and the personification of natural forces'.[39] She suggests that Lessing may be parodying the Rhodesian historical romantic fiction of writers such as Gertrude Page, Cynthia Stockley and Sheila MacDonald, who write about love among the pioneer trekkers set against an exoticised African backdrop.[40] Thus Visel rescues the novel from earlier critical condemnation of its problematic association of Moses, the black African character, with mythopoeic natural symbolism (see chapter 2). She compares it instructively to a range of writing by both white and black Zimbabweans, including Peter Godwin, Ian Holding and Alexander Kanengoni, which also makes symbolic connections between the power of nature and the ownership and control of land. Given the worsening political and economic situation in Zimbabwe and the ways in which it could be argued that discourses about land and its reapportionment under Mugabe's regime uncannily echo the colonial era[41] it is important not to separate out Lessing's work as an irrelevant relic of this period.

In the racially segregated Southern Rhodesia of the 1940s Lessing has claimed that [the Communists] 'were the only people I had ever met who fought the colour bar in their lives'.[42] She became a Communist 'emotionally if not organizationally' in 1942[43] and it is important to recognise that her involvement with Communism grew out of a wish to challenge white supremacy as well as an interest in how socio-economic conditions and hierarchies of social class operate in particular societies. Lessing has remarked that

> Marxism looks at things as a whole and in relation to each other – or tries to … A person who has been influenced by Marxism takes it for granted that an event in Siberia will affect one in Botswana. I think it is possible that Marxism was the first attempt, for our time, outside the formal religions, at a world-mind, a world ethic.[44]

Lessing suggests here that for her, at its best, Marxism was a way of thinking: that it provided a perspectival shift that allowed her to see connections and adopt a world view. There are striking similarities between her remarks here and her understanding of her identity as an 'exile' and as a writer/observer as she explores them in *In Pursuit,* where she examines and also challenges her own privileged detachment from those around her. Lessing concludes her assessment of Marxism in the preface to *The Golden Notebook* with the reflection that it 'went wrong, could not prevent itself from dividing and sub-dividing, like all the other religions, into smaller and smaller chapels, sects and creeds'.[45] Tensions between distance and involvement, analysis versus engagement and connection versus fragmentation are key to her experience as a second-world writer as well as to her understanding of Marxism and writing.

In Britain in the 1950s Lessing was a part of the Angry Young Men literary scene, which she discusses in *Walking in the Shade*.[46] She was the only female contributor to Tom Maschler's 1957 collection *Declaration,* which also included Osborne's 'They Call It Cricket' and essays by Colin Wilson, John Wain and Lindsay Anderson.[47] She described the work of the Angry Young Men as 'an injection into the withered arm of British literature',[48] although subsequently she claimed that 'The Angry Young Men was a creation of the media, invented by the newspapers, and never had any basis in fact'.[49] She was on the editorial board of the *New Reasoner,* which became the *New Left Review* (again, she has subsequently claimed that her role was negligible).[50] She claims she only officially joined the Communist Party in 1951 in London.[51] Her involvement with Communism is discussed in most detail in the first and second volumes of her autobiography, *Under My Skin* (1994) and *Walking in the Shade*, and in fictionalised form in *A Ripple from the Storm* (1958), *The Golden Notebook* and *The Sweetest Dream*. Like many others, she left the British Communist Party in December 1956, after the Twentieth Party Congress of the Communist Party of the Soviet Union, in which Kruschev denounced Stalin.

Lessing's experience of Communism was undoubtedly formative, although she has attempted to distance herself from it since, claiming that she only had 'about two years of the pure "being a Communist" in Southern Rhodesia. It disappeared very fast because I was married to a 150% Communist, Gottfried Lessing. That cures you very quickly.'[52] Many accounts of involvement with the Communist Party in the period from the 1930s to the 1950s exhibit similar patterns of enthusiasm followed by disillusionment.[53] Paul Foot argues that this generates a familiar trajectory, where the 'former socialist [grows] into a petulant reactionary'.[54] Whether or not Lessing quite fits this pattern is certainly arguable, but what is undoubtedly important is the effect that an engagement (sometimes admittedly critical) with Communist thought had on her writing practice. Nick Bentley makes clear that Lessing's experimental construction of *The Golden Notebook* made an important contribution to debates on the Left about the politics of form occurring in the 1950s and early 1960s. Writers and critics as various as Georg Lukács, Raymond Williams and Bertolt Brecht were also interested in the relationship between literary form and radical politics and the connection between subjective experience and socio-economic structures.[55] Probst Solomon suggested earlier that without the experience of 'shifting continents' Lessing might not have 'hit upon the technique of the simultaneous notebooks'. I would suggest that her engagement with Communism was also crucial in enabling her to 'hit upon' that 'technique'.

The Golden Notebook is undoubtedly Lessing's best-known novel and it was singled out by the Nobel committee as 'a real breakthrough' that 'belongs to the handful of books that informed the twentieth-century view of the male–female relationship'.[56] Described as an 'epicist of the female experience' in the press release announcing that she had been awarded the Nobel prize for literature,[57] the association between Lessing's work and feminism has been a close but not always a happy one. *The Golden Notebook* certainly made a significant contribution to women's liberation, as was widely recognised after the award of the Nobel was announced. Writing in *The Observer*, Robert McCrum positions the novel as 'a seminal [sic.] classic of early feminism';[58] *The New York Times* claims that it 'inspired a generation of feminists'.[59] However, Lisa Allardyce also acknowleges that Lessing has made many efforts to 'shake off' the 'mantle' of 'Britain's elder stateswoman of feminism'.[60] In recent years Lessing has been particularly critical of the direction she perceives feminism to have taken; at the Edinburgh Books Festival in 2001 she made various controversial pronouncements about the supposed failings of feminism. Lessing was quoted by *The Guardian* as follows:

> I find myself increasingly shocked at the unthinking and automatic rubbishing of men which is now so part of our culture that it is hardly even noticed ... Great things have been achieved through feminism. We now have pretty much equality at least on the pay and opportunities front, though almost nothing has been done on childcare, the real liberation. We have many wonderful, clever, powerful women everywhere, but what is happening to men? Why did this have to be at the cost of men? I was in a class of nine- and 10–year olds, girls and boys, and this young woman was telling these kids that the reason for wars was the innately violent nature of men. You could see the little girls, fat with complacency and conceit while the little boys sat there crumpled, apologising for their existence, thinking this was going to be the pattern of their lives.[61]

Clearly the signifier 'feminism' means many different things here: Lessing alludes to the liberal feminist objectives of the early second wave of feminism, with its emphasis on equality of opportunity, equal pay and the importance of child-care provision. Some of the assumptions of radical feminism about women's essentially nurturing, pacifist nature as opposed to innate male violence are challenged. Although there is a sense that Lessing is aligning herself with the 'backlash' argument that feminism has 'gone too far' – to the detriment of masculine identity for example – she does not express the concern for the future of family life of many neo-conservative writers on the evils of feminism.[62]

Lessing rejects the idea that feminism merely means including women in patriarchal structures without changing them (although she also seems to think that inclusion is an important first step). She challenges the idea that feminism can confine itself to the reversal of stereotyped gender hierarchies. She also suggests that feminism has to challenge gendered assumptions about men as well as women in order to be genuinely transformative. It is clearly possible to see Lessing's views as in keeping with the 'third wave' of feminism, which, according to Gillis, Howie and Munford, 'does not seek to provide a uniform theory of feminism – this would go against what feminism is',[63] and yet also 'does not (indeed, cannot) reject or ignore earlier concerns, [the concerns of the second wave] but is keen to navigate ways forward through those debates'.[64] However, it is also possible to view her thinking here as plain wrong-headed: is the 'rubbishing of men' really dominant in our supposedly ironic, 'overloaded' millennial culture?[65] Is Lessing not merely exhibiting a liberal suspicion of radical causes?

We might wish that Lessing talked of feminisms rather than feminism; that she was more rather than less specific in her comments about its history and achievements, that she worked from within the term rather than distancing herself from it. She shares her suspicions, however, with a writer like Virginia Woolf.[66] While this in itself is not a defence of her position, it does connect her with other writers who have expressed concern about the way language and terminology get incorporated by those they were initially intended to challenge. Gayle Greene explains Lessing's difficulty with feminism thus:

> I think I know why Lessing never became involved with organized feminism. In the late sixties, when the women's movement emerged as a social and political force, Lessing

> was in her late forties. She had lived through a period of intense political involvement in her twenties and thirties, the kind of engagement difficult to repeat in one's forties. She had charted feminist quest throughout the fifties, in the Martha Quest novels, and had revolutionized female literary expression in the early sixties, with *The Golden Notebook*. By the time feminism consolidated itself into a movement, in the late sixties, Lessing had moved on to other things.[67]

She continues: 'she is not a feminist writer in any simple way, yet I persist in believing that she is deeply feminist … in envisioning (and indeed, helping to bring about) what Rich terms a "profound transformation of world society and human relationships"'.[68]

We can think of *The Golden Notebook*'s technique of the simultaneous notebooks as related to Lessing's experience of 'shifting continents' (as Probst Solomon suggests) and as a way of engaging with different ideas about the ideology of form. We can also view it as a way of conceptualising the multiplicity of feminine identities and the multiplicity of feminisms.

As Lessing herself said in the preface to *The Golden Notebook*, written ten years after writing it, she might get three letters a week about the book, '[b]ut one letter is entirely about the sex war … [t]he second is about politics … [t]he third letter, once rare but now catching up on the others, is written by a man or a woman who can see nothing in it but the theme of mental illness'.[69] Many critics, as Nick Bentley suggests, have seen the novel as marking 'a turning point, or break' in Lessing's work and as 'pointing towards her "inner space" fiction of the later sixties and seventies'.[70] However, the interest in subjective experience – particularly in those intense subjective experiences that are at variance with mainstream definitions of normality – has always been present in Lessing's work. In *In Pursuit*, for example, 'Doris' spends some time articulating her response to the confusing, humdrum atmosphere of post-war London and its characteristically 'local', un-metropolitan feel. In this environment she cannot tell one corner of a street from another and is shocked at, but interested in, the 'provinciality' of women like Flo and Rose, who hardly ever travel further than their own neighbourhood.[71] The suggestion that perceptions of the city are precisely that – perceptions – is clarified in a scene where Miss Privet takes the narrator to Trafalgar Square. Before the trip, Miss Privet and 'Doris' have been discussing their tastes in reading; Miss Privet tells 'Doris' that she is fond of Defoe's *Journal of the Plague Year* and Pepys's diaries. She concludes: 'I often read a bit of his *Diary* and then walk over the streets he walked and think about things' (218). That our experience of the city and the environment is formed through what we have read is clear; the point is extended to include other art forms, particularly the visual arts. Having shown 'Doris' a print of Monet's 'Charing Cross Bridge', Miss Privet remarks that '"That's London" … "But you have to learn to look"' (218). She offers to take the narrator to her favourite place in London, but only if the light is right.

As they stand on the steps of the National Gallery, the vision of London that they share is thus already framed by their discussion of Defoe, Pepys and Monet:

> It was a wet evening, with a soft glistening light falling through a low golden sky. Dusk was gathering along walls, behind pillars and balustrades. The starlings squealed overhead. The buildings along Pall Mall seemed to float, reflecting soft blues and greens on to a wet, shining pavement. The fat buses, their scarlet softened, their hardness dissolved in mist, came rolling gently along beneath us, dissembarking a race of creatures clad in light, with burnished hair and glittering clothes. It was a city of light I stood in, a city of bright phantoms. (218)

The sense of transience (within ten minutes the light has changed and they both leave), fluidity and spectrality proves Lessing's point: places and spaces (even those, like London, that have accrued agreed symbolic capital as the centre of empire, for example) are open to alternative, subjective interpretations. Her allusion to the journal and diary form of Pepys and Defoe (in a text the genre of which is itself unstable) refers us deliberately to ideas about the 'personal' and the intersection between private and public cultural forms, as does the reference to Monet and impressionism. Lessing's early fiction often invests in similar moments of what we might call epiphany, where intensely personal perceptual shifts generate moments of revelation that challenge accepted definitions of normality and the distinction between the 'internal' world of the protagonist and the 'exterior' social environment.

Throughout the 1960s and 1970s, however, Lessing became more and more interested in such occasions of rupture, particularly where they contest conventional ideas about sanity. Like Michel Foucault's *Madness and Civilisation* (1961) Lessing's work emphasises that ideas about mental illness are socially constructed and context dependent. More particularly, some critics have connected her writing, particularly in this period, with what later became known as the 'anti-psychiatry' movement, as it tends to be represented by the work of R. D. Laing.[72] Marion Vlastos, for example, summarises Laing's argument in *The Divided Self* (1960) as follows: 'the mad person embodies in grotesquely exaggerated forms society's self-division ... in the heights and depths of his nature the mentally ill individual participates in those realms of existence that conventional man has either denied or never known'; she continues: 'Laing believes it is essential to understand the mad person as symptom and as victim of a sick society and finally as prophet of a possible new world'.[73] She also stresses the similarity between Laing's and Lessing's critical attitude to the power dynamic inscribed in the conventional doctor–patient relation (see chapter 3). Both Lessing and Laing see the family as important in explaining the experience of mental illness. In *Sanity, Madness and the Family* (1964) Laing argued that close study of the family could provide a way to understand schizophrenia and in novels like *The Four-Gated City* and *The Fifth Child* (among others) Lessing demonstrates the connection between the claustrophobia of the family and mental breakdown or perceived disability.

Lessing's attraction to mysticism and Orientalism in this period develops from her interest in the writings of Idries Shah, author of *The Way of the Sufi* (1968), who is widely credited with popularising Sufi literature and thinking in the West. Sufism is often understood as the mystical tradition and movement within Islam, although, according to Ann Scott, both Shah and Lessing refuse such a summative definition because Sufism cannot be viewed as a 'mystical system designed to produce ecstasy and based on theological concepts'.[74] One of Lessing's key essays on the subject of Sufism is entitled 'In the World, Not Of It', first published in 1972. She begins the essay by claiming 'that East must ever be East and West must be West is not a belief which is subscribed to by Sufis, who claim that Sufism, in its reality, not necessarily under the name, is continuously in operation in every culture'.[75] Müge Galin notes that 'academic scholars of Islam in the West have in the past created as their object of study something they call "traditional" Islam or "authentic" Sufism, dismissing practitioners such as Idries Shah, who have tailored their message to a Western audience, as not worthy of serious study'.[76] Galin notes the continuities between this view and Edward Said's understanding of Orientalism as 'the problem of fixing/freezing Eastern culture at one particular point and putting it on a pedestal to be studied (and worshipped or attacked) by those in the West'.[77] Lessing's attraction to Sufism appears less in any theology and more in the forms her work adopts. For Scott, for example, mysticism in Lessing's fiction is not about 'the literal advocacy of a particular set of beliefs about the nature of reality, space–time categories, transcendence, and so on; but about defamiliarisation, a writer's attempt to make use of a form of language, a way of looking at narrative, or an interpretative framework as a whole which the Sufi tradition seems to have provided'.[78]

Lessing's long engagement with the question of literary form in fiction has often made her work difficult to categorise and therefore unpopular. Publishers, book sellers and even academics like to be able to make clear distinctions between realism and more 'experimental' texts, between different genres and between the highbrow/literary and the lowbrow/popular novel. It is certainly the case that her work has run the gamut of forms and modes and often initiated developments in the novel genre. Lessing's early fiction is broadly realist (although the stresses and strains in her adoption of this mode become more visible when writing from the vantage point of hindsight, after reading *The Golden Notebook* and her other novels in the speculative fiction and gothic genres for example). She has acknowledged her debt to the nineteenth-century European and Russian realist novelists, wanting, even when writing *The Golden Notebook*, to emulate the way that Tolstoy and Stendhal 'described the intellectual and moral climate of a hundred years ago, in the middle of the last century'.[79] Writing in 1957, in 'The Small Personal Voice', she claims that 'for me the highest point of literature was the novel of the nineteenth century, the work of Tolstoy, Stendhal, Dostoevsky, Balzac, Turgenev, Chekhov; the work of the great realists' and argues that the realist novel is 'the highest form of prose writing'.[80] She also remarks that as a child she 'read Dickens and had only to look around me (the old Southern Rhodesia) to see what he described'.[81] In 'The Small Personal Voice' she stresses the importance of 'commitment' and the need to find in fiction a 'resting point, a place of decision, hard to reach and precariously balanced' between the individual and the collective.[82]

However, Lessing's periodic and deliberate choice of what I call in chapter 5 'minor' genres does suggest a more nuanced position in relation to realism than might be implied on a casual reading of this comparatively early essay. Her attraction to speculative fiction and remarks about the genre's position in the literary canon and amongst readers, critics, publishers and book sellers are indicative. In 'Between the Fax and the Fiction', Lessing demonstrates how scientific ideas 'permeate our thinking and our vocabulary';[83] she rejects the 'two cultures' argument that assumes a hard and fast separation between the arts and sciences. In this article she implicitly refers to C. P. Snow's well-known contention in his 1959 Rede Lecture, *The Scientific Revolution and the Two Cultures*, that the arts establishment wrongly dismisses scientific culture, but she also demonstrates how the very notion of 'two cultures' has its origins in outmoded 1940s and 1950s binary thinking that is itself derivative of the Cold

War. She concludes: 'At first, the readers of science fiction were few, and they were afficionados of the ideas and not the writing, which was crude. That time has gone. Yet, while large numbers of people everywhere read science fiction some are still furtively addicted because of the unrespectability of the genre.'

Lessing's engagement with science is serious: Clare Hanson suggests that 'Lessing responds to and interrogates the models of inheritance developed by twentieth-century science, in the context of her own longstanding preoccupation with questions of motherhood and inheritance.'[84] However, her reputation as a science fiction writer is mixed (see chapters 4 and 7). The fact that Lessing does not sit easily in any genre suggests her discomfort with the concept itself. Certainly, Lessing would now reject any hierarchisation of literary modes or genres and would not necessarily associate particular ways of writing with certain political positions. In *Walking in the Shade* she argues that:

> Once, all our storytelling was imaginative, was myth and legend and parable and fable, for that is how we told stories to and about each other. But that capacity has atrophied under the pressure from the realistic novel, at least to the extent that all the imaginative or fanciful aspects of storytelling have been shuffled off into their definite categories. There are magical realism, space fiction, science fiction, fantasy, folklore, fairy stories, horror stories, for we have compartmentalized literature as we do everything. On one side realism – the truth. On the other, in another box, imagination – fantasy.[85]

One way to connect the disparate parts in the Lessing corpus is to re-interpret them, as I do in chapter 6, as life writing. Whether classified as novel, essay, memoir or official autobiography, Lessing has been attracted to autobiographical forms and has been preoccupied with the blurred dividing lines between fact, truth and fiction. In an essay entitled 'A Reissue of *The Golden Notebook*', written when she was working on *Under My Skin*, she concludes that 'fiction is better at "the truth" than a factual record. Why this should be so is a very large subject and one I don't begin to understand.'[86] In *Under My Skin* itself she describes her novel, *The Memoirs of a Survivor* (1975) as 'an attempt at an autobiography', but continues, sadly, that 'no one was interested. Foreign publishers simply left it off the title page, and soon no one remembered to put it on reprints in English. People seemed embarrassed. They did not understand it, they said.'[87] In the preface to her 2001 novel, *The Sweetest Dream*, Lessing teases the reader by admitting that she has written the novel as a replacement for the third volume of her autobiography in order not to cause 'possible hurt to vulnerable people'. In the same preface, however, she refuses to accept the idea that she has 'novelised autobiography'.[88] Her last work, *Alfred and Emily* (2008), is about her parents' lives. The first half is speculative, imagining their lives as if the First World War never happened; the second half is a memoir.

The generic instability of life writing returns us to *In Pursuit of the English*, where this chapter started. I argued earlier that this text's uncertain status as, at one and the same time, memoir, autobiography, essay, novel and documentary, deconstructs ideas of 'Englishness' (including the author and narrator's own claims to this term) and also challenges the narrator's privileged position as a writer/observer of others. *In Pursuit* stresses the necessity of involvement rather than escape in order to enable a creative engagement with people, histories (both personal and political) and ideas. What is apparent in the enormous variety of Lessing's writing is the importance, for her, of engagement with the world. As a contemporary world writer, Lessing's work still demands the same kind of engagement from its readers.

2

Going 'home': exile and nostalgia in the writing of Doris Lessing

Doris Lessing's key novels of the period 1945–60 examine the years leading up to the Second World War and the early to middle years of the war itself. Like Lessing, her heroines, Mary Turner and Martha Quest, grow up in a British colony in Africa in this period. The umbrella title of the five-volume novel sequence focusing on Martha is *Children of Violence*. This is indicative not just of Lessing's preoccupation with the war, but also of her wider analysis of its connection with the violence of the colonial encounter. The sharpest irony for Lessing is occasioned by the patriotic willingness of white 'Zambesians' (Southern Rhodesians) to fight with England against Hitler, the 'monster across the seas ... whose crimes consisted of invading other people's countries and forming a society based on the conception of a master race'.[1] Lessing makes a controversial comparison here between British and German imperialism. In her fiction, she frankly details the uncertainty in the immediate pre-war period about who exactly the adversaries would be. In *A Proper Marriage*, when asked what he will do when the war starts, Solly Cohen remarks: '"I shall be a conscientious objector if they turn the war against the Soviet Union, and I shall fight if it's against Hitler"' (57). Lessing demonstrates that the enemy fluctuates in the popular press also: 'the newspaper had warned them that an enemy (left undefined, like a blank in an official form to be filled in later as events decided) might sweep across Africa in a swastikaed or – the case might be – hammer-and-sickled horde' (114). The 'monstrosity' of Hitler's

Germany is persistently seen as relative rather than absolute when set alongside the Soviet Union and the history of British colonialism. Lessing's attitude to the war in her novels of the 1950s is complex. It is never unequivocally negative because it begins a process that ultimately splits apart white British colonial supremacy and fragments stable pre-war conceptions of race and gender. Lessing's novels in this period mark the tentative emergence of more plural, fluid notions about race and gender and the interconnections between them, which force their way through the 'crack in the white crust'[2] of a strictly segregated society.

A narrative voice that might almost be characterised as nostalgic for those aspects of the war that created an impulse for decolonisation is important in the novels of this period; this is not a straightforward longing for the past but a critical and creative nostalgia. Dennis Walder suggests that: 'in many colonial and post-colonial writers, there is in fact a dialectic between different forms of nostalgia … producing a more informed and self-reflexive relation with the past, with many pasts. Doris Lessing's … African work, offers a suitable case for treatment.'[3] The critical or creative nostalgia[4] of the fiction can be instructively compared with the narrative perspective in Doris Lessing's 1957 essay, *Going Home*, which details her first return to Southern Rhodesia (now Zimbabwe) after an absence of eight years.[5] At the time of Lessing's visit, Southern Rhodesia had become part of the Central African Federation (1954–63) with Northern Rhodesia and Nyasaland (now Zambia and Malawi). 'Partnership' between black and white was, despite continuing racial segregation, the official rhetoric of the white government. Both Federation and Partnership were suspected as attempts to prolong white supremacy against emerging nationalist movements (the Southern Rhodesian African National Congress (SRANC) was formed from various protean groups in 1957). As Christine Sylvester suggests: 'SRANC capped a period of increasing unrest about the cynical half-measures of racial partnership.'[6] Federation was also intended to collapse the differences between Southern Rhodesia and the historically more independent Northern Rhodesia and Nyasaland. Colin Stoneman argues that Federation was 'strongly opposed by the blacks, particularly in the latter two countries' and that it 'operated greatly to the benefit of the industrial economy of Southern Rhodesia'.[7] Lessing herself remarked, several years later, that 'the Central African Federation ... was a last-ditch attempt by the whites to preserve their position'.[8] *Going Home* thus appears to occupy an unusual historical moment of stasis and consolidation of colonialist forces, which, I will suggest, is apparent in its narrative voice.

Going Home situates 'home' as a wandering site of nostalgia, exile and alienation. At the opening of the essay, Lessing attempts to construct a romantic African landscape, which can unite people of all races and political persuasions. She begins by acknowledging that after a year of 'horrible estrangement' in London, a 'nightmare city'[9] of cold, damp and weak sunlight familiar to us from *In Pursuit of the English*, it has finally become her home. Of her return to Africa Lessing writes that she had 'turned myself inwards, had become a curtain-drawer, a fire-hugger, the inhabitant of a cocoon' (8). Yet, confronted with the heat and light of Africa the adjustment 'outwards' again is easy because 'this was my air, my landscape, and above all, my sun' (8). However, ownership of the landscape can only ever be provisional in a country where white people are the descendants and beneficiaries of settler-invaders: 'Africa belongs to the Africans; the sooner they take it back the better' (8).

The growing awareness of 'usurped ownership' is also key to one of Lessing's early African stories, 'The Old Chief Mshlanga' (1951), in which the narrator, a young white girl, gradually becomes aware of the history of imperial conquest that forms her environment. She initially thinks that 'this is my heritage, too; I was bred here; it is my country as well as the black man's country; and there is plenty of room for all of us, without elbowing each other off the pavements and roads'.[10] In *Going Home*, Lessing also suggests: 'a country also belongs to those who feel at home in it' (8) and expresses the utopian hope that 'the love of Africa the country will be strong enough to link people who hate each other now' (8). However, by the end of the short story, the girl narrator comes to admit that 'I had learned that if one cannot call a country to heel like a dog, neither can one dismiss the past with a smile in an easy gush of feeling, saying: I could not help it, I am also a victim.'[11] The girl acknowledges that she cannot simply repudiate her status as the beneficiary of colonialism through individual acts of friendship with native African people. The fraught histories of ownership of land fight against the strong metaphorical sense of it as an emotional home for the narrator. In *Going Home* Lessing wonders whether 'this passion for emptiness, for space, only has meaning in relation to Europe' (9). It is only by comparison that the emotional pull of Southern Africa acquires this specific resonance and sense of emotional attachment. Acknowledgement of relativity and specificity in relation to colonial histories and racial difference questions any absolute understanding of the landscape of Africa as 'home' for the narrator, or anyone.

As *Going Home* progresses the narrator is forced to confront further her status as exile and alien. She is refused entry to the Union of South Africa, discovering that she is a prohibited immigrant on arrival at Jan Smuts airport. She is then informed that she was only granted permission to enter Rhodesia after intervention from a senior official and that if she attempts to visit Northern Rhodesia and Nyasaland (part of the Federation) she will be deported. Lessing writes: 'to be refused entry into a country one knows and loves is bad enough; but to be told one is on sufferance in a country one has lived in nearly all one's life is very painful' (82). Lessing manages to visit Northern Rhodesia, but not Nyasaland, before returning to London, at which point she is informed that she is now prohibited from entering the Federation. These events render her homeless and alien, a status she also occupied during the war because of her marriage to a German refugee. Regular reporting to the Aliens' Office was, according to the narrator, a 'useful apprenticeship' (105) for this post-war experience. *Going Home* concludes: 'I don't feel very optimistic. I don't see how the next decade can be anything else than stormy, bitter and unprofitable' (233). The title *Going*

Home thus becomes increasingly ironic as the reader progresses through the essay. Losing a secure sense of home is regretted by the narrator and associated with loss of faith in a secure identity. This regret for home and self is explicitly related to the uneasy political situation in Rhodesia in the 1950s.

In the early volumes of *Children of Violence* Lessing often attempts to construct a home in the female body; she then self-consciously demonstrates the capacity for failure of such a project, given the body's overdetermination by the structures and codes of history, race, gender, class and sexuality. In *Martha Quest* (1952), for example, the teenaged Martha is clearly a product of her family situation and social environment. She understands the influences that have formed her and is aware that her body is a site of conflict and contestation. Martha's mother's concern with English middle-class values and their inscription on Martha's body bears the weight of history: of her moral exhaustion with England after the First World War, but also her determination to support the final flourishes of the British Empire. This can be seen in the following passage, where Martha's mother responds negatively to her desire to wear less child-like clothes:

> Her mother said that girls in England did not come out until at the earliest sixteen, but better still eighteen, and girls of a nice family wore dresses of this type until coming out. That she herself had not 'come out', and that her family had not by many degrees reached that stage of *niceness* necessary to coming out, was not enough to deflect her. For on such considerations is the social life of England based, and she was after all quite right in thinking that if only she had married better, or *if only* their farming had been successful, it would have been possible to arrange with the prosperous branch of the family that Martha should come out.[12]

The First World War has in fact destroyed the kinds of values to which Mrs Quest clings;[13] Martha is the victim of her mother's unresolved feelings about the huge historical changes she has witnessed.

Martha's awareness of her own body and its (failed) potential as a source of revelation, of epiphany even, is stressed in one particular scene where she is walking back home from the station one evening. During this moment, Martha is almost painfully self-aware. She is aware of her seemingly endless capacity to analyse: ('she must *not* analyse, she must not be conscious' (73)); she is aware of the religious and literary tradition of which such moments are part: ('words like *ecstasy, illumination*, and so on ... suggest joy. Her mind having been formed by poetic literature (and little else), she of course knew that such moments were common among the religious' (74)); and most of all she is aware of her body: 'She felt the rivers under the ground forcing themselves painfully along her veins, swelling them out in an unbearable pressure; her flesh was the earth, and suffered growth like a ferment; and her eyes stared, fixed like the eyes of the sun' (74). In the end, though, the moment makes her understand 'her smallness, the unimportance of humanity' (75); it only partially confirms the body's potential for revelation and suggests that such potential may only be accessible via the falsities of nostalgia: 'the wave of nostalgia made her angry. She knew it to be a falsity; for it was a longing for something that never existed, an "ecstasy", in short' (75). Martha learns to be suspicious of her body's capacity to act as a source or home for revelation and critical of the nostalgic literary tradition that has instructed her thus. At the same time, however, the moment consciously rewrites the literary tradition of the moment of epiphany in new ways. It focuses on difficulty and nihilism in a new African environment of mealies, bucks and bush, rather than the traditional self-affirming Wordsworthian 'spots of time', set in the English pastoral landscape that forms part of Martha's reading of 'poetic literature'.

In the second novel in the quintet, *A Proper Marriage* (1954), Martha is engaged in the prescribed role of white middle-class colonial wife and mother. Her body is even more significantly the site where ideological matrices of gender, race and nation coincide, as is apparent in Dr Stern's expert manipulation of her pregnancy; it is also, again, a putative space of resistance to those discourses. That these contradictions are foregrounded by the experience of pregnancy and maternity is clear in an important episode in the novel where the heavily pregnant Martha and her friend Alice, who is also pregnant, swim naked in a muddy pot-hole in the vlei. Emerging from their dissatisfaction with their husbands, marriages and impending motherhood, the scene, like the moment of revelation in *Martha Quest* discussed above, engineers a sense of the female body (in this case the pregnant female body) as a home or source of authenticity and site of resistance to imposed discourses of maternity. Maternal colonial discourses depend, as Victoria Rosner suggests, on strict separation between the domestic, cultured, feminine, white space of the house and the wild, patriarchal, African space of the bush. While the latter was viewed, in accordance with pioneer mythology, as empty space in need of cultivation, the former was seen as the 'ground of white separatism'.[14] However, as Pat Louw demonstrates, Lessing's attention to spatiality in the African stories often focuses on the 'crossing of boundaries in colonial space to construct complex subjectivities'.[15]

Just such a crossing of boundaries takes place in this scene. Alice and Martha divest themselves of their clothes and run into the bush, revelling in the pleasurable sensation of the wet grass and the rain stinging their naked bodies. Martha nearly falls into a pot-hole and then deliberately jumps in, followed by Alice. She experiences a 'moment of repugnance' and then 'loosened deliciously in the warm rocking of the water' (177). She is surrounded by images of fertility and the pot-hole itself, a 'gulf ... gaping like a mouth, its red crumbling sides swimming with red water', above which 'the long heavy grass almost met' (177), clearly resembles the female genitals and womb. Martha feels her unborn child 'protected from the warm red water by half an inch of flesh' (178). This moment of close relationship between Martha's body, her unborn child and the muddy waters of the pot-hole suggests the possibility of a *jouissant* or even *abject* subversion of the codes of colonial maternity, which, as we have seen, are focused on keeping boundaries secure and interior and exterior apart. Afterwards, Martha feels that 'that plunge into the wet soiled veld seemed to her exaggerated and unpleasant', even though it leaves her 'free and comfortable … relaxed and tired' (179). Nicole Ward Jouve argues that 'mud is where Martha defends herself, her strong body, against the inroads of convention' but notes that 'the disappearance of mud from the universe of the novels is bound up (runs parallel with) the disappearance of the home'.[16]

A Ripple from the Storm (1958) constructs the loss of the home in very different ways. In this text, set during the war, the colony is being used to train the British airforce, the arrival of which has disturbed many of the certainties of Zambesian society, including previously secure sexual, racial and class categories. Martha is at this point fiercely engaged in left-wing politics (in an environment broadly sympathetic to Communism and the Soviet Union as 'Our Allies' against Hitler) and much of the novel deals with the activities and alliances of the nascent Communist group in the colony. However, an important episode in the middle of the text tells of the experiences of one of the British air crew, a fitter named Jimmy who is a member of the Communist group, as he struggles to adapt himself to the colony's way of life. Returning to the RAF base after an argument at the Communist group meeting, the men joke '"back to the concentration camp"' (144) and this joke begins an extended series of metaphors comparing the RAF base and Jimmy's wider part in the military machine to imprisonment in a concentration camp. Once Jimmy is back at the base, he begins to chafe against his 'imprisonment' and persuades one of the African camp guards to lift a broken bit of perimeter fence and let him 'escape'. The freedom of lying in the grass outside the camp is a revelatory epiphany for him, which is severely disturbed by the discovery that the grass is full of insects, which are also crawling all over him. As Ward Jouve puts it: 'in RS [*A Ripple from the Storm*], mud, grass, lush "singing" African grass, is given to a passing character, Jimmy, *not* Martha'.[17]

After this initial and important experience of abjection and displacement, Jimmy decides to take the opportunity to visit the Native Location and the Coloured Quarter, partly as a challenge to

Communist group decisions against this. When he arrives in the Location, he is struck by the fact that the perimeter fence is rusty and much lower than the RAF camp fence. He concludes: 'fences, fences, everywhere you look, concentration camps everywhere and fences. He thought of the concentration camps in Europe and without any feeling of being alien' (154). Reluctantly admitted to a room in the Location, he concludes: 'I feel at home here. This is the only place in this bloody country I've felt at home' (155). Jimmy makes putative attempts here to equate the Location with 'home', but also to place the experiences of exile and alienation as universal. These impulses arise from a feeling of working-class solidarity with black Africans (as he says later, watching men and women from the Location cycling to work: 'at home I'd join in, I'd be one of them' (163)) and a sense of the global existence of economic exploitation. However, his confidence in finding a home in shared oppression is only short-lived. His host's obvious fear forces Jimmy to recognise that his white skin makes him an extremely dangerous (in fact prohibited) house-guest and thus profoundly separates him from the people in the Location. Jimmy then visits the Coloured Quarter and attempts to find somewhere to sleep for the night, but the woman, a prostitute, will only let him into her home if he pays for sex. The only (unofficially) sanctioned relation between 'coloured' woman and white man in the colony is that of prostitute and client.

Jimmy's superior position in the hierarchies of gender and race and his position in the RAF fragment his notions of home, which are based on an attempt to recapitulate his subordinate class position in Britain: 'just because I've got a white skin … He remembered his uniform – he was doubly separated from them' (163). Indeed, all the events of the night are triggered by his exploitation of the black camp guard, who would doubtless have borne the brunt of the punishment if he had been discovered enabling Jimmy's 'escape'. Jimmy is forced to accept his own position as part of the white elite in the colony and recognise the provisional nature of home for its black populace, whose civil rights are non-existent. In *A Ripple from the Storm*, concepts of home and exile are split and fragmented, as they are in *Going*

Home. Overall, the narrative displays a sense of the futility and inevitability of what happens to Jimmy that resembles the tone of *Going Home*: immediately after the events just described the airmen who attend the Communist group are posted from the colony as the result of a terrified black informant involving the local magistrate. However, the memorable episode of Jimmy's 'escape', like Martha's epiphanies in the previous two novels, occupies a disruptive and subversive space in relation to those naïve certainties that function elsewhere in the text (such as the Communist group's reliance on economic explanations and class categories which substantially ignore gender and race). In addition, rather than solely creating a sense of nostalgic regret on the part of the narrator, the fragmentation of securely established ways of perceiving subjectivity is seen as productive, generating what Said terms the exile's 'contrapuntal' vision, where 'habits of life, expression, or activity in the new environment inevitably occur against the memory of these things in another environment'. He argues that there is a 'unique pleasure in this sort of apprehension, especially if the exile is conscious of other contrapuntal juxtapositions that diminish orthodox judgement and elevate appreciative sympathy'.[18]

Lessing's work of the 1950s is permeated by the mobility of concepts like home, exile, refugee and alien. Yet Jimmy's night-time excursion in *A Ripple from the Storm* suggests, in addition, a further important way in which home is defined in Lessing's work of this period: as a place apparently removed from, yet actually underpinned by, inter-racial sexual desire. Jimmy is seeing a woman from the Coloured Quarter, against the agreed rules of the Communist group. Jimmy views this relationship as one of class solidarity: '"I've got myself a real working girl, a girl like myself"' (141). Anton, the leader of the group asks:

> 'Would it help matters if every single man here married an African or a coloured girl tomorrow – not that it would be possible. Or if we all took coloured mistresses? There's nothing new about white men sleeping with coloured and African girls. Is there? The basic problem is economic and not social.' (140)

Jimmy's use of the term 'working girl' implies prostitution to an early twenty-first-century reader; indeed, in the episode we have just examined, Jimmy finds that despite his efforts to relate to 'coloured' women as equals and friends, the only relationship that is possible is one that combines and conflates the sexual and the economic: '"How much?" she said … Jimmy, his throat thick, half with lust and half with a longing to cry, said, "But listen, I just wanted to … "' (162).

Lessing's work in this period acknowledges and analyses the workings of what Robert Young has termed 'colonial desire'. Young's aim is to demonstrate that notions of racial difference have always been bound up with inter-racial desire: 'racial theory, which ostensibly seeks to keep races forever apart, transmutes into expressions of the clandestine, furtive forms of what can be called "colonial desire": a covert, but insistent obsession with transgressive, inter-racial sex, hybridity and miscegenation'.[19] The term 'hybridity' has been famously used by Homi Bhabha (and others subsequently) to suggest the mutual implication of colonising and colonised voices, which ultimately enables the contestation of colonial discourses by revealing their lack of purity, or inevitable 'contamination' by the colonised voice.[20] However, for Young, the term 'hybridity' carries with it echoes of nineteenth-century racial theories about inter-racial sex and miscegenation (the 'fertile fusion and merging of races'[21]), which makes it a more suspicious term than theorists like Bhabha allow: 'there is no single, or correct, concept of hybridity: it changes as it repeats, but it also repeats as it changes'.[22]

What strikes any reader of Lessing's writing of this period is her willingness to address the controversial place of sexuality in the colonial encounter. Her concern with desire between white and black bodies complicates simple categorisation of bodies as racially separable (Chennells terms this the myth of the 'gulf' between black and white races).[23] It also again suggests that the body (as the site of sexual dissidence) can be the source or 'home' for challenges to colonial values and ideologies. Anthony Chennells argues that Rhodesian settler novelists began by being 'unexpectedly relaxed about miscegenation between white men and black women, which shows how widespread it was', although this tolerance disappears after the First World War.[24] The myth of 'black peril' – the fear amongst white people of sexual attacks by black men on white women – was also widespread. Murray Steele suggests that part of the myth was a belief that such attacks were a revenge response to white men's sexual relations with black women.[25] Noting the absence of 'black peril' in settler fiction, Chennells suggests that 'one can only hazard a guess at why so prominent a public issue was made a central concern only by Lessing'. Lessing is 'the only novelist who registers the hysteria of the settler belief that all black men are potential rapists' and the only novelist 'whose tone [in dealing with 'black peril'] is one of a perfectly poised detachment'.[26] In fact, Lessing's interest in deconstructing the myth of 'black peril' is part of a wider concern with a spectrum of 'dissident' colonial sexualities. In her collected African Stories sexual relationships between white men and black women are central to '"Leopard" George' (1951) and 'The Antheap' (1953), but other stories concern adultery and incestuous relationships in the white settler-invader class ('Old John's Place' (1951) and 'Winter in July' (1951)) and the predicament of juvenile 'spares' or 'town wives' – young black girls who occupy an informal 'second wife' status to black men working as servants in white middle-class homes ('A Home for the Highland Cattle' (1953)). In every case, the sexual relationships concerned are necessary to the functioning of colonial society and simultaneously transgressive, disturbing and capable of calling it into question.

In 'The Antheap', for example, the white boy, Tommy, the son of a mine manager, uncovers the truth about miscegenation when he befriends Dirk, the 'mixed race' son of the white mine-owner and one of his black mine workers. As he gradually learns the lessons of what Ann Stoler usefully terms 'carnal knowledge and imperial power' and is made aware of the 'affective grid of colonial politics',[27] he feels 'as if he were part of a conspiracy of some kind that no one ever spoke about. Silence. His real feelings were growing up slow and complicated and obstinate underneath that silence'.[28] These complicated feelings and the impossibility of verbalising them generate a growing interest in communicating through sculpture and art; Tommy models Dirk, Dirk's mother and the mine itself, in the soil and clay of the compound. He also teaches Dirk to read and lends him his school books, so that Dirk soon outstrips him academically. At the end of the story, having impressed a local artist/scholar with his work, he permits Macintosh, the mine-owner, to pay for his university education to study art, thus allowing him to express his quasi-paternal feelings for him. However, he also exacts a price: Macintosh must also pay for Dirk's education as an engineer and acknowledge, at least financially, the son he is unwilling to see as his own. The silences at the centre of colonial society recur at the end of the story:

> And so he left them and went back to his house, an angry old man, defeated by something he did not begin to understand.
>
> As for the boys, they were silent when he had gone.
>
> The victory was entirely theirs, but now they had to begin again, in the long and difficult struggle to understand what they had won and how they would use it.[29]

As Julie Cairnie suggests, 'Ultimately, there is a great deal of uncertainty about the boys' future relationship'; she continues: 'we never know if their subversive fraternity develops or withers'.[30] However, the silences have generated an art that the local artist describes as having 'quite a modern feeling';[31] it is also an art that can be challenged by those it depicts. Dirk asks Tommy why the sculpture shows him 'writhing out of the wood like something struggling free';[32] he repudiates, perhaps, the crude attempt to present him as part of, even oppressed by nature. In this final conversation about art and Tommy's insistence that he will 'do it [the sculpture] again'[33] there is a challenge to oppressive patterns of colonial desires and the attempt to forge new relationships.

In *Martha Quest* we are presented with several scenes concerning 'black peril', including a heated conversation between Martha and her mother about whether or not she should be allowed to walk to the station:

> 'What would happen if a native attacked you?'
> 'I should scream for help,' said Martha flippantly.
> 'Oh, my dear ... '
> 'Oh, don't be ridiculous,' said Martha angrily. 'If a native raped me, then he'd be hung and I'd be a national heroine, so he wouldn't do it, even if he wanted to, and why should he?'
> 'My dear, read the newsapapers, white girls are always being ra – attacked.'
> Now, Martha could not remember any case of this happening; it was one of the things people said. She remarked, 'Last week a white man raped a black girl, and was fined five pounds.'
> Mrs Quest said hastily, 'That's not the point; the point is girls get raped.'
> 'Then I expect they want to be,' said Martha sullenly; and caught her breath, not because she did not believe the truth of what she said, but because of her parents' faces: she could not help being frightened. (57)

This passage makes a number of dangerous suggestions: first, that inter-racial desire is a routine part of colonial discourse and secondly, that it is permissible (if illicit) only in the case of the white man for the black woman. Thirdly, Martha implies that the black man's desire for the white woman is phantasmatic: a displacement of its opposite: the white woman's desire for the black man, or the white man's fear of/desire for that possibility. Ironically, when Martha makes the trip to the station, she is actually propositioned by Mr McFarline, a white mine-owner and prospective Member of Parliament whose native compound 'was full of half-caste children, his own' (58).

The prohibition of inter-racial sex in Southern Rhodesia was enshrined in the Immorality and Indecency Suppression Act (1903), which made sexual intercourse between an African man and a European woman illegal. In the 1950s proposals headed by women's groups were made to extend this prohibition to sexual relations between European men and African women, but these amendments were not successful. Indeed, the fact that the then Prime Minister Garfield Todd voted against the amendments was widely unpopular and led to the defeat of his government.[34] The existence of legislation to prevent inter-racial sex between white women and black men but not between black women and white men suggests, like the passage from *Martha Quest*, that the real taboo is the white man's simultaneous fear of and attraction towards a stereotyped black male sexuality that is irresistible to white women (and, by implication, to white men).

It is in her first novel, *The Grass is Singing* (1950), that Lessing most explicitly tackles the elaboration and deconstruction of colonial desire. The novel examines the complex discourses that generate and are generated by the murder of a white woman by her black servant. The novel resembles classic crime fiction, in that it opens with the newspaper announcement of the murder and then unravels what lies behind it, concluding with the murder itself. However, this analeptic narrative structure, where story and plot are at odds, is not merely about playing with suspense. It is designed to encourage an examination of the *discursivity* of the events told in the novel. The newspaper account of the murder is followed by summaries of how it would have been interpreted throughout the country and then, more particularly, by those in 'the district' who knew Mary Turner and her husband.

By virtue of its careful choice of narrative mode, Lessing manages to convey both the pressure of agreed opinion and the pressures that disturb that opinion. Both are clear in the opening chapter because much of it is from the point of view of an outsider, Tony Marston, who, like Jimmy in *A Ripple from the Storm*, is just out from England and adjusting to the new environment and its conventions. For Tony, although 'logical enough'[35] the explanation for the murder 'could not be stated straight out, like that, in black and white' (21). He repeats this later: '"this case is not something that can be explained straight off like that. You know that. It's not something that can be said in black and white, straight off"' (27). This apparently casual turn of phrase evokes the myth of the gulf between the black and white races and associates this with logic in order to suggest all the ways in which that racist logic has been questioned by the murder. Mary's dead body is the source of all the apparently illogical (although, to repeat, actually logical enough) blurrings and 'greyings' of the discourse of racial incommensurability. First we see this through the eyes of Charlie Slatter, a neighbour and farmer who has been called in to help deal with the murder:

> Now a curious thing happened. The hate and contempt that one would have expected to show on his face when he looked at the murderer, twisted his features now, as he stared at Mary. His brows knotted, and for a few seconds his lips curled back over his teeth in a vicious grimace. (19)

A few pages later we see Tony's shock at an identical expression of hatred and disgust from the local policeman: 'the faces of the two men as they stood over the body, gazing down at it, made him feel uneasy, even afraid ... This profound instinctive horror and fear astonished him' (23). Mary's abject body reminds them that, as Lessing puts it later: '"white civilisation" ... will never, never admit that a white person, and most particularly, a white woman, can have a human relationship, whether for good or for evil, with a black person'. She continues: 'once it admits that, it crashes, and nothing can save it' (30). Mary's dead body represents the crossing and overlapping of racial and gender boundaries. The choice of the word black 'person', which, unlike white 'person' remains unqualified by gender, suggests that the white female desire for the black man must remain implicit.

Indeed, that desire is only ever implicit in the text. The exact nature of the relationship that develops between Mary and Moses is never concrete, although it is suggested in various ways. Lessing describes it in terms of the emergence of the personal (178), which makes visible the power relation between the two and unsettles it. Throughout the text, scenes where this power dynamic becomes visible and is then questioned focus on elaborating those connections between race, sexuality and economics that underly it. Mary's sudden marriage to Dick Turner ends her life as a single, independent woman who works in an office in town and lives with other single women in a 'girls' club'. The recognition that she is unable to adjust to the lonely life on the farm is the surface concern of much of the text. Lessing also explores the predicament of women not suited to farm life in a short story of the period, 'The De Wets Come to Kloof Grange' (1951). Mary's abrupt decision to marry is precipitated by overhearing gossip about her 'old maid' status which focuses on the phrase: '"She just isn't like that, isn't like that at all. Something missing somewhere"' (48). Mary repeats this phrase, highly suggestive of 'frigidity', to Tony Marston when he asks why she allows Moses to dress and undress her (232). The attempt to 'prove' herself a sexual woman attaches to Moses because of his increasingly explicit refusal of the power she has over him as a member of a 'superior' race. As the novel progresses, Moses instead asserts his superiority over her in gender terms. In the first key interaction between them, he flouts her orders by stopping work to drink water. In the second, he stops washing when he notices her watching him. Both instances involve his refusal of her gaze at him and his return of that gaze. After Mary whips him for pausing to drink, we are told that 'for a moment, the man looked at her with an expression that turned her stomach liquid with fear' (147); in the second scene Lessing writes:

> A white person may look at a native, who is no better than a dog. Therefore she was annoyed when he stopped and stood upright, waiting for her to go, his body expressing his resentment of her presence there … She felt the same impulse that had once made her bring down the lash across his face'. (176–7)

Unlike her ineffectual husband, whose submissiveness she enjoys but also despises, Moses is 'a man stronger than herself' (156), whom Mary needs but also fears. As Lessing later writes:

> There was now a new relation between them. For she felt helplessly in his power. Yet there was no reason why she should … her feeling was one of a strong and irrational fear, a deep uneasiness, and even – though this she did not know, would have died rather than acknowledge – of some dark attraction. (190)

Mary's submissiveness is simultaneously arousing and frightening precisely because it plays around with and disturbs her racial 'superiority', suggesting, as Young argues, the covert involvement of inter-racial desire with racial categorisation in the colonial encounter. This is apparent in Charlie Slatter's comment to the Sergeant at the beginning of the novel: '"Needs a man to deal with niggers ... Niggers don't understand a woman giving them orders. They keep their own women in their right place"' (27). The white man admires the black man for one thing only – his imagined sexual control over black women – and that fantasy underpins the colonialist project. As Lessing writes of Tony Marston: 'he had read enough about psychology to understand the sexual aspect of the colour bar, one of whose foundations is the jealousy of the white man for the superior sexual potency of the native' (230). 'The basic problem' is not, as Anton expressed it in the earlier quotation from *A Ripple from the Storm*, 'economic and not social' (or sexual) but, as Young puts it, that we have ignored the fact that inter-racial sexual desire is inseparable from the economic motive for colonialism.

The point of view that is absent from the text is that belonging to Moses. We are never party to his perspective on events, nor to his motivation for the murder, both of which have to be surmised from how others react to the little that he says. Critics have found this a problematic aspect of the novel. Margaret Moan Rowe notes that he is presented as 'sexual energy rather than as a person'.[36] Lorna Sage relates his 'blankness' to issues of representation: 'how much, that is, can one find others in oneself'.[37] Perhaps most well known is Eve Bertelsen's argument that *The Grass is Singing* relies, rather problematically, on 'an idea of nature and consequently Africa as quintessentially savage, a symbol of uncontainable energy, a collection of dark, extreme forces that are constantly threatening to run out of control, to reassert themselves and claim some primitive ascendancy'.[38] Bertelsen also claims that it is not merely particular characters, but also the narrator, who 'blithely invokes "the savage mind," "the savage sun," "the savage heat," and "the savage and antagonistic bush"'.[39] Moses's murder of Mary becomes, according to

Bertelsen, emblematic of the bush's revenge, from, as it were, the 'heart' of darkness: his own voice is silent. Interviewed by Bertelsen for her book in 1984, Lessing admitted that she had made Moses 'less of a person than a symbol' but could not have written differently, since 'at that time ... I'd never met Africans excepting the servants or politically, in a certain complicated way'. She concluded, however, that 'now I've changed my mind again. I think it was the right way to write Moses, because if I'd made him too individual it would've unbalanced the book. I think I was right to make him a bit unknown.'[40]

I would argue that this 'erotic silencing' of Moses explicitly suggests the powerlessness of his voice and its overdetermination by discourses of colonial desire. However, one of the things Mary finds in her new personal relation with Moses is that he asks her questions, on one occasion about the progress of the war. This forces Mary to recognise that the war is more than 'a rumour, something taking place in another world' (191). It forces her to realise the specificity and impermanence of her own situation, or, as Bhabha might put it, the 'contamination' of the colonial voice by the colonised voice and thus the possibility of its contestation. Thus, *The Grass is Singing* elaborates and deconstructs the workings of colonial desire in order to suggest how the society in which it functions will ultimately be rendered unstable. The disturbances effected in the text by the relationship between Moses and Mary and her murder certainly work towards the 'crash', as it was earlier termed, of 'white civilisation'. As Sage later writes: 'Moses "is" the future'.[41]

Going Home stages a comparable scene of colonial desire in far less subversive ways. Lessing writes in the essay of meeting two white women on the boat coming to Britain in 1949. Known as 'Durban society girls' (21), they are on a trip to Europe, funded by the wealthy family of one of the women, Camellia, who has recently been widowed. Two years later Lessing sees the girls in Trafalgar Square with a black man. The passage continues:

> That was in 1951. In 1953 I was walking along the edge of the sea in the south of France, and there was the young man I had seen in Trafalgar Square with an extremely beautiful

> black girl ... Then I saw that the beautiful negress was in fact Camellia. (22)

A few years later, Lessing sees a photograph in a South African society magazine of Camellia marrying a white South African in a society wedding. Although this is partly a 'passing' narrative, which is structured around the simultaneous denial and attraction of the dynamic of inter-racial sexual desire, this story also suggests the flexibility of racial categorisation. Yet it ends by positioning that mutability as entirely subject to economic imperatives: it is Camellia's uncle who provides the money for the trip and when that runs out she is forced to return home and resume a 'white' identity and marriageable status. The far more negative reading of racial 'hybridity' and colonial desire in *Going Home* resembles the dourly stripped down interpretation of exile and homelessness in the essay. It is striking that Lessing's novels of the post-war period are more optimistic about the subversive possibilities contained in such testings of colonial discourses.

The tone of *Going Home* might appear to 'fit' the static and depressed mood of the 1950s. In addition to Lessing's growing disillusionment with Communism, she was also aware of the consolidation of colonialist forces in Southern Rhodesia and was analysing what Sage refers to as 'blocked passive British post-war culture'.[42] Lessing's essay emphasises that the latter are interdependent. As Taylor notes, the essay (along with *In Pursuit of the English*) stresses 'the role that colonialism played in the construction of a dominant British national identity'.[43] The difference in the tone of the novels is therefore striking. Although the narrator is often ironic about her characters' beliefs and involvements, there is an important sense of nostalgia for the fluidity and impermanence generated by the war and the inroads this made into colonial identities, discourses and power structures. The body also offers the potential, however limited, for challenges to colonial and patriarchal discourses. The narrator of *A Ripple from the Storm* comments of Jimmy and a friend:

> They also felt that after the war things could not possibly go on as they had before. They had jeered at the Atlantic Charter, and greeted the patriot speeches of the high-ups

> about better times coming after the war with a steady contempt as bait for suckers, the suckers being themselves. But all the same ... [ellipsis original] things could not go on as they had; and the victories of the Red Army in some way proved this. (147)

Is this difference in tone between fiction and essay generated by their generic differences, or by the question of distance? Georg Lukács argues, after all, that the novel, more than any other genre, is the form of transcendental homelessness.[44] Elizabeth Maslen, comparing *Going Home* and *A Ripple from the Storm*, suggests that the answer lies elsewhere. She argues that the point of view of *Going Home* (written the year after the visit it describes) is close to the events described in the text, whereas the viewpoint of the novel 'seems to reflect a narrative viewpoint of 1958 rather than of the time in question'.[45] She comments on the ironic detachment that this allows in the novel, but forgets that distance can also generate a nostalgic relation. Subsequent editions of *Going Home* contain an endnote under the heading 'Eleven Years Later' which uses a more nostalgic tone when discussing the Southern Rhodesian Communists in the 1950s: 'it is no accident that the only group of people who knew the Federation ... was dangerous nonsense, that Partnership ... was a bad joke, were Socialists of various kinds' (247).

Admittedly Lessing is often suspicious of certain kinds of nostalgia; Roberta Rubenstein suggests that 'the past ... is entirely equivocal for Lessing'[46] and that she acknowledges 'the impossibility of perceiving an unproblematic perspective in relation to either past times or places'.[47] In *A Ripple from the Storm* Martha dreams a dream that had 'the peculiar nostalgic quality which she distrusted so much, and yet was so dangerously attractive to her' (95). The dream is of a country, which Martha assumes must be England, wondering 'how can I be an exile from England when it has nothing to do with me?' (95). Yet nostalgia for a fictionalised and self-constructed 'home' can, as Rubenstein admits, involve 'emotional resolution' and 'transformative significance',[48] however partial these may be. We may speculate that the absence of this nostalgic distance is part of the reason why Lessing suppressed her 1956 novel *Retreat to Innocence*, which is about the impact of a Czech refugee writer on a conventional upper-class English girl. Clearly, as we will see in the next chapter, what Walder (after Boym) views as a creative and critical relation to nostalgia[49] is crucial in *The Golden Notebook* (1962), although by the time of writing this novel Lessing had found many additional devices with which to explode conventional notions of home, subjectivity, gender and race. Through the 1950s, however, creative nostalgia is a key element, which allows Lessing to begin to create an unease in her use of the realist form. Nostalgia for the uncertainties of the war, generated by distance, can therefore provide Lessing with a home, but that 'home' can only ever putatively exist in the act of writing and reading.

3

The politics of loss: melancholy cosmopolitanism

What must strike any reader of Lessing's 1962 novel, *The Golden Notebook*, is the extent to which its protagonist, Anna Wulf, has been affected by the experience of loss. In the first section of the conventional realist frame novel *Free Women*, Anna asks Molly: '"Well, don't you think it's at least possible, just possible that things can happen to us so bad that we don't ever get over them?"'.[1] She mentions failed marriages, broken relationships, single parenting and years spent in the Communist Party as painful instances of 'bad things'. Instead of struggling with pain, Anna seems to suggest that it might be better to admit failure and accept the sense that one's life has been useless. She concludes: '"After all, Molly, it's not much loss is it, a few people, a few people of a certain type, saying that they've had it, they're finished"' (66). Anna's attempt to convince herself that her pain and that of other women like her represents 'not much loss' is belied by the experience of reading the entire novel and by Lessing's continuing preoccupation with the idea of loss in her later novels, *Briefing for a Descent into Hell* (1971) and *The Memoirs of a Survivor* (1974).

What have the protagonists in these novels lost? As a 'free woman' Anna has made a conscious decision to live outside patriarchal familial, domestic and emotional structures. In *The Memoirs of a Survivor*, the narrator experiences the collapse of civilised society and the nuclear family. *Briefing for a Descent into Hell* detaches its protagonist from family and sanity through an extended process of mental breakdown and amnesia. In all three novels political engagement is severely challenged or actually disappears. In *The Golden Notebook*, particularly, a meaningful idea of national identity is also significantly lost. More important than all these, however, is the fact that the central characters in all these novels have lost a worthwhile relation to writing and language itself. Lessing remarked on the experience of writing *The Golden Notebook* as follows: 'The actual time of writing, then, and not only the experiences that had gone into the writing, was really traumatic. It changed me.'[2] The link made here between traumatic loss, writing and subjective change is one that David L. Eng and David Kazanjian explore further in *Loss: The Politics of Mourning* (2003). They suggest that 'avowals of and attachments to loss can produce a world of remains as a world of new representations and alternative meanings'.[3] In other words, the sense of subjective violation and transformation that occurs during the process of writing about loss can be creative, both for the writer and the writing itself. In this chapter I want to explore how, in her work in the 1960s and the early 1970s, Lessing rewrites the experience of loss as potentially creative, productive and transformative. In her vision of what I am calling a 'melancholy cosmopolitanism',[4] Lessing challenges the closed-off, paranoid legacy of the Cold War in the 1950s. In *Memoirs* and *Briefing* she further develops the distinction between the claustrophobic, nostalgic relation to loss that is characteristic of mourning and the creative work of melancholia. In the context of the late 1960s and early 1970s, however, it is only in the metafictional world of the novels, rather than the characters' lived experience, that this creative relationship to loss can exist.

Lessing writes in the preface to *The Golden Notebook*, written nearly ten years after the novel's publication in 1971, that 'it described many female emotions of aggression, hostility, resentment. It put them into print. Apparently what many women were thinking, feeling, experiencing, came as a great surprise' (9). Ella, the central character in *The Shadow of the Third*, Anna's draft novel that appears in the yellow notebook, believes herself to be 'very normal, not to say conventional' (164) and considers her rejection of an unhappy marriage to be a necessary moral decision required by her idea of being true to herself. She resents the fact that other women view her, with a 'mixture of envy and hostility' (164), as refusing ordinary sexual morality and other men view her as fair game sexually. For the 'free women' of this novel, the loss of conventional sexual and domestic structures – trying to live in a new way – tends to mutate into occupying outsider status or becoming pariah figures: the mistress, the marriage wrecker, the gay divorcee and the single parent.

In *The Memoirs of a Survivor*, the narrator is surrounded by the gradual and progressive breakdown of 'civilised', industrialised society and the nuclear family. She takes in a young girl, Emily, who is brought to live with her by a faceless official. The narrator's relation to Emily is partly maternal, but she also stands as a kind of double, who generates, in the alternative world the narrator discovers beyond the living room wall, a sequence of painful, personal family scenes. These scenes occupy a strange status between personal memory, imaginary recreation and psychoanalytically inflected dreamwork or analysis of a typical family romance. The overriding sensation during these scenes is the intense feeling of loss: specifically, the girl's loss of the mother figure:

> Between the little girl's hot, needful, yearning body, which wanted to be quieted with a caress, with warmth, wanted to lie near a large, strong wall of a body, a safe body which would not tickle and torment and squeeze; wanted safety and assurance – between her and the mother's regularly breathing, calm body, all self-sufficiency and duty, was a blankness, an unawareness; there was no contact, no mutual comfort.[5]

Supplanted in her mother's affections by a baby brother who provides (in Freudian terms), the phallus the mother lacks, the child is offered instead the 'tickle, torment and squeeze' of a relationship with the father. On his behalf, 'guilt', 'appeal', 'astonishment' and 'incredulity' (80) at the mother's license of a suggestively incestuous – but apparently normal – relation dominate. In what the narrator calls the 'personal scenes' beyond the wall, Lessing lays bare the mechanics of the nuclear family with its focus on Oedipal relations and concomitant loss of mother-daughter connection.

In the 'everyday' world of the novel, Emily embarks on a relationship with Gerald, and they attempt to establish a home for the increasing numbers of vagrant children who roam the streets and live underground. Their attempts to institute cooperation and a sense of community are resisted: Emily becomes an unwilling authority figure, who resents the apparently inevitable intrusion of hierarchy. The narrator muses on the persistence of 'stale social patterns' and 'the old thoughts, which matched the patterns' (121). Anna regrets the loss of status and power accorded those within an accepted domestic structure, but both she and Emily also resent the fact that it seems difficult if not impossible to move outside those structures. As the novel nears its conclusion, however, the message about the loss of the normative family darkens. The children who have never lived in family structures have become feral, killing 'because of a whim, a fancy, an impulse. Inconsequence' (183). Inconsequence, the narrator tells us, is 'a new thing in human psychology. New? Well, if it had always been there, it had been well channelled, disciplined, socialised. Or, we had become so used to the ways we saw it shown that we did not recognize it' (183). While the narrator is reluctant to accept the idea that the breakdown in conventional domestic arrangements represents some kind of reversion to primitive atavism, she is uncertain whether or not the children's way of life is something 'new' or merely something unfamiliar. The novel asks the reader to connect the loss at the basis of the Edwardian nursery scenes beyond the wall with the inability to create new, flexible domestic structures outside it. Gayle Greene summarises the point Lessing makes here well: 'Human beings produced by the prison of the family are incapable of making a free society'.[6]

Charles Watkins, the protagonist of *Briefing for a Descent into Hell*, also loses any sense of relation to his family. An academic who experiences what we might conventionally describe as some kind of mental breakdown, he suffers from amnesia for a substantial proportion of the novel and is unable to recognise his wife or remember their life together. At the end of the book, he is offered a number of alternative living arrangements: to return to his family or live with a friend from before his illness, or to move into another hospital. He is strongly discouraged from what he really wants: to move into a flat with another patient. Rather than endure any of these alternative domestic arrangements, he agrees to undergo electric shock treatment, which has the effect of restoring his memory and effecting a 'cure'. The medical personnel treating him speculate that 'it is possible that your home or your wife or your children set you off in the first place'[7] but Charles does not agree with this diagnosis.

Briefing, like *The Golden Notebook*, is deeply concerned with the protagonist's experience of losing conventional sanity. Lessing suggests in the preface to *The Golden Notebook* that it was where she first wrote at length about 'this theme of "breakdown", that sometimes when people "crack up" it is a way of self-healing, of the inner self's dismissing false dichotomies and divisions' (8). In these terms then, the characters exchange their sanity for a more profound sense of connection: the emerging awareness of the connections between disparate parts of experience is key to mental breakdown in both texts and also to Lessing's 1973 novel, *The Summer Before the Dark*, in which the protagonist, Kate Brown, reaches a mid-life crisis point and 'permits herself a kind of breakdown ... following her own inner line of growth, even if apparently in outward disarray'.[8] Both Anna and Charles experience, as if it is their own, the subjective identity of other people. As Lessing puts it in the preface, Anna and Saul 'hear each other's thoughts, recognise each other in themselves' (7–8). However, this kind of realisation cannot be sustained without excising the individual from the realm of the 'normal' and 'sane'; therefore it cannot be permanent. Both novels therefore express the return to the world of conventional mental 'health' as a kind of loss: before his shock treatment returns him to 'normality', Charles Watkins experiences this as a nagging urge to remember something important.

In *Memoirs* the relation between fragmentation and connection, sanity and insanity is experienced at the collective level of the social world of the novel. The mental 'health' of the narrator is not explicitly questioned by herself or anyone else; unlike Anna and Charles, she is not 'in therapy' or receiving medical treatment of any kind. It is not possible to dismiss her experience as subjective: the society around her is sick. Pollution, breakdown of civic and social structures and urban degeneration are the norm. This loss is experienced as something to be endured and coped with; it is often so gradual that it is not noticed. The narrator's experience of the world behind her living room wall begins, like Charles Watkins's 'descent', as a personal journey, but the novel concludes by offering a genuine alternative to the redundant external world, when all the characters, even the feral children, are offered 'the way out of this collapsed little world into another order of world altogether' and 'the last walls dissolved' (190). This conclusion is the most interesting in relation to the idea of loss, because the necessity for return to an everyday world associated with sanity and mental and civic 'health' is refused. The loss associated with return to that world (represented in the ironic, dry frame narrative of *Free Women* in *The Golden Notebook*, the arid discourse of the academic lecture in *Briefing* and Kate's decision to dye her hair again and resume her 'proper' feminine persona in *The Summer Before the Dark*) is here overtaken by a different kind of loss: the loss of the 'real' world of the novel itself. In the preface to *The Golden Notebook*, Lessing argues that 'nothing is personal, in the sense that it is uniquely one's own' and that 'the way to deal with the problem of "subjectivity" … is to see him [the individual] as a microcosm and in this way to break through the personal, the subjective, making the personal general' (13). What changes and develops in *Memoirs* is the way she chooses to express that understanding. Individual experience is no longer merely in an analogous or expressive relation to the social world but instead expands sufficiently to overtake and subsume it.

The Golden Notebook is also deeply concerned with the loss of meaningful political engagement. In the preface, Lessing claims that she chose to set the novel amongst Socialists and Marxists because it is in this environment that the great intellectual debates and 'the movements, the wars, the revolutions' (11) have occurred. She also discusses the gradual dilution and absorption of Marxist ideas to the extent that 'something so thoroughly absorbed is finished as a force' (11). The 'finishing' of Marxism as an effective political force but also as a meaningful belief system is something that preoccupies Anna throughout the novel. As more emerges about Stalinist atrocities during Anna's four years as a member of the British Communist Party she acknowledges that she misses the tone of 'simple, friendly respect' for 'Uncle Joe', feeling that without it 'a dream would be dead – for our time, at least' (273). It is significant that her loss when she leaves the Party is more often identified in terms of changes in 'tone' or 'atmosphere' than in relation to a change in particular political beliefs or attitudes. This is apparent in the 1955 and 1956 sections of the red notebook that are concerned with a sudden renewal of Anna's engagement with Communism. At this point in the novel, Anna becomes involved with a group wishing to form a new 'really British CP' (395) that is untainted by Stalinism and can start afresh, having broken all ties with 'foreign Communist Parties' (394). She mentions her interest in this group on 13 November 1955 and starts her diary entries again on 11 August 1956, having spent the intervening time deeply enthused and engaged with this group's ideas. Her resumption of the diaries, signifying her break with this group and loss of belief in their endeavour, occurs as a result of a joke made by someone at a meeting:

> the truth usually comes out in just such a speech or a remark ignored at the time, because its *tone* is not that of the meeting. Humorous, or satirical, or even angry or bitter – yet it's the truth, and all the long speeches and contributions are nonsense.
>
> I've just read what I wrote on the 13 November last year. I am amazed at our naivety. Yet I was really inspired by a belief in the possibility of a new honest CP. I really did believe it was possible. (395)

The sense that the tone has changed marks Anna's loss of a meaningful engagement with politics; the grief occasioned by this loss is frequently described in terms of fragmentation and breaking. People leaving the CP are described as 'broken hearted' twice in the entry for 20 September 1956 (395) and Anna earlier describes her need for the Party as 'a need for wholeness, for an end to the split, divided, unsatisfactory way we all live. Yet joining the Party intensified the split' (157).

In *Briefing* and *Memoirs* there is little explicit focus on party politics and yet the loss of political engagement (more broadly conceived) is still significant. In *Memoirs* there remains a class of officialdom, represented in the novel by the narrator's neighbours, the Whites, who still work in some capacity for the remnants of government and are able to access facilities that are unavailable to everyone else. This bureaucracy is self-perpetuating and entirely remote from the lives of the ordinary people, but this state of affairs is accepted rather than mourned. The absence of concern at the loss of any belief in political representation or involvement necessitates the abandonment of the 'real' world at the end of the novel. In *Briefing* Charles Watkins writes a memoir of his time as a member of an allied forces group parachuted into Yugoslavia to support Tito's Partisans during the Second World War. It later emerges that Charles was never in Yugoslavia (although his friend, Miles Bovey was) and yet the memoir is vivid, engaging and seemingly authentic. The fact that this memory may be genuine, if (paradoxically) not his own, is significant: in this novel and *The Golden Notebook* Lessing is interested in how memories of politically engaged pasts are owned, made use of and written.

In *The Golden Notebook* memories of previous political enthusiasms are focused on those sections of the black notebook that deal with the events surrounding a group of friends in a Communist group in Southern Africa during the Second World War. The loss of political engagement is intimately linked to the experiences of loss occasioned by the colonial encounter throughout the Mashopi hotel sequences of the novel. As Victoria Bazin suggests, this part of the novel is 'charged with a sense of loss, of unrequited love, of tragic absurdity and intense eroticism' and 'it is at the Mashopi that the group collectively loses its commitment to the Communist Party'.[9] The Communist group is fighting Fascism but also trying to fight white privilege, but as people who themselves benefit from that privilege while attempting to dismantle it, they often find themselves in an ambiguous and difficult relation to both native Africans and white settlers. They begin to spend weekends at the Mashopi hotel, an oasis of Englishness in the middle of the Southern African bush. Their attraction to Mashopi suggests that one significant loss for the group is a straightforward relation to English culture and identity, which they can no longer believe in yet hanker after in a self-conscious manner. Their relation to romanticised ideas of Africa is equally partial. After one of the happiest and most erotic encounters in Anna's life, when she makes love with Paul, the doomed British airman, in the African bush surrounding the hotel, they notice Bushman paintings, 'fresh and glowing even in this faint light, but badly chipped. All this part of the country was covered with these paintings, but most were ruined because white oafs threw stones at them, not knowing their value' (148). The image of an authentic native culture boorishly damaged by the invasive power of ignorance is commented on by Paul, who terms it a '"fitting commentary"' although he cannot find '"the right words to explain why"'(148). Knowing that their position in relation to the country is a consequence of British imperialism, Anna is unable to luxuriate in her love of the African landscape without questioning her right to do so. However, as Marxists, the group must also be suspicious of African nationalism, which Party doctrine dismisses as a 'right wing deviation' (99). The loss of straightforward ideas about ownership of land and belonging to nation is part of the atmosphere of the Mashopi sequences.

In addition to the experiences of loss detailed above, the central characters in these novels appear to have lost something that Lessing suggests is even more important: a meaningful relation to writing. Anna Wulf is living off the proceeds of a novel, *Frontiers of War*, but she struggles with writer's block throughout *The Golden Notebook*. Despite producing extensive diaries and notebooks and possibly authoring *Free Women*, according to the notebooks she feels unable to write another novel because she has lost her belief in the value and purpose of art and literature. In the preface, Lessing writes that the reasons for the block are 'linked with the disparity between the overwhelming problems of war, famine, poverty, and the tiny individual who was trying to mirror them' (12). Whether or not literature can ever 'mirror' reality is, of course, a question that is debated in the novel by Anna herself (both in conversation and in the notebooks) and also in the writing practice of the text.[10] Any unequivocal sense of the value of art and literature is lost to Anna and this loss is painful: 'I am incapable of writing the only kind of novel which interests me: a book powered with an intellectual or moral passion strong enough to create order, to create a new way of looking at life' (76). Anna is also haunted by the fear of inauthenticity and nostalgia in her writing, particularly in those sections of the novel concerning the Mashopi hotel that relate to her colonial past and provided the 'material that made *Frontiers of War*' (149). She is aware that, as Bazin puts it, 'her own account of the past, with its emphasis upon tragic loss, reflects a longing for the social and racial hierarchies of empire rather than a critique of them'.[11] Her fear of the influence of nostalgia dominates these sections but does not avoid the recrudescence of nostalgia itself. Bazin argues that 'even in the retelling Anna cannot eradicate the nostalgia and finds herself failing again to describe events without infusing them with the sense of loss and longing of nostlagia'.[12]

The narrator of *The Memoirs of a Survivor* has also lost a straightforward relation to the practice of writing. She writes tentatively and doubtfully: never sure whether she is presenting a version of events with which others would agree. The novel's opening suggests this provisionality:

> We all remember that time. It was no different for me than for others. Yet we do tell each other over and over again the particularities of the events we shared, and the repetition, the listening, is as if we are saying: 'It was like that

> for you, too? Then that confirms it, yes, it was so, it must have been, I wasn't imagining things.' (7)

The confident statement that 'it was no different for me than for the others' is progressively undermined by the very need for repetition, which actually serves to question rather than confirm the narrator's memories. Rosenfeld notes the play between the pronouns 'we' 'me' and 'it', which suggests 'the tensions that govern relations among the individual, the collective and the environment'.[13]

The authorship and ownership of memory are also important in *Briefing for a Descent into Hell.* In this novel, Charles Watkins's loss in relation to writing is something the reader becomes conscious of as part of the reading process; it is not, however, something he is aware of himself or able to acknowledge by the end of the novel. This is an important distinction between *Briefing* and *The Golden Notebook* and *Memoirs.* The novel consists of medical notes, conversations (represented as dramatic dialogue) between the medical profession and the patient, Watkins's account of what he experiences when unconscious under heavy sedation, and letters between family, friends and acquaintances and the doctors treating him. Towards the end, we also read the 'memoir' about Yugoslavia that he is encouraged to produce as a kind of therapy intended to help him recover from amnesia; at another point we also read a word-for-word account by an acquaintance of a lecture he once gave. The account of the 'descent into hell' or Watkins's experience when unconscious, although narrated in the first person, does not have the status of a notebook, diary or concrete object read by others in the text in the way that Anna's notebooks do. Neither, however, does the entire text consist of a personal recollection in the way that *Memoirs* does. Instead the novel is a hybrid of both forms, where certain of the inner narratives appear to have a kind of objective or authorised status and others do not. By the end of the novel, Charles is 'cured'; in a letter to his Head of Department, he remarks: 'I seem to be in full possession of my faculties again' and associates this with a return to giving lectures: 'I do remember all about the lecture series. I feel quite well enough to undertake them' (250). Having undergone electric shock treatment, Charles returns to conventional consciousness and loses awareness of his alternative 'inner space' explorations. His narration of these is now lost to him and accessible only to the reader.

That Lessing found the experience of writing *The Golden Notebook* traumatic has already been noted. David L. Eng and David Kazanjian explore the link between traumatic loss, writing and subjective change in *Loss: The Politics of Mourning* (2003), where they argue that the fluctuations in identity that occur during the process of writing about loss can be creative, both for the writer and the writing itself. Eng and Kazanjian's reassessment of loss as potentially productive is part of a more sustained engagement with ideas about the experiences of mourning and melancholia that they undertake in *Loss*. They draw on, but question, Freud's distinction between 'healthy' mourning, in which libido is gradually withdrawn from the lost object and the mourner is able to accept its loss, and 'pathological' melancholia, in which the mourner is unable to detach from the lost object and move on from it.[14] Eng and Kazanjian note Freud's tendency in 'Mourning and Melancholia' (1917) to 'cast doubt on the inevitability of this distinction' despite using it and suggest that 'a better understanding of melancholic attachments to loss might depathologize those attachments, making visible not only their social bases but also their creative, unpredictable, political aspects'.[15] They make use of Judith Butler's understanding, in *The Psychic Life of Power* (1997), that melancholic attachments are in fact constitutive of the psyche, in order to claim that an attention to melancholia might produce a 'counterintuitive apprehension of loss as creative'.[16] Julia Kristeva's assessment of melancholic grief as suggesting 'the signifier's flimsiness' is re-interpreted as suggesting its 'flexibility' and its 'palimpsest-like quality'.[17] In other words, melancholic writing can produce 'a realm of traces open to signification', 'an extended flexibility, an expanded capacity for representation'.[18]

The essays in *Loss* are concerned, as Judith Butler suggests in her afterword, with writing about different kinds of loss that have been generated by the experiences of genocide, slavery, exile and colonisation. Eng and Kazanjian argue that the modern and postmodern eras have been characterised by war, genocide and (neo)colonialism.[19] These are, of course, as we have just seen, also Lessing's preoccupations in her work of this period. The kind of productive melancholia that Eng and Kazanjian define in *Loss* does seem to be an appropriate way of describing Lessing's writing about the linked processes of war, imperialism and colonisation and their resistance in the twentieth century. In fact, a number of writers and critics have associated melancholia with experiences of postcoloniality, exile and cosmopolitanism. Paul Gilroy's *Postcolonial Melancholy* (2005) argues that contemporary British culture can be characterised by what he terms its 'postimperial melancholia', or an 'inability even to face, never mind actually mourn, the profound change in circumstances and moods that followed the end of the empire and consequent loss of imperial prestige'.[20] Gilroy's reading of melancholia here is, unlike Eng and Kazanjian's, consistent with Freud's explicit positioning of it as pathological. He proposes that 'the infrahuman political body of the immigrant'[21] is forced to bear the weight and act as the focus of this unresolved traumatic loss in contemporary British society. Only when postimperial melancholia is replaced by 'conviviality', defined as the 'processes of cohabitation and interaction that have made multiculture an ordinary feature of social life in Britain's urban areas',[22] will this pathology be resisted. Gilroy believes conviviality is a more useful tool for cultural and political analysis because of its distance from identity-based politics. In the current climate Gilroy believes melancholia is definitely a negative condition; when he mentions the term 'cosmopolitanism' it is merely to discuss its cooptation by Western powers, which use what Gilroy terms an 'armoured' cosmopolitanism to 'justify intervention in other people's sovereign territory on the grounds that their ailing or incompetent national state has failed to measure up to the levels of good practice that merit recognition as civilized'.[23]

Gilroy's suspicion of the concept of cosmopolitanism is shared by those, including, at times, Lessing herself, who associate the term with a luxury of mobility and refusal of national affiliations only available to the privileged. This cosmopolitanism 'from above' has been challenged, however, by writers who understand it as capable of more critical potential, especially when specifically 'located and embodied'.[24] In fact, what has been variously termed 'critical' and 'discrepant' cosmopolitanism can be intimately connected to, or indeed a consequence of, marginality.[25] In an essay on Jorge Luis Borges, Dominique Jullien suggests that 'the Argentine writer's marginal status with respect to the Western tradition is what paradoxically enables him to play freely with all world literature'; in other words, 'the artist's marginality is a prerequisite for his universality'.[26] If we extend the argument, we can argue that critical cosmopolitanism exists in a productive relation to the rewriting of and engagement with loss that Eng and Kazanjian describe. Jullien's analysis focuses on the function of translation in a Borges short story and essay. The concept of translation in these works functions to question the notion of originality: translation is inevitably a failure in the sense of fidelity to the original, but the melancholic recognition of that failure, or loss is also capable of generating new meanings in 'the fertile play of mistranslations'. These 'melancholy words in praise of misreading'[27] suggestively connect the experiences of cosmopolitanism, writing and melancholia.[28]

In Lessing's work of this period we can certainly read the preoccupation with loss as ultimately creative, productive and transformative (in Eng and Kazanjian's terms 'melancholy') rather than (again in their terms) as representing the prematurely foreclosed cultural work of mourning. It is also the case that in *The Golden Notebook*, *Briefing* and *Memoirs*, a nostalgic relation to the past and to loss is viewed as characteristic of mourning, whereas a melancholic relation to it is associated with cosmopolitanism. Lessing's recognition of the culturally productive critical value of melancholy cosmopolitanism is a consequence of her reading of the particular social and political contexts of the 1950s (in *The Golden Notebook*) and the late 1960s and early 1970s (*Briefing* and *Memoirs*). Critics writing about *The Golden Notebook* have tended not to focus closely on the decade of the 1950s as particularly relevant to the interpretation of the novel; however, many of the issues it discusses are very much a product of 1950s culture.[29] In addition to the fact that Anna's diaries note many historical events of the decade, for example the electrocution of the Rosenbergs, the Korean War, the war in Quemoy, she is also preoccupied by the emergence of the Cold War in a post-nuclear society, the death of Communism and the rise of McCarthyism, the relation between decolonisation and nationalism, the growth of the suburbs, trends in psychiatry and psychotherapy, and changes in art and culture (seen in television, film, magazines and fashion).

Anna notes that during the 1950s the Cold War ended wider interest in Communism and made it 'suspect instead of fashionable' (80). In a diary entry of 3 January 1952 she dates this shift in attitudes to 'the last two or three years', commenting that 'the atmosphere of this country has changed dramatically' (155). It is now 'tight, suspicious, frightened' and Anna believes 'it would take very little to send it off balance into our version of McCarthyism' (155). Anna meets many American Communists who have moved to Britain to escape McCarthy; she and Molly call this group 'The Colony' (64). However, she also meets other Americans who are shocked to discover that she is a Communist. Edwina Wright, an American TV producer interested in adapting *Frontiers of War*, reacts with fear:

> She sits, opposite me, breathing fast, her eyes uncertain, her pink lips, rather smeared now, parted. She is thinking: next time I must be careful to make enquiries. She is also seeing herself as a victim – that morning I had read through a batch of cuttings from the States about dozens of people sacked from their jobs, being grilled by Anti-American committees, etc. She says breathlessly: 'Of course things are quite different here in England, I realize that ... ' Her woman of the world mask cracks right across, and she blurts out: 'But my dear, I'd never have guessed in a thousand years that ... ' This means, I like you so how can you be a Communist? (266–7)

Perhaps drawing on this experience in 'The Shadow of the Third', Anna has Ella tell an American lover, Cy Maitland, that she shares a house with a woman who is a Communist. Having just argued that he agrees with McCarthy, because '"we can't have the Reds taking over"' (294), he reacts to her proximity to the red peril with confusion: '"I know things are different here with you. I don't get it, I don't mind telling you that"' (294). What is common to both scenes and developed throughout the novel is Lessing's understanding that the Cold War polarises thinking. Edwina's shock is the result of being forced to admit that it is possible to like someone associated with something as alien as Communism. Cy's awareness that things are 'different' in England, where Communism is still more acceptable than it is in the US, also disturbs the secure positioning of Communism as 'other' to Western, democratic, capitalist values. Later in the novel Saul Green also emphasises how McCarthyism divides writers into those who 'fell into a conformity of being "red" under pressure from McCarthy', and those who 'became respectable and fell into a conformity of anti-Communism' (494). Anna realises that the same refusal of any middle ground could have happened in the UK 'if the heat had been turned on even a little harder' (495). Later, she has a vision 'of the world with nations, systems, economic blocks, hardening and consolidating; a world where it would become increasingly ludicrous even to talk about freedom, or the individual conscience' (496).

This atmosphere of 1950s Cold War post-nationalism is an important context for Lessing's interest in melancholy cosmopolitanism. In part, Anna shares what Robbins suggests is 'the general form of the case against cosmopolitanism on the left': that it constitutes 'a privileged and irresponsible detachment … doomed to … mere aesthetic spectatorship'.[30] Anna's resistance to writing on the grounds of its futility in the face of the state the post-war world is in suggests just this kind of thinking. She also shares the classic Marxist suspicion of cosmopolitanism's role in sustaining global production and international commerce.[31] The many attempts to adapt *Frontiers of War* are an example of this kind of imposition, packaging and selling of cultural uniformity. Many of those who want to film the novel seem to be keen to change the setting or the characters in order to make the supposedly essential qualities of the story more accessible (but in fact to iron out the uncomfortable sexual and racial tensions in the story). However, she recognises in the CP a refusal of the commercial imperatives of the literary world that helps her to resist the further corruption of her novel *Frontiers of War*. Equally, however, Anna is disturbed by the new stress in fiction on reportage, or what she calls 'information about areas of life we don't know' (75). She writes that:

> The novel has become a function of the fragmented society, the fragmented consciousness. Human beings are so divided, are becoming more and more divided, *and more subdivided in themselves*, reflecting the world, that they reach out desperately, not knowing they do it, for information about other groups inside their own country, let alone about groups in other countries. It is a blind grasping out for their own wholeness, and the novel report is a means towards it. (75)

Her thinking here suggests an unwillingness to accept the extreme parochialism of the contemporary novel because of its purely local relevance. This tension between the local and the global in relation to art and culture is clearly a response to the 'hardening and consolidation' of the wider political culture of the 1950s, in which, as Brennan suggests, many writers were interested in the creation of a federated Europe, a world state and the promotion of English as a *lingua franca*.[32] More than that, it constitutes a central tension for the novel, but interpreting this tension as melancholic allows us to recognise that it is productive because it is generative of the novel itself. In the preface to *The Golden Notebook*, Lessing positions the novel in the European tradition and regrets the 'intense parochialism' (13) of British culture. Immediately afterwards, she claims that Marxist readers of the novel were capable of 'intelligent criticism' because 'Marxism looks at things as a whole and in relation to each other – or tries to' (14). She admits that this attempt at a 'world-mind, a world ethic' failed and describes this failure in terms of the division and subdivision into 'smaller and smaller chapels, sects and creeds' (14). The tension expressed here between the global and the local is regretted, but is actually intrinsic to the novel's construction of a melancholy cosmopolitanism.

In this context of post-war post-nationalism, the relation between emergent African nationalism and decolonisation is immediately discomfiting. In the Mashopi hotel sequences of the novel, Paul twice predicts that future African nationalist movements will, of necessity, embrace Capitalism (101, 381). In 'Free Women 4', Anna attempts to convince Marion that African nationalist movements are hampered by their derivative relation to British politics and will be judged on whether the buses run on time; or, in other words, whether they meet British standards of 'efficiency' and 'democracy'. Her efforts with Marion and Tommy are focused on preventing them from 'cheapening' (452) the struggle for independence in the press. This concern is connected with her knowledge that she was culpable of the same nostalgic inauthenticity in *Frontiers of War* and in the Mashopi hotel sequences. If, as has already been suggested, *The Golden Notebook* associates nostalgia with the premature foreclosure of mourning, then the crucial question is whether or not Anna's Mashopi sequence, or indeed the novel as a whole, is capable of a productive, self-conscious, melancholic engagement with the colonial past. Bazin suggests that the return to realism in the Mashopi sequences 'not only reflects upon past events but attempts to examine the ways in which the account of those events reproduces the ideologies of empire the narrative itself sets out to expose and critique'.[33] The existence of this narrative as a fragment or extract within the novel itself 'becomes a way of dissecting the backwards glance characterising post-war British culture';[34] for Bazin this dissection 'confirms that the novel itself is capable of disrupting such nostalgic gestures'.[35] As we saw in chapter 2, it is also possible to see the melancholic rewriting of nostalgia as 'positive, creatively reflective … a form of nostalgia that, paradoxically, looks ahead, to the future'.[36]

Another important feature of the 1950s that is present throughout the novel is suburbanisation and its attendant gender norms. Anna summarises and parodies the middle-class male attitude to wife, family and home as follows: '"Please be sorry for me, I have to get home to 16 Plane Avenue and the dreary labour-saving house in the suburbs … the little house at 16 Plane Avenue and the missus"' (59). The connection she makes between housing design, town planning and sexual politics is continued in *The Shadow of the Third*. Ella travels to her employer, Dr West's house, a journey which involves 'miles in all directions, this ugliness, this meanness. This was London – endless streets of such houses' (168). Equally important, however, is Ella's sense that these suburban streets are filled with misery and wretchedness because of the psychological effects of this way of living. Ella's job on a woman's magazine involves answering the letters to the medical column that are too personal, or too 'neurotic' (to borrow the doctor's vocabulary), for him to answer. She connects the sprawling suburbs with fear, ignorance and loneliness and concludes: 'On the surface everything's fine – all quiet and tame and suburban. But underneath it's poisonous. It's full of hatred and envy and people being lonely' (178). The fact that it is predominantly women who are experiencing this fear and loneliness makes clear the gender inequalities at the heart of the separation of public and private spheres in the 1950s. The letters Ella has to answer are all from women and the doctors who pass them on to her and dismiss them are all men.

It is no coincidence that the important male characters in *The Golden Notebook* are doctors and that they are either dismissive of mental illness (Dr West) or are specialists in it: Paul Tanner is a neurologist and psychiatrist; Cy Maitland is a brain surgeon with a particular specialism in the leucotomy. Both these men are experts in their fields and yet their relationships with women are dysfunctional. Cy's marriage is sexless and he is extremely naïve about women's sexual desires. Paul Tanner has a relationship with Ella and yet she understands that he values the security and respectability that his marriage represents. He has to position her as a 'pretty flighty piece' and move to Nigeria in order to break off the relationship. Ella concludes that 'probably they were all like this, all in fragments, not one of them a whole, reflecting a whole life, a whole human being; or, for that matter, a whole family' (205). This sense of fragmentation reaches its apotheosis in the discussion of the leucotomy, when Cy states that he has '"cut literally hundreds of brains in half"' (294). When Ella expresses her concern that people '"are never the same again"' he admits '"it is pretty final"' (294).

The dominance of invasive and surgical treatments for mental illness in the 1950s is clearly associated in the novel with patriarchal control of women and with new ideas about suburban domestic space.[37] Lessing has Anna counter this ideological formation through a developing understanding of a more cosmopolitan relation between the home, hospitality, the family, domesticity and mental health. Anna's understanding of ideas of foreignness and otherness are key here and draw on her psychoanalytic sessions with Mother Sugar. In a similar way, in *Strangers to Ourselves* Julia Kristeva makes use of the intellectual resources of psychoanalysis in order to argue that 'uncanny, foreignness is within us: we are our own foreigners, we are divided'.[38] Kristeva, as Varsamopoulou suggests, 'can only feel comfortable when everyone else is like her: a foreigner; that one can only feel at home when no one feels at home'.[39] Anna's experiences with Saul Green at the end of the novel suggest exactly this kind of unhomeliness and breakdown. Her breakdown coincides with her inviting Saul into her home and corresponds with his. Lessing suggests in the preface to the novel that 'they "break down" into each other, into other people, break through the false patterns they have made of their pasts, the patterns and formulas they have made to shore up themselves and each other, dissolve' (7). Saul tells Anna that '"This is an extraordinary room. It's like a world"' (531). Anna's hospitality is reluctant: initially she is persuaded to let her spare room to Saul as long as she doesn't have to engage with him and she makes all kinds of stereotypical assumptions about him because he is American. The tensions between homely domestic space and foreign 'other' in fact elaborate precisely the movements between the home and the world in cosmopolitanism.

Anna refuses the more conventional symbolic association between the home and the nation and demonstrates how the 'most powerful of cosmopolitan perceptions and ethical actions emerge within dramas of home'.[40] The gendering of this process is also important; clearly there are exploitative and abusive elements in Saul Green's sexual behaviour with Anna and other women. However, Lessing is determined to suggest that this is a productive experience (which allows Anna to begin writing again) precisely because it loosens up fixed attachments to gendered and national norms. In a discussion of the South Asian Cold War writer, Santha Rama Rau, Burton claims that the heroine of her novel *The Adventuress* (1970) is 'among the first of a new generation of postcolonial heroines who find themselves adrift in the wreckage of the post-war world'.[41] I believe Anna is an earlier example of these preoccupations and also, like Rama Rau's heroines, suggests the importance of 'the move from a Britain-centred world to an American-centred world which the global Cold War produced'.[42] Lessing's decision to make Anna's most important lover an American exile from McCarthy is no accident.

What Anna learns in her psychoanalytic sessions with Mother Sugar is to develop a melancholic relation to pain and loss, which means accepting their part in her life and in the world as a whole; she also comes to understand how she can begin to create from these fragments. Initially Anna goes to Mother Sugar because she is unable to feel; the process of her analysis focuses on allowing her to own what she frequently terms 'joy in destruction'. Initially Anna refuses pain because her relation to it is only the nostalgic relation of mourning. She tells Mrs Marks that 'that sad nostalgic pain that makes me cry is the same emotion I wrote that damned book out of', concluding 'the root of that book was poisoned' (219). She dreams repeatedly of an anarchic principle of destruction, variously imaged as a dwarf, or sometimes an object. In an early dream the object is a casket that she believes contains something precious but instead contains 'a mass of fragments, and pieces … from everywhere, all over the world' (230). These fragments transform into a small, green, jewelled crocodile, allowing her to cheat the businessmen who have bought the casket. This transformation of pain and fragmentation into a consumable object clearly reminds us of

Anna's massaging of her experiences in Southern Africa into *Frontiers of War* and the Mashopi sequences.

In recurrences of the dream, the principle of 'joy in spite' gradually becomes more human, mutating from a Russian vase into an elf, a dwarf, a deformed old man or woman and then into a human being she knows and recognises. Finally, during her relationship with Saul, Anna dreams the dream and she herself is the dwarf figure and feels 'terrible joy' and on waking 'joy and peace' (518). In order to acknowledge the joy of pain and destruction it is necessary for Anna to accept fragmentation and splitting; in Eng and Kazanjian's terms she must admit 'a world of remains as a world of new representations and alternative meanings'.[43] This acceptance is of course apparent in *The Golden Notebook* in a number of ways: in its structure, its repetitious quality, where events and thoughts are written about more than once in different ways and characters double and proliferate and in its inclusion of fragments of all kinds.

More specifically, however, this acceptance is also apparent in the number of allusions to the nuclear bomb. In March 1950 Anna pastes a clipping about the 'H-Bomb' hairstyle into her diary. On the day she decides to leave the British Communist Party, she has a conversation with Jack about the implications of atomic energy, using it as an example of the increasing segmentation and specialisation of the post-war world and the impossibility of living as a whole person. With Mother Sugar she also insists on the unique aspects of living in the 1950s by alluding to the H-bomb exploding (415) and in a later therapy session uses the same image as an example of the worst thing that could happen, insisting that Mother Sugar would still see the 'creative aspects' (478) of such destruction. At the end of the novel during her experience with mental breakdown, Anna dreams of Mashopi again but this time the group of friends witnesses the explosion of an H-bomb, which was 'unbelievably beautiful, the shape of death' (536). These allusions not only place the novel securely in its Cold War context but also indicate the importance of a melancholic relation to loss in Lessing's work in this period. The bomb is perhaps the ultimate example of fragmentation, splitting and destruction: if, finally, even this must be acknowledged and put to work creatively in forming Anna as writer and, indeed, the novel itself, then we must accept the tremendous energy that Lessing's engagement with loss represents in this novel.

Critics have tended to view *The Golden Notebook* as a turning point in Lessing's engagement with realism.[44] Certainly the combustibility of the realist mode is more visible in *Landlocked* (1965) and *The Four-Gated City* (1969), the two volumes of *Children of Violence* Lessing produced after that novel. In *Landlocked* Martha is waiting to divorce her husband, leave Southern Africa and move to England. Her attachment to the Communist group has ended, the British airmen are gradually leaving the colony and she experiences a transformative love affair. Dreams and the pressures of Martha's unconscious life create a parallel existence that disrupts the surface of her daily existence and the realist surface of the text. This is also an important strategy in *The Summer Before the Dark*. There is significantly more chronological dislocation, key events are not narrated in the text and there is more stylistic disruption, with increasing use of parentheses and ellipses to create a provisional and awkward style. In *The Four-Gated City* Martha arrives in London and becomes integrated into the life of a large middle-class family as housekeeper, secretary and surrogate wife and mother. Again, Lessing includes the oppressive and paranoid atmosphere of the 1950s, during which the members of the family suffer as the relatives of a defected Soviet spy. The novel concludes with an appendix that describes social breakdown of the kind we see in *The Memoirs of a Survivor*, culminating in a series of nuclear and chemical accidents that destroys the Western world. The deliberately awkward transformation of this novel from realist *bildungsroman* to science fiction clearly suggests Lessing's need to push her own questioning of realism as far as she can.

In *The Golden Notebook*, Lessing's move away from realism is part of a wider critical examination of the fictional processes associated with the ideologies of empire. Her rejection of mourning and nostalgia and development of an ethic of melancholy cosmopolitanism are elaborated in more detail in the very different context of the early 1970s in *Briefing for a Descent into Hell* and *The Memoirs of a Survivor*. Lessing explores issues such as anti-psychiatry, mysticism and Orientalism, extraordinary psychic phenomena, social breakdown and the beginnings of environmentalism that interested many writers and thinkers in the late 1960s and 1970s (see discussion in chapter 1).[45] The possibility that humanity is not alone in the universe and speculation about the nature of 'alien' species and their relation to humankind is also a preoccupation. Lessing's continued interest in mental illness and in alternatives to conventional psychiatric treatments is apparent in *The Four-Gated City*. Martha's time with Lynda Coldridge, the wife of Mark, the head of the family with which Martha becomes involved, allows her to come to terms with mental disruption and her growing psychic powers. In *Briefing*, however, these are the central subjects of the novel. In this novel doctors known only as 'x' and 'y' disagree over the causes and diagnosis of Charles Watkins's breakdown and amnesia and prescribe different, conflicting treatments that are based more on their preference and on a sense of competition with each other than on efficacy. In the afterword, Lessing tells the story of various responses to a film script she had written about a man whose 'senses were different from the normal person's ... who experiences everything differently from "normal" people' (251). A number of film makers considered the project, but all wanted to know what was wrong with the protagonist; Lessing then sent the script to a neurologist and a psychiatrist. Both offered 'skilled', 'compassionate', 'authoritative' but 'quite different' (252) diagnoses.

Marion Vlastos notes the similarities and differences between Charles Watkins's 'descent' and that of Jesse Watkins - a patient of the 'alternative psychiatrist' R. D. Laing's, whose 'journey' during a psychotic episode is detailed in *The Politics of Experience* (1967).[46] In *The Divided Self*, Laing remarks that 'the therapist must have the plasticity to transpose himself into another strange and even alien view of the world'.[47] The vocabulary of strangers and aliens may be metaphorical, but it is telling. Lessing's interest in the remodelling of the therapeutic relationship in this period necessitates a genuinely cosmopolitan engagement with the other, without complete loss of the self. In this sense, *Briefing*, unlike *The Golden Notebook* and *Memoirs*, does, as we have seen, ultimately represent a very bleak failure: Vlastos suggests that 'finally, Charles lacks the courage, or the imagination, to *be* fully schizophrenic, to recognise his strange simultaneous existence in both worlds and to explore its meaning'.[48] Rather than suggesting that this is a matter of Charles's personal courage, Lessing shows that the treatment he receives and the entire framework in which mental illness is understood at this point in history fail the patient because they insist on instituting mourning at the expense of melancholy cosmopolitanism.

Lessing's attraction to mysticism and Orientalism in this period develops, as we saw in chapter 1, from her interest in the writings of Idries Shah, author of *The Way of the Sufi* (1968). Her suspicion of the idea 'that East must ever be East and West must be West' ('In the World, Not Of It')[49] suggests an ethics of cosmopolitanism understood as being 'at home in the world'[50] that displays a growing awareness of the importance of mobility between terms like East and West, the rational and the mystical, the local and the global, the self and the stranger, the self and the world, and the homely and the unhomely. One of the two epigraphs in *Briefing* comes from *The Secret Garden*, by Mahmud Shabistari. The extract develops the notion of 'the world within a grain of millet's heart' and concludes 'therein two worlds commingled may be seen'.[51] The dizzying perspectival shift between the miniature and the gigantic respects the existence and co-dependency of both.

For Lessing (and for many other writers and thinkers in this period[52]) changing the thinking process means taking seriously the possibilities occasioned by extraordinary psychic phenomena, as we see in the conclusion of *The Four-Gated City*, where there is a grain of hope after social collapse in the birth of several children whose paranormal powers far exceed the weak abilities of Martha and Lynda, who are viewed as an interim stage in human evolution. In *Briefing* the reader is encouraged to believe that as part of his experience of mental illness, Charles Watkins has been able to access Miles Bovey's memories of his time in Yugoslavia in the Second World War and remember and write about them as if they are his own. In *Memoirs* we have, similarly, to accept as entirely credible the narrator's ability to pass through the wall of her living room into another realm of perception and existence. We also have to accept that humanity is being watched over by benevolent, Godlike creatures. The female Presence in *Memoirs* (who is the exiled rightful inhabitant of the world beyond the wall) is sensed by the narrator as early as her second visit, although she accepts that she may have been reflecting back this memory from the point at the conclusion of the novel where 'everything ended' (16), all the characters in the novel join the Presence and 'the last walls dissolved' (190). During Charles's descent in *Briefing* we witness a conference of the gods who watch over the Earth and realise that Charles, along with Rosemary Baines and Frederick Larson, may be one of the gods who has forgotten his mission during his descent to Earth and rebirth in human form.

The evidence of social breakdown and changes in attitudes to authority figures in the early 1970s is present in different ways in both novels.[53] In *Memoirs*, as Greene suggests, we are offered the 'spectacle of the destruction, the collapse, of all systems – social, economic, political, ecological' (143) and the creation of new fictional forms to accommodate that vision (142). In *Briefing* the focus is on mental breakdown but on the understanding that 'individuals become sick because the world is sick'.[54] In Lessing's work in this period this sickness begins to be presented as an organic illness, not only in the body politic but in the physical organism of the Earth itself. By the end of *Memoirs*, for example, the air and water are polluted and have to be filtered. The second of the two epigraphs to *Briefing for a Descent into Hell* is from Rachel Carson's *The Edge of the Sea* (1955); like Shabistari's poem discussed earlier, it explains the existence of a 'miniscule world of the sand grains … of inconceivably minute beings … so small that our human senses cannot grasp its scale'. Carson is better known for her *Silent Spring* (1962), which has become known as 'the founding text of modern environmentalism'.[55] Carson's work can be seen as part of 'an ethos of resistance to the nature of Cold War politics, the intensification of the arms race, and the uses of science in the face of increased abuses of natural history'.[56] Lessing's work in the early 1970s, then, is clearly still responding to changes that she traces back to the Cold War.

If, as we have seen, *The Golden Notebook* establishes an important distinction between the nostalgic mourning of empire and the melancholy cosmopolitanism of post-national post-war culture the two later novels develop the implications of that distinction further. In *Briefing*, as we have seen, Charles's decision to undergo electro-convulsive therapy and his return to 'normality' effectively close off productive and creative engagement with madness and loss. For Lessing this decision, although no fault of his own, represents the work of mourning. In *Memoirs* the narrator's experiences of the 'personal scenes' in the nursery beyond the wall also stand for the claustrophobic, nostalgic relation to loss of mourning, as opposed to the impersonal scenes beyond the wall, which suggest a melancholic relation to loss that incorporates breakdown and fragmentation. This is clear in two scenes in the novel: the first where the narrator sees Emily as a small girl being punished for playing with and eating her own excrement:

> This scene – child, cot, sunlit room – diminished sharply, dwindled in the beam of my vision, and was whisked away to be replaced by the same scene made smaller, reduced by the necessity to diminish and so to contain pain; for suddenly there were heavy clanging steps on the stone, a loud angry voice, slaps, heavy breathing – there were low mutters and then exclamations of disgust, and the child yelling and screaming, first in anger, and then … in despair. (129)

Emily's abject pleasure (she is 'absorbed'; 'oblivious'; shrieking in 'triumph and joy' (129)) in crossing the boundaries between the clean and the dirty, consumption and expulsion is sternly refused by her mother, who forcefully reinstates those divisions, leaving Emily crying, with 'the miserable lost sound of incomprehension' (129). The mother's imposition of control is, however, echoed in the way the narrator experiences the scene, as it dwindles and shrinks and is finally replaced by 'the same scene made smaller', which is necessary in order to 'diminish and so to contain pain' (129). The impulse to control and diminish pain by miniaturising it is contrasted with an experience in a scene a few pages later when the narrator watches Emily cry after her friend June leaves without saying goodbye. Emily's grief here is a woman's rather than a child's grief, 'intolerable' 'painful' (150), 'as if the earth were bleeding' (151). The child is at some subjective level 'untouched' by the experience of pain and retains a secure sense of identity: '*Me*, it is *me* sitting here, to whom this frightful injustice has occurred' (150). However, the adult woman refuses to demand justice and embodies 'the finality of the acceptance of a wrong' (151). This kind of melancholic grief accepts pain and allows it to confront and challenge the basis of individual subjectivity; it also contains within it the 'yell of laughter, which is every bit as intolerable as the tears' (151). This acceptance of laughter within grief is akin to Anna's acknowledgement of 'joy in destruction' in *The Golden Notebook*.

In order for Anna to acknowledge the joy of pain and destruction it is necessary, as we have seen, that she should accept fragmentation and splitting; in Eng and Kazanjian's terms she must admit 'a world of remains as a world of new representations and alternative meanings'.[57] This is also the case in both *Briefing* and *Memoirs*. Both novels contain images of fragmentation as positive, but the relation between whole and part is now stressed more clearly. In *Briefing*, Charles clears the debris from a stone circle and uncovers geometrical patterns 'that suggested flowers and gardens and their correspondence with the movements of the sky' (55). Later on, he has a vision of the Earth viewed from space as composed of particles and fragments that 'seemed stationary, motionless' but

> moved, but in set patterns, so that looking down at one fragment of this crust of matter, smaller than the tiniest of grains of sand or dust of pollen, it seemed that even the curve made by a journey of a group of such items from one continent to another was a flicker of an oscillation in a great web of patterning oscillations and quiverings. (93–4)

Memoirs shares this interest in fragmentation as part of a pattern or design. The narrator finds behind the wall a room with a carpet with an intricate design that needs to be brought to life by adding patches of material that match the design (72). The impulse to see patterns and connections in destruction and fragmentation, or the whole in the part, is, according to Vlastos, key to the work of both Lessing and R. D. Laing: 'For Lessing, as well as for Laing, fragmentation, compartmentalization, splitting is seen as *the* essential problem of the makeup of our individual lives and of our society'.[58] The solution to the problems occasioned by splitting is not the imposition of a design, however, but the acceptance of fragmentation and destruction and their incorporation in creative cultural work.

In *Briefing* and *Memoirs* such creative work cannot take place in the everyday worlds of the novels (which is in marked contrast to *The Golden Notebook*) but does occur in the structure and form of the texts themselves and the reading experience as process. This change can be connected with Lessing's interest in Sufism and the effect of the Sufi teaching story. For Scott, mysticism in Lessing's fiction is, as we saw in chapter 1, about 'defamiliarisation, a writer's attempt to make use of a form of language, a way of looking at narrative'.[59] In *Briefing* and *Memoirs* Lessing uses fictional form in the spirit of the Sufi teaching story as 'a means, rather than an end … intended to change the form of the thinking process itself'.[60] Altering the thinking process in *Memoirs*, for example, involves unsettling the reader's sense of generic stability. The novel is clearly a speculative fiction, but Rosenfeld suggests that *Memoirs* is more than that: it is also a metafictional commentary on the different sub-genres of speculative fiction (the utopia, the dystopia, the post-apocalyptic and the arcadian).[61] If we also take seriously the statement that the novel is, as Lessing calls it, 'an attempt at autobiography', in which the individual reflects on her past, we can recognise that the novel's structures are 'seemingly antagonistic'; speculative fiction is forward looking and autobiography is backward looking. This antagonism is, according to Rosenfeld, intended to suggest the 'limitations of translating consciousness into prose'.[62]

In effect then, *Memoirs* resembles *The Golden Notebook* in that its very structure and narrative practice reflect on the impossibility of any straightforward relation to reality, the past and subjective experience. The loss of that certainty is mourned, but in a way that creatively generates new forms of fiction. The collage of inner texts in *Briefing* serves a similar purpose: it questions how we ascribe authority and credibility to different kinds of writing and different accounts of experience. The characters' growing awareness of the design and purpose behind fragmentation and destruction is severely limited in *Briefing* and *Memoirs* to realms of experience that are finally inconsistent with the everyday worlds of the novels. The everyday world of *Memoirs* collapses and in *Briefing* Charles recovers his identity but loses his memory of his 'descent'. Lessing encourages the reader to turn to the structure, form and experience of reading the texts themselves to find the most creative work of melancholia generated by an acceptance of loss. The metafictional world of the novels becomes the 'world of new representations and alternative meanings'[63] generated by the melancholic relation to remains. In *The Golden Notebook* it is still possible for Lessing to articulate a creative relation to loss at the level of the protagonist's lived experience in the everyday world as well as in the form of the text itself. This distinction is an important one that clearly connects to Lessing's sense of the very different contexts of the 1950s and the 1970s and the opportunities that they offer to the artist and writer. The 'hardening and consolidation' that Anna witnesses in the Cold War culture of the 1950s generates an alternative in the ethic of melancholy cosmopolitanism that she produces; by the 1970s that culture has turned inward, as has Lessing's own ability to challenge it.

4

The voice of authority?

In 1979, Doris Lessing made the transition to new worlds, publishing *Shikasta*, the first novel in her *Canopus in Argos: Archives* quintet (1979–83) and her first novel written entirely in the speculative mode. Science fiction (SF) has always involved extrapolation, so in what ways is writing about new worlds a way of writing about our own? What is the best way of voicing the relation between the familiar and the unfamiliar? Does SF require a different voice or narration? If it does, how might that make a writer like Lessing rethink her authorial and narrative voice when she returns to realism? How might it impact on her attempt to write about a subject like terrorism? In the *Canopus in Argos: Archives* series and in *The Diaries of Jane Somers* (1984) and *The Good Terrorist* (1985) questions of voice are central.

When discussing her own voice, or style, in an interview with Eve Bertelsen, Lessing was asked about something she had once said about 'deliberately "roughening" your style or avoiding perfecting a particular style'.[1] She replied:

> About perfecting style, what I meant was that if a writer perfects his or her own style, that style becomes a prison. Because style is a way of thinking. The style is not something abstract, it's feeling. So if you become a highly stylised writer, to my mind that is a prison which you impose on yourself. It doesn't mean to say that I haven't used many different styles; I have used different styles for different books. For example, in this new series that I've written [*Canopus*] there's a different tone of voice in every book.[2]

Lessing suggests here that style and voice cannot be separated from content and that there is no such thing as a characteristic authorial style or voice. She tested out these premises in her work in this period.

'What would we do if we found a new world?':[3] postcolonial feminist science fiction'

There is a valuable body of feminist critical work on women's speculative and fantastic fiction, which has convincingly elaborated some of the reasons why women writers have turned to these genres and found them fruitful. SF offers women writers the chance to rewrite conventional patriarchal and heteronormative wisdom about the way we conceptualise and organise women's understanding of, amongst other things, embodiment, gender, sexuality and family. As Virginia Tiger suggests: 'feminist and feminocentric novelists … have adopted the fantastical mode in part because it permits the representation of fluid rather than static gender relations'.[4] She also notes that 'the imaginative restructuring of social and political roles by women often involves transformed familial structures' and the severing of the link between sexuality, reproduction and their institutionalisation in marriage and heterosexuality.[5] Feminist SF also makes explicit questions of gender and genre or form. In the introduction to *Where No Man Has Gone Before: Women and Science Fiction*, Lucie Armitt argues that whereas much male-authored SF is marked by the idea of 'escape from', women writing SF tend to focus more on 'escape *into* … an alternative reality within which centrality is possible'.[6] She also stresses the importance of defamiliarisation as a strategy for SF writers of both genders. The idea of escape and the attempt to disturb the familiar are both key to Lessing's speculative fiction.

More recently, critics have begun to work towards a definition of postcolonial science fiction. This work, like much feminist work on SF, has also addressed the role that science and technology play in the genre. Women's understandable suspicion of techno-science is shared by the writers of postcolonial SF, according to Claire Chambers, who suggests that Amitav Ghosh's 1996 SF novel *The Calcutta Chromosome* deploys fiction to contest and contextualise the truth claims of Western science.[7] Reid also believes that representations of technology are key to postcolonial SF, claiming that 'it is the genre's fascination with technology that identified it as a literature of empire, but it is science fiction's technological imagination which provides the means of questioning the association between technology and the Western world views that supposedly underpin the genre'.[8] She suggests that postcolonial SF can begin to imagine different technological legacies that have not been influenced by Western paradigms.

Critics have, then, clearly begun to define postcolonial science fiction and have for some time found the category feminist SF useful. This chapter makes a claim for Doris Lessing's *Canopus in Argos: Archives* as postcolonial feminist SF. It is the *ironic* possibilities that can be generated by moving into new worlds that go some way towards defining 'postcolonial feminist science fiction'. Is any world ever 'new' and in what sense is humanity bound to endless repetition? In what ways are patterns of repetition linked to patriarchal, heterosexist and colonialist social and intellectual structures? Is it possible to find in images of return, repetition, allusion and home new ways of thinking about identity and new ways to write (speculative) fiction rather than suggestions of entrapment? Can postcolonial feminist SF be 'voiced' in new ways that defamiliarise familiar ways of thinking and suggest alternatives?

Avtar Brah's term 'diaspora space' is a useful one in relation to postcolonial feminist science fiction, which both writes about and actually constructs such space. Brah defines diaspora space as the site where concepts of border, location and dislocation collide, where multiple subject positions come into contact and where the licit and illicit meet. She writes: 'what is at stake is the infinite experientiality, the myriad processes of cultural fissure and fusion that underwrite contemporary forms of transcultural identities'.[9] More controversially, Brah suggests that diaspora space can pertain to those cultures and peoples whose identity is constructed as indigenous just as much as to those characterised by migration; she writes: 'the diaspora space is the site where *the native is as much a diasporian as the diasporian is the native*'.[10] Brah admits that her definition of diaspora space leaves her open to accusations of relativism (and to the criticism that she may well be de-emphasising strongly entrenched power structures that disempower migratory subjects). However, the appeal of her thinking is that it refuses rigid distinctions between the dominant and dominated, centre and periphery, and majority and minority. It also allows for what she refers to as a kind of '*theoretical creolisation*' that she argues borrows from feminist work, as well as from 'analyses of colonialism, imperialism, class, and gay and lesbian politics'.[11] This makes sense of my intersectional term feminist postcolonial science fiction. Brah also notes, usefully for literary critics, that diaspora functions through narrative, remarking that 'multiple journeys may configure into one journey via a *confluence of narratives* as it is lived and re-lived, produced, reproduced and transformed through individual as well as collective memory and re-memory'.[12]

The five novels in the *Canopus in Argos: Archives* construct an entire cosmic order where three super-powers, the benevolent and wise Canopus, the bureaucratic and technocratic Sirius, and the evil and wicked Shammat intervene in the destinies of less advanced planets, peoples and cultures. The first novel in the sequence, *Shikasta*, is about the long pre-history, history and future of a planet that is recognisably like Earth and the loss and eventual recovery of the planet's sense of one-ness and unity with Canopean Purpose. The second novel, *The Marriages between Zones Three, Four and Five* (1980), concerns three of the concentric zones that surround *Shikasta* and the marriage between the Queen of Zone Three and the King of Zone Four, a marriage which is demanded by an all-seeing deity (presumably Canopus) as a necessity for the health of each zone in order to encourage understanding and aspiration and to open up frontiers. *The Sirian Experiments* (1981), the third novel, was nominated for the Booker Prize. It is narrated from the point of view of an official in the Sirian Colonial Service who manages processes of redeployment and resettlement of people throughout the galaxy. As the novel progresses the narrator gradually learns how differently the rival power, Canopus, treats supposedly less advanced peoples and cultures and begins to question the entire colonial project of the Sirian empire. *The Making of the Representative for Planet 8* (1982), the fourth novel in the series, is about the population of a planet that experiences an ice-age and how the people gradually learn to adjust, under Canopean guidance, to the abandonment of a physical life in the body and individual personality. The final novel, *The Sentimental Agents in the Volyen Empire* (1983), examines the 'rhetorical diseases' that affect those involved in colonisation and nationalist movements in the Volyen empire.

The books received extremely mixed reviews both from the literati and SF fans and pleased hardly anyone. Looking at those literary reviews, it seems that part of the problem was the mere fact that Lessing had made a move into speculative fiction, which in the 1970s and early 1980s was still considered by many to be a somewhat cranky lowbrow genre. Another issue was the fact that she somehow hadn't done SF 'properly': this wasn't 'hard' or 'techno' SF but was variously described as 'social science fiction' or 'anatomy' (after Northrop Frye and with a nod to *Gulliver's Travels*).[13] Many readers felt disturbed by what they perceived to be the implicitly reactionary politics of the series; the need for the individual to exist in harmony with Canopean Purpose does, according to this interpretation, turn Canopus into a benevolent colonial dictatorship. These criticisms were often subsumed in the larger issue of Lessing's style and narrative voice in the series. Clare Hanson remarks on the reaction to the series as follows:

> A *TLS* [*Times Literary Supplement*] review of *The Sirian Experiments*, for example, begins, magisterially, 'Doris Lessing employs the science fiction genre purposefully, but not well', and the critic then goes on, interestingly, to attack Lessing's style: 'misplaced participles abound, singulars and plurals are confused, sentences are made

> verbless quite unnecessarily and there is much too much reliance on those magic triple dots'.[14]

The possibility that Lessing is purposefully adopting the dull, verbose, grammatically poor style of the colonial official in the novel seems not to occur to the reviewer. In fact Lessing's narrative voice is nothing if not self-conscious: in the *Canopus* sequence two novels are narrated from the perspective of the colonisers, two from the colonised and one a mixture. When written from the colonisers' point of view, the narrative consists of collections of official documents and reports, in an attempt to discourage identification with the values and perspectives therein: the style adopted is 'dry and bureaucratic', as Lessing suggests herself in the interview with Bertelsen:

> *The Sirian Experiments* is written from start to finish in a, I hoped, rather dry and bureaucratic style, written by a bureaucrat. I make a point of saying that, because I notice that some critics haven't even noticed that, and said the style of the book was bureaucratic and pedantic. I thought no, they can't be that stupid, but alas they are![15]

Hanson's discussion of reviews of the *Canopus* series continues:

> there is a nicely comic juxtaposition in the *TLS* of 3 June 1983 of a review of *The Sentimental Agents* in which it is claimed that Lessing is 'no longer capable' of seeing the irony of her position as an ex-colonial writing of a benevolent imperialism – and an advertisement below for *The Diary of a Good Neighbour* by Jane Somers – 'Likeable, readable and often funny, with good points to make and a warm heart at the centre of them'.[16]

To the *TLS* reviewer Lessing had adopted the voice of the benevolent imperialist unself-consciously. At this time the fact that Lessing created the likeable readable voice of Jane Somers as well as the benevolent imperialist was known only to a few.

It is difficult to reconstruct SF fans' responses to the series at the time, but an interesting discussion on the internet forum *The Valve* that took place when Lessing was awarded the Nobel prize gives a sense that the *Canopus* series never quite fitted genre fans' expectations either. Provoked by Harold Bloom's assessment of the last fifteen years of Lessing's work as 'unreadable … fourth rate science fiction',[17] the first contributor raises the issue of Lessing's place in the SF community and concludes that 'Lessing is regarded as marginal by most of genre fandom'.[18] This comment provoked some disagreement from other contributors to the forum and an attempt to link her *Canopus* series with work by other writers such as Olaf Stapledon, but one contributor referred to *Shikasta* as 'unreadable' and 'un-science-fiction like'.[19]

Lessing's *Canopus* series explores a number of issues characteristic of postcolonial feminist SF. First is her suspicion of techno-science and interest in ecology, defined by Jane Glover as 'many different parts, working together, in an evolving dynamic equilibrium', or 'a world view that perceives all of life as an interconnected web or single living being'.[20] In the third volume in the *Canopus* series, *The Sirian Experiments*, science is, according to David Waterman, 'one of Lessing's major targets of criticism, especially the institution of science as it is used to support the war machine, justify colonial expansion and establish authority, all under the control of a special elite class of technocrats'.[21] The narrator, Ambien, recounts (initially without any sense of discomfort) the continuous intervention of the Sirian empire in other cultures and less technically advanced native populations. The experiments of the title are often barbaric: one example that is particularly so is Ambien's account of the Lombi experiment. The Sirian empire cannot seem to work out why it is that the mere appearance of Sirian colonisers on a planet leads inevitably to the rapid social evolution of the native inhabitants. In some cases this social progress is unwelcome; as Ambien remarks: 'We did not want to discover, and then colonise, planet after planet of savages or semisavages who then it seemed almost at once, would become privileged citizens. In short we needed a reservoir or bank of populations whom we could use for ordinary, heavy, undifferentiated work.'[22] The Sirians select the Lombi people as suitably adaptable for hard labour and space lift them from their native planet to another planet where they are put to work. The colonial service officials who monitor them are instructed not to show any evidence of their 'superiority'. After five years' hard labour, during which time some die as a consequence of what Ambien defines as 'Mal-Adaptation due to Life Disappointment', the Lombis are then space lifted to another planet, where the Sirian officials are bemused to discover that they appear to believe that they have returned home and exhibit strange symptoms of joy: weeping, laughing and dancing. Ambien remarks: 'We had not known that these animals wept; no mention had been made of it' (39). After several more moves to different planets and regions of planets and a period unobserved by Sirius, Ambien sends in a group to observe the Lombis and assess their stage of development. The observers are stunned to find that the Lombi have developed a highly advanced oral literature and calendar of festivals to remember their homeland formally, despite the fact that 'none of them remembered, as individuals, their capture from their home planet and subsequent events' (44). The focus on home, both as folk memory and as projected future place of return, has become key to this people's diasporic culture in ways that were completely unanticipated by Ambien. The irony is that the Sirian attempt 'not to interfere' has actually had unintended consequences; as Waterman suggests: 'when discussing such large-scale biosocial experiments, in which entire populations have been transplanted, even a natural habitat becomes the laboratory ... wherein the role of the experimenter must not be discounted'.[23] As the novel progresses, Ambien begins to realise the brutality of the supposedly neutral, objective, scientific method used in the Sirian colonial service, which she becomes capable of criticising and ultimately rejecting.

The second novel in the *Canopus* sequence, *The Marriages between Zones Three, Four and Five,* also evidences Lessing's rejection of techno-science and interest in eco themes. Jayne Glover claims that 'Lessing addresses relationships between human beings, between humans and animals, between humans and nature or the environment, and between the human and the spiritual. Her approach is "ecological" in that she seems to propose that there is an intricate web of interrelationships between the earthly or natural, the animal, the human, and ultimately the spiritual.'[24] The marriage at the centre of the novel has been ordered because something is not in harmony in both zones. Animals are dispirited and have stopped conceiving and both zones are permeated by a stale, inward-looking, depressed quality. As representatives of their realms or zones, the Queen of Zone Three, Al·Ith and the King of Zone Four, Ben Ata, must marry, despite the great differences in their respective cultures. Zone Three seems to be typically feminine: in touch with emotions and spirituality, with open sexual and kinship systems and political structures. Zone Four at first appears to epitomise patriarchal clichés: it is militaristic, barbaric and territorial. It is not merely Zone Three that has things to teach Zone Four, however. Zone Four's secret women's festival teaches Al·Ith the importance of aspiration, of 'looking up' (the festival involves enforced cloud-gathering, thus challenging the Zone Four laws that forbid looking at the sky). At the end of the novel, Ben Ata is ordered to leave Al·Ith and marry Vahshi, the Queen of Zone Five, a realm of hunter-gathering, tribal, warlike people; it is from their desert songs that another message comes about the importance of aspiration beyond mere contentment. The novel closes with continuous movement between the zones, rather than closed frontiers, and what Lessing refers to as 'lightness', 'freshness', 'enquiry', 'remaking' and 'inspiration' rather than 'stagnation'.[25] Al·Ith is now able to make a move upwards into Zone Two, the insubstantial zone of fire, spirits and dancing shapes.

Glover's article explains the points of correspondence between this novel and a number of different eco-feminist ideas such as the link between the ill-treatment of women, animals and the natural world and the questioning of dualistic thinking. It is equally clear that Lessing's attraction to ecology and suspicion of techno-science are just as much a result of her interest in non-Western cultural and spiritual forms. As Lessing herself stated, 'the best scientists … always come closer and closer to the mystical'.[26] Shadia Fahim recognises that Lessing's stress on the balance between inner and outer modes of perception and her continued interest in equilibrium owe much to Sufi thought.[27] Müge Galin examines how the *Canopus* series is modelled on the Sufi teaching story and places Lessing 'between spirituality and science' and 'somewhere between the Eastern and Western traditions'.[28] Perrakis concludes that the marriage of East and West in this work 'is offering a model for cooperation and interchange between nations'.[29] Lessing's Southern African upbringing also has a part to play in her challenge to conventional Western science and also explains why her SF can read as oddly unlike many other examples of the genre. Perhaps, as Adam Roberts, writing on *The Valve* internet forum discussing Lessing's SF work, claims, she is attracted by the emphasis on magic and spirits in African oral culture and the challenge it offers to Western scientific theories.[30] Lessing's Southern African upbringing may well explain the allusion to magic and spirits in her SF work, which he elsewhere suggests is 'in conflict with the materialist emphases of contemporary science'.[31]

Positive transformations of identity and sexuality are also present in Lessing's *Canopus in Argos* series. In *The Marriages between Zones Three, Four and Five*, as we have seen, Lessing rewrites the relationship between the genders as an exploration of particular spaces or zones and insists on the necessity of dialogue and movement through and between these spaces for the health and aspiration of all. In the fourth novel in the sequence, *The Making of the Representative for Planet 8*, she borrows, as she explains in the afterword, from Scott's expeditions to the Antarctic to construct the story of a planet that experiences an ice-age. The people on the planet spend most of the narrative waiting and expecting to be space lifted by Canopus to a warm and pleasant planet, but Canopus cannot keep this promise. Instead, some of those on the planet give up and die quickly while others gradually learn to adjust, under Canopean guidance, and become 'the representative' of their planet, abandoning a physical life in the body and individual personality. On planet 8, individuals are defined by and named according to their role or function and thus from the first individual identity is understood as malleable. Johor, the Canopean guide who helps the stricken people adjust to the new climate, encourages them to develop this fluid conception of identity further. Towards the end of the novel, shortly before the people who become 'the representative' undergo a physical death and transformation, one of them struggles towards a new conception of identity, one that we might define as gesturing towards a diasporic space, in Brah's sense of the term:

> It seems to me that the wholes or groups or collectives need not be geographically close or contiguous, but that perhaps an individual who has precisely the same feeling of herself or himself as I do when waking in the dark out of a deep dream, knowing nothing of his or her past, or history, all memories gone too, for just that brief space – this individual might be one I never meet, might be living in a city on the other side of the planet where I have not been, nor ever will go now ... my loneliness is softened when I reflect that in saying *I, here I am, here is what I am,* this feeling or sensation or taste of me – I speak for ... but I do not know how many. For others, that is certain. In that feeling of me-ness, is, must be, a sharing, must be a companionship.[32]

The sense of identity as a shared experience of dislocation amongst a trans-national group is suggested here in an intensely metaphorical way through the conceit of crossing the border between an individual physical existence and a collective spiritual one.

As well as her suspicion of conventional techno-science and her interest in transformations of identity and sexuality, Lessing is drawn to the maternal imaginary. It is clear that many colonial narratives rely on metaphors of paternity – founding fathers for example – or of conquest of the female body as virgin territory. It is equally the case that diasporic cultures often make use of metaphors of return and home that are often implicitly maternal. Lessing makes explicit the metaphorical connections at work in these narratives and creatively rewrites them in her work. *The Marriages between Zones Three, Four, and Five* is concerned with the maternal imaginary. As Phyllis Perrakis suggests, 'Lessing's novel can be seen as a revisionist account of the Demeter/Kore (or Persephone) myth ... common to women's rebirth fiction'.[33] In the classical myth, Persephone has wandered away from her mother Demeter and is raped and abducted by Pluto to live in the Underworld. Demeter searches for her daughter everywhere and finally asks Zeus for her return. Perrakis demonstrates that 'Al·Ith's mythic descent and return [into zone three] involves mothering adequately herself and others, and then ... she is able to master the challenges of playing daughter to herself and others'.[34] She also suggests that Lessing rewrites the myth by including Ben Ata or Pluto's experience in the narrative, noting that although woman-centred myths are key to the novel Lessing also gives a voice to the masculine principle as if to suggest that the spiritual development of both genders is inter-dependent.

The prominence of the maternal imaginary in Lessing's texts is linked to a stress on circularity, return and repetition, not only at the level of plot, but also in terms of form or narrative structure. The first way in which this manifests itself is through the focus on millennial time scales that suggest beneath superficial differences deep patterns of repetition across different planets, solar systems and galaxies. In *Shikasta,* for example, Lessing finally returns the planet to its unity with Canopus; she ends the last volume in the quintet with three dots: the story is unfinished. In terms of identity, too, repetition is important. Once the entire *Canopus* quintet has been read, the reader has to balance a sense of the futility of the repetitious thoughtless brutality of the Sirian and Volyen empires with the more hopeful prospects for change and transformation generated in *Marriages, The Making of the Representative for Planet 8* and, to a lesser extent, *Shikasta.*

This play on the idea of repetition is also apparent in the creative use of intertextual allusion, not so much to other SF writing but to classical literature, myth and religious texts. Lessing draws, in *Shikasta* alone according to the preface, on the Old Testament, the Apocrypha, the Epic of Gilgamesh, the Torah and the Koran, and elsewhere in the series, as we have seen, on classical mythology and Sufi teaching stories. She seems to be suggesting that not only is there no 'new found land', there are also no new stories under the sun. Discussing the importance of Martha's vision of the city in the *Children of Violence* series in the interview with Eve Bertelsen, Lessing remarks on its long history in different cultures and religious traditions:

> Marxism took over a lot of utopian ideas … these ideas of harmony and happiness and equality … comes [sic.] from religion. Utopias long pre-date Marxism. The idea of paradise and heaven comes from Christianity … it predates even Christianity. It's the old Golden Age theme.[35]

When asked where Martha gets these visions from, Lessing replied: 'From literature of course. Her books, her house was full of books.'[36] Lessing looks to intertextual allusion, circularity and repetition as creative, palimpsestic strategies.

It is clear that in her speculative fiction of this period Lessing is trying to find 'new worlds' and new narratives in different ways: deconstructing the rhetorical voices of colonialism and imperial conquest and suggesting their links with certain narrative patterns and structures of progress and development. Lessing redefines progress in terms of a narrative transformation towards positive instead of negative forms of repetition, acknowledgement and allusion. The narrative voices in the series construct a 'creolised' (to borrow from Brah) parody of colonial rhetoric and suggest ways to displace it creatively. Lessing's postcolonial feminist science fiction constructs what Brah might define as a diaspora space. Lessing suggests, like Brah, that the condition of humanity is inevitably diasporic, while also acknowledging that entrenched power structures make that experience much more visible and less comfortable for some than others. As the ultimately 'homeless', diasporic or interstitial genre, postcolonial feminist science fiction, which draws on so many sources and influences, is the appropriate space in which to undertake such a project.

The 'Jane Somers' hoax: aging, gender and the literary marketplace

In 1983 (the same year of publication as *The Sentimental Agents in the Volyen Empire*, the final *Canopus* volume) Doris Lessing published *The Diary of a Good Neighbour*, which was quickly followed in 1984 by a sequel, *If the Old Could*. Both novels used the name 'Jane Somers', which purported on the book jacket to be 'the pseudonym of a well-known woman journalist'. Using this pseudonym, she had submitted the manuscript of the first novel to her usual publishers, Jonathan Cape and Granada, who both rejected it, Granada arguing that 'it was too depressing to publish'.[37] The novels were, however, accepted and published to moderate critical acclaim by Michael Joseph, who had published her first novel, *The Grass is Singing*, in 1950. Once genuine authorship was acknowledged, both novels were eventually republished in 1984 in one volume as *The Diaries of Jane Somers*, with a new preface by Lessing that discussed the reasons for her literary imposture. Lessing's 'play' with the literary establishment and the publishing industry has become one of the most well-known literary hoaxes. It is clear that even as early as the 1980s Lessing was preoccupied by questions relating to the marketing and reception of literary fiction and by questions of authorial and narrative voice. She chose to explore these issues by crossing the border of authorial identity and writing in a different voice.

The Jane Somers hoax clearly raises a number of interesting issues about authorship, canonicity and literary production that critics have to some extent addressed.[38] More commonly, however, *The Diaries* has been celebrated for its provocative treatment of aging, gender and the body, a subject which has until recently received little serious treatment in fiction, despite growing concerns about an aging population at the close of the twentieth century.[39] Very few critics have made any connections between the issues raised by the hoax and the subject matter of the novels. In fact, there is an integral relationship between the two: Lessing specifically questions the expectations of and 'proper' role for women authors entering the third stage of life. The novel achieves this by making use of a generic and formal complexity that masquerades as naïve realism. What is striking is that the issues raised by the hoax and the novel itself anticipate a growing body of criticism precisely concerned with the relationship between gender, race, authorship and commercial culture.

Janna, the heroine and narrator of *The Diaries*, is an ambitious, confident career woman who works for a woman's magazine called *Lilith*. She is 49 in the first novel and in her early 50s in the second. At the opening of the first novel she acknowledges that she is emotionally repressed and self-centred. Having been 'in denial' since her husband's and her mother's deaths (both from cancer), she unexpectedly befriends an old lady in her 90s named Maudie Fowler. Getting to know Maudie allows Janna to confront her own fear of aging, death and decrepitude and engages her in the domestic labour of caring for the elderly: 'women's work' that she admits was for her previously invisible and unimaginable. The novel is visceral in its descriptions of filth and poverty, and its focus on the maintenance of the body and the domestic environment is one of its most memorable elements. Janna is obsessed with style, image and grooming, which is related to her job in the women's magazine industry but is also an aspect of what Judith Butler might term her 'performative' construction of femininity.[40] Maudie's filthy home, incontinence and physical frailty allow Janna to re-evaluate this aspect of her identity. As the novel develops and Janna's time spent caring for Maudie increases she begins to curtail her elaborate grooming of her own clothes, body and interior décor:

> And I see that I did *not* write down, in Janna's day, about going to the loo, a quick pee here, a quick shit, washing one's hands … All day this animal has to empty itself, you have to brush your hair, wash your hands, bathe. I dash a cup under a tap and rinse out a pair of panties, it all takes a few minutes … But that is because I am 'young', only forty-nine.
>
> What makes poor Maudie labour and groan all through

> her day, the drudge and drag of *maintenance*. I was going to say, For me it is nothing; but the fact is, once I did have my real proper baths every night, once every Sunday night I maintained and polished my beautiful perfect clothes, maintained and polished *me*, and now I don't, I can't. It is too much for me. (Ellipses in the original)[41]

Janna's emphasis here is not only on what is excluded from our understanding of femininity but also on what is excluded from *writing*: what she did '*not* write down' (but actually of course did).

Lessing's literary imposture can, of course, be read as an attempt to circumvent the restrictions or cross the borders of what Foucault would term the 'author function', or to stage what Roland Barthes might refer to as the 'death' of 'Doris Lessing'.[42] In her preface to *The Diaries* she alludes to both aims: 'I wanted to be reviewed on merit, as a new writer, without the benefit of a "name"; to get free of that cage of associations and labels that every established writer has to learn to live inside' (5). And yet, rather perversely for those who might wish to align her with a poststructuralist suspicion of essentialist ideas about authorial identity, Lessing gives the impression that she was delighted when some readers *were* suspicious and recognised her writing:

> What is it that the perspicacious recognise, when they do? After all, Jane Somers's style is different from Lessing's. Each novel or story has this characteristic note, or tone of voice – the style, peculiar to itself and self-consistent. But behind this must sound another note, independent of style. What is this underlying tone, or voice, and where does it originate in the author? It seems to me we are listening to, responding to, the essence of a writer here, a groundnote. (7)

Yet Lessing's attraction to traditional Romantic conceptions of the author as the creative origin of the text is complicated if we compare it with her discussion of the reception of the *Canopus* series in the interview with Eve Bertelsen in 1984. Bertelsen mentions that 'people often misread the tone when you're deliberately creating a satirical narrator, and say "Lessing is being bureaucratic." Several critics take up the problem of a narrator who seems to be "above it all." In *The Sentimental Agents* … they feel that somehow the narrator is a bit smug'.[43] Lessing replied:

> *The Sentimental Agents*? Because it's a social satire, it's in the tradition where there're no real characters at all, they're all cardboard cutouts aren't they? As my dear Bob Gottlieb of Knopf said, 'Doris! Where is your characteristic deep note?' I said, 'You can't have a characteristic deep note in this kind of book, it's a different tradition.' They're looking for something that can't be in that particular genre.[44]

Lessing seems to suggest that 'groundnotes' and 'deep notes' are not universal and unchanging. As the preface to *The Diaries* continues, Lessing goes on to argue that even if such a groundnote existed, it would be unlikely to be recognised in a work *even if her name were attached.* To the reading public, the figure of the novelist Doris Lessing has a label: 'she is a writer about the colour bar (obsolete term for racism) – about Communism – feminism – mysticism; she writes space fiction, science fiction. Each label has served for a few years' (5). Such labels may, particularly as time passes, bear less and less relation to the 'groundnote' or 'essence' of Lessing's own sense of her authorial identity/voice; yet publishers rely on such labels to promote fiction, which, in circular fashion, further reinforces readers' expectations.

Lessing discusses in the preface some of the commercial imperatives that shape this process, such as literary prizes and the short 'shelf lives' of books by unknown authors as opposed to the construction of celebrity status for well-known authors. Her arguments would seem to support Foucault's contention that the author function arises alongside and is an intrinsic part of a modern commercial culture 'once strict rules concerning author's rights, author–publisher relations, rights of reproduction, and related matters were enacted'.[45] Yet several recent studies have demonstrated that the 'commerce' of literature has existed quite happily alongside anonymity and pseudonymity. John Mullan, for example, suggests that 'if we reopen once celebrated cases of anonymity, can we see how, for their first readers, an uncertainty about their authorship could give new and original works of literature a special voltage?'[46] Mullan's study of anonymous and pseudonymous publications concludes that a work that 'appears without its true author's name' has a paradoxical effect: it 'sends not just critics but ordinary readers off in search of the author'.[47] Mullan does, however, acknowledge the importance of one historical development: 'Anonymity became much less common in the twentieth century';[48] he claims that an important reason for the shift away from anonymous publication is that 'the business of selling authors became inextricable from the business of selling books'.[49] In *Marketing Literature: The Making of Contemporary Writing in Britain* Claire Squires claims that 'the last two decades of the twentieth century underwent an intensification in the marketing activity surrounding literary fiction. This intensification came about through a variety of factors including the increased financing available to publishing, conglomeration and globalisation and competition at all levels.'[50]

In fact, Lessing recognises in the preface that in adopting a pseudonym she does not *escape* the commercial constraints of modern literary production so much as exchange one set of constraints (those of a well-established literary celebrity) for another (a woman journalist who has made a first attempt at breaking into the world of 'literary' fiction publishing). It would appear then that Lessing's intentions were more complex than merely to point out how grubby economic motives taint and corrupt the purity of the novelist's artistic imperative. In choosing to publish pseudonymously she aimed to examine the nature of authorship and the authorial and narrative voice and point out the connections between gender, age, genre and literary and other kinds of production. In doing so she was in advance of a steadily increasing critical interest in the relationship between the publishing and book-selling industry and the literary work itself.

Pierre Bourdieu's examination of ideas about taste, distinction and the 'field' of cultural production is extremely relevant here. In 'The Field of Cultural Production; or, the Economic World Reversed,' first published in English in 1983, the same year as the first volume of *The Diaries*, he claims that 'the work of art is an object that exists as such only by virtue of the (collective) belief which knows and acknowledges it as a work of art'.[51] The belief in the work's value is produced by 'critics, publishers, gallery directors and the whole set of agents whose combined efforts produce consumers capable of recognising the work of art as such'.[52] The job of critics is to explore this process and inevitably, for Bourdieu, such an exploration means recognising that the literary or artistic field is subject to change, rather than static; it can be defined as 'a *field of forces*, but it is also a *field of struggles* tending to transform or conserve this field of forces'.[53] Elaborating on the metaphor of struggle and force, he later uses an analogy that is particularly suggestive, arguing that the field of cultural production can be characterised by the 'extreme permeability of its frontiers'.[54] Defining the borders, frontiers or limits of the field involves the attribution of cultural respectability or capital to particular texts and authors; the border, although permeable, is extremely contested.

However, whereas ideas about gender, race and national identity are not central in Bourdieu's analysis, his approach is, as Mary Eagleton argues, 'equally applicable to female authors of the twentieth and twenty-first centuries'.[55] Indeed, McDermott argues that 'one significant strand' (of the most recent feminist criticism) 'focuses on the relation between women's literature and the marketplace: the culture of literary prizes, the connection between (post)feminism and popular fictional forms such as 'chick lit,' and the celebrity culture surrounding particular female authors'.[56] As early as 1998, the collection *Writing: A Woman's Business* aimed to consider 'the issues of consumerism as they affect women's position in a commercial environment, where issues of gender frequently disturb the always fraught transmission from imaginative creation to printed page'.[57]

When considering Lessing's strategy in adopting a younger woman journalist's authorial voice or persona interesting contrasts can be drawn with other twentieth-century fakes and impostures. In a number of well-known recent cases of imposture that occurred in Australia white writers have assumed minority ethnic authorial identities. Critics have claimed that in these cases those who feel threatened by affirmative action policies and increasingly visible cultural differences have been tempted to adopt a minority ethnic pseudonym and writing identity. In the case of Australian imposture, therefore, 'it is questions of cultural and racial difference, rather than sexual or gender difference, which preoccupy those who feel themselves to have "lost out" in the cultural changes of post-war Australia'.[58] The adoption of a faked Jewish diasporic identity has also been important in some of the most well-known instances of ersatz holocaust testimony such as Binjamin Wilkomirski/Bruno Doessekker's *Fragments: Memories of a Childhood 1939–1948*. In both cases it has been argued that the 'commodified authenticity' of contemporary authorial identity is what is being tested.[59] The fact that, as Sue Vice puts it, 'ethnicity may be taken for personal identity'[60] in contemporary literary culture (and indeed in culture more widely) has arguably led to the creation of an 'alterity industry' that leads to the 'global commodification of cultural difference' that Huggan terms the 'postcolonial exotic'.[61] It would perhaps not be too much of an exaggeration to say that Lessing was quite early in sensing this alteration in the publishing climate (or, in Bourdieu's terms, the literary field) that other writers and critics have subsequently begun to address.

Cynthia Port claims that

> the questions about economies of moral and material value raised throughout *The Diary of a good Neighbour* – What is a good life? A good neighbor? A good investment? – are mirrored by the questions about aesthetic value introduced by the novel's anonymous publication … Whereas the fashion cycle venerates that which is youthful and new, the publishing industry banks on the accumulated symbolic capital of successful authors. Indeed, by masking her identity in a cloak of youthful anonymity, Lessing restages the plot of the novel, demonstrating the usually underappreciated value of accumulated age and experience. At the same time, however, she calls attention to the

> dangers of rapid cycles of obsolescence and disposal, which skew estimations of aesthetic and moral value.[62]

However, is it the case that the publishing industry always 'banks on the accumulated symbolic capital of successful authors'? The 'venerat[ion] of that which is youthful and new' would seem to apply to women writers and postcolonial writers much more than to white men. Diana Wallace also suggests that 'it is ironic, however, that she [Lessing] could only make visible the issues of women's aging and death through the mask of a pseudonym.' She continues: 'there is also a further irony in the fact that, at least in Britain, Lessing, despite her reputation as an internationally-acclaimed writer, seems to be becoming more invisible with age'.[63]

In order to understand Lessing's connected aims in moving from speculative fiction to tackle the subject of aging and gender in *The Diaries* via the adoption of the pseudonym we need to be aware of what was happening to her reputation in the early 1980s and also to think about the literary field at that time. In 1983, when *The Diary of a Good Neighbour* first appeared under the name Jane Somers, Doris Lessing was 64, four years older than the official retirement age for women and roughly half way between the ages of Janna (her narrator) and Maudie. As we have seen, earlier that same year she had completed her sequence of five science fiction novels *Canopus in Argos: Archives*. In the preface to *The Diaries* she reflects on the unpopularity of her move away from realism and into science fiction thus: 'some reviewers complained they hated my Canopus series, why didn't I write realistically, the way I used to do before: preferably *The Golden Notebook* over again' (5). What is interesting here is the fact that many critics have taken this comment to mean that *The Diaries* marks a return to realism.[64] Yet it would seem that if this is a return it is an extremely complex and perverse one: *The Diaries* is about as realist as *The Golden Notebook*. In fact, as is also true of that novel, Lessing makes use of a number of metafictional techniques in order to 'stage' her 'realism' for the reader. Her intention is to question the commercial constraints that push certain authors towards particular kinds and genres of literary production and to challenge the association between realism, 'authenticity' and women's writing. She does this in full knowledge of the limitations and problems of realism as a form and anticipates many women and postcolonial novelists' turn away from realism and towards other modes and genres such as magic realism, gothic and postmodernism.

In terms of the literary field in the early to mid 1980s, it is worthy of note that Margaret Atwood and Jeannette Winterson were yet to publish *The Handmaid's Tale* and *Oranges are not the Only Fruit* (which both appeared in 1985) and that Angela Carter would publish *Nights at the Circus* the following year. Three extremely significant feminist texts which adopt elements of science fiction, fantasy and gothic and question the relation between fact and fiction/history and literature appeared after Lessing's experiment with pseudonymous publication. In terms of prize culture in the UK, The Booker prize for 1983 went to J. M. Coetzee for *Life and Times of Michael K.* and in 1984 it went to Anita Brookner for *Hotel du Lac,* apparently just the kind of modest middle-aged feminine novel that Lessing is satirising. Lessing herself was nominated in 1981 for *The Sirian Experiments,* the third volume in her *Canopus* series, but lost out to Salman Rushdie's *Midnight's Children,* a classic magic realist postcolonial text. She was nominated again in 1985 for *The Good Terrorist,* but she did not win for either her science fiction or her 'social realism'. It might therefore be claimed that in writing *The Diaries* and adopting the pseudonym Lessing wanted in her own way to test out issues of genre, particularly by stretching the limits of realism and challenging the supposition that it is the appropriate genre for older women novelists to use.

The first element of Lessing's self-conscious 'staging' of realism in *The Diaries* is, obviously, the adoption of the diary form. *The Diaries* begins with the narrator's 'summing-up of about four years' (13). In this section she tells us briefly about her life before meeting Maudie and their first few meetings. She then decides, 'Now I am going to write day by day, if I can' (38), although finding the time to write becomes more difficult as the text progresses and Janna states that she often has to choose between writing and grooming her body, clothes and flat. Within the text, Janna often attempts to write from the perspective of someone else, usually Maudie, to think herself into her consciousness, or to record what she imagines a day in her life might be like. She also records from memory conversations with Maudie, usually Maudie's memories of her earlier life. This focus on various forms of life writing – the diary and the auto/biography being prominent among them – suggests a number of things. First, it makes clear Lessing's wish to acknowledge the importance of those supposedly 'minor' forms of writing. Secondly, she wants to alert readers to the gendering of such forms: to make clear their association with gendered notions of authenticity. Third, the 'fictive' or 'self-conscious' artfulness of life writing (rather than its transparent reflection of reality) is stressed in order to question how we define realism in literature and highlight its inevitable exclusions.

Lessing's use of a first-person narrator is also part of an attempt to make the reader question the status of *The Diaries* as a realist text, partly because it is intimately connected with the adoption of the pseudonym and the whole question of authorial and narrative voice. Lessing has used the first person relatively infrequently in her novels and commented in the preface that it might be liberating to do so (5). Her strategy here was to satirise the unthinking conflation of the narrator with the author in the reading and promotion of realist texts (particularly those written by women and writers of colour) by insisting on the similarities between the narrator, Janna and the *supposed* author, Jane Somers. This was achieved by stating on the book jacket that 'Jane Somers' was the pseudonym of 'a well-known woman journalist', which led, as Lessing explains, to the novel being reviewed in women's magazines rather than the broadsheets (7–8). The novel is more than superficially affected by the choice of narrator. Lessing comments: 'It was more than a question of using the odd turn of phrase or an adjective to suggest a woman journalist' (6). Janna's conservative, image-conscious, consumerist values pervade the novel even though she has to reassess them once she meets Maudie.

Of course, Janna is herself an author of other texts in other genres than the diaries. While keeping the diary she also writes magazine articles for *Lilith* and plans and writes a historical novel called *The Milliners of Marylebone*, which is a heavily romanticised version of Maudie's life-story. (Janna writes: 'Oh, I know only too well why we need our history prettied up. It would be intolerable to have the long heavy *weight* of the truth there, all grim and painful' (149).) She plans a romantic fiction novel called *Gracious Lady* about a Victorian lady philanthropist and considers writing a critical book called *The Contribution of Boredom to Art*. She has apparently nearly finished 'another serious sociological-type book called *Real and Apparent Structures*' (172) and a book called *Fashion Changes*. When Maudie goes into hospital Janna plans a book on the lives of the ward maids. The sheer extent of her productivity is surely some kind of ironic joke on Lessing's part. During the course of the novel Janna works full time for Lilith, which often involves trips abroad to fashion shows, cares for Maudie and begins to do the same for other elderly women as the novel progresses, writes her diary and produces these other works, both academic and fictional. Of course work (or production of all kinds) is the subject of all this writing. Of the novel she plans about the ward maids in hospital, Janna writes:

> I want to write about these ward maids, the Spanish or the Portuguese or Jamaican or Vietnamese girls who work for such long hours, and who earn so very little, and who keep families, bring up children, and send money home to relatives in Southeast Asia or some little village in the Algarve or the heart of Spain. These women are taken for granted. The porters are paid well in comparison; they go about the hospital with the confidence that goes with, I would say, not being tired. I know one thing, these women are tired. They are tired. They are so tired they dream of being allowed to get into bed and to stay there sleeping for weeks. They all have the same look, of a generalized anxiety, that I recognise; it comes from just keeping on top of things … How do I recognise this look? For I cannot remember seeing it before. I have read about it? No, I think it comes from Maudie. (248)

The fact that Janna 'has not read about' the look of anxiety and tiredness that accompanies these women's work emphasises the absences in the literature that Janna is involved in consuming and producing. She comments that 'that is what I would like to write, but a novel of this kind is hardly the same task as one about those gallant milliners or the sentimental lady' (249). A few pages later, reading the newly published *Milliners of Marylebone* to herself, she thinks: 'How I did enjoy making Maudie's relentless life something gallantly light-hearted, full of pleasant surprises ... Maudie would love her life, as reconstructed by me' (252). Having sanitised Maudie's life in the lowbrow women's genre of romantic fiction, it could be argued that even though she fails to write her novel about the lives of ward maids, saying that 'Reality is clearly too much for me' (317), *The Diaries* itself provides just the kind of 'reality' about women's work that other genres or modes fail to accommodate.

Novelist Maggie Gee, discussing her experience of the contemporary marketplace in 1998, remarks:

> my books are all very different from each other, and I have noticed that those of my books which deal with war or murder, which can be crudely categorised as male topics, receive far more attention and literary respect than those which deal with families or children or love or sex. Yet for me these are all great themes, themes from which you can make serious literary works, themes which demand the same careful attention to structure and form and style.
>
> Nevertheless, if I write a book about love, it is very likely to be reviewed in company with other books by women, and in a particular way. If there is 'love interest' in the foreground of a work by a woman, reviewers cannot see what else is there; immediately the book is categorised as women's romance. The act of reviewing is too often an act of domination or colonisation, and critics start to map their territory by categorising consciously or unconsciously in terms of gender.[65]

In a suggestive metaphor comparing reviewing to colonial categorisation of subordinate cultures and peoples (that can be instructively compared with Bourdieu's conception of the 'permeable frontiers' of the literary field), Gee suggests that women's writing about domestic and emotional labour is often unthinkingly conflated with the category of 'popular' fiction and reviewed as such. Certainly, according to the preface, part of the intention of Lessing's hoax was to test whether 'Jane Somers', an author whose authorial identity was already deemed 'lowbrow' (as a well-known woman journalist whose previous novels had been big-selling romances), could break down the border between popular and 'literary' fiction (8). The hoax thus suggests questions about gender and definitions of art that are explored by Mary Eagleton in *Figuring the Woman Author in Contemporary Fiction*. Eagleton draws on Pierre Bourdieu's distinction between the aesthetic disposition, 'the capacity to consider in and for themselves, as form rather than function', and the popular aesthetic, 'based on the affirmation of the continuity between art and life, which implies the subordination of form to function'.[66] Eagleton claims that what distinguishes contemporary women's writing is its refusal of this opposition.[67] This involves not merely a revaluing of the popular but a challenge to the border between popular and dominant; lowbrow and highbrow. It also incorporates the idea that women's work of all kinds can have a status as art and that usefulness can co-exist with an object's status as an artform.

More recently, other contemporary writers have also examined how the border between the popular and the literary is constructed and policed in relation to gender, race and nation, with particular reference to questions of form and ideas about authenticity. Maggie Gee continues her discussion of women's writing in the marketplace by claiming that 'women writers suffer from a lack of attention to style and even more particularly to form. Form is something that critics apparently only expect to find in the work of male literary writers ... Women "write *about*" – by which I mean that reviewers look first at our subject matter. Men simply "write" – a primary, literary activity.'[68] Similarly, bell hooks suggests that black women writers become ghettoised into autobiographical realism because publishers are reluctant to publish postmodernist or formally experimental writing by

African American writers.[69] Moving on from Bourdieu's point about the absence of attention to form in the popular aesthetic, Gee makes the important point that questions of style and form are *ignored* in reviewers' assessments of women's fiction. Clearly this is something that happened in reviewers and critics' responses to *The Diaries* and the speculative fiction. *The Diaries* were read, as we have already seen, as marking a welcome, if somewhat naïve return to realism once Lessing's authorship was acknowledged; certain volumes of *Canopus* were merely seen as dull and verbose.

Absence of stylistic experimentalism, or 'the formal', does not, however, always accompany the equation of the authorial persona with the narrator. Where the 'absence' of style or form is a feature of the popular, the conflation of author and narrator (and the concomitant commodification of authenticity) tends to happen more in assessments of 'literary' fiction. As Lisa Appignanesi explains, it is often easier to resist the call for and constraints of authenticity when writing popular commercial fiction. She explains her decision to write in popular genres in precisely these terms: 'one of the differences between literary and popular fiction ... is this: that in literary fiction writers seek an authentic voice. I on the other hand, write in order to play out a masquerade.'[70] It is striking that pseudonymous publication is often associated with 'serious' writers 'slumming it' in genre fiction, as if it provides an escape from the constraints of writing within the framework of authenticity and the limitations of 'writing from experience'.

By making Janna a prolific author, who apparently writes serious academic books and romantic fiction as well as the diary we are reading (which also, of course, is a biography or memoir of Maudie Fowler), Lessing attempts to refuse distinctions between the popular and the dominant aesthetic. She also points out how gendered those distinctions are and how heavily they are policed by commercial literary culture. For Janna, this is all writing and it is all work. Those often unvalued genres associated with women, such as romantic fiction, the diary and the autobiography, may have more to say about women's lives and work, more that is real, in fact, than the kinds of realism readers might expect from an elderly woman writer such as Doris Lessing. Lessing points out the things that the mode of literary realism tends to exclude (for example the body, the abject, the aging process, domestic and emotional labour of many kinds). In doing so, she makes us rethink realism as a transparently authentic mode of expression appropriate for elderly women writers' reproduction of their lives. With almost flagrant exaggeration, Lessing seems to be saying: 'If you want realism then this is what it means for countless elderly women.' It makes for a disturbing read.

The strategies Lessing has used in the content, form and publication of *The Diaries of Jane Somers* are intimately connected in order to ask pertinent questions about authorship, commercial literary culture, aging and gender. In the preface to the *Diaries* Lessing recounts that when asked why there had been so little promotion of the first novel, the American publisher responded that 'there was nothing to promote, no "personality", no photograph, no story' (8). The Jane Somers hoax allowed Lessing to cross the borders of the authorial persona and voice; in doing so she was at the forefront of an increasing body of work by both writers and critics that examines the relationship between race, nation, gender, authorship and commercial literary culture. In setting up the hoax, Lessing contends that the cult of the celebrity author is in fact profoundly gendered and ageist, pushing older women writers towards the repetitious reproduction of realist novels that sit comfortably with readers' expectations.

The voice of terror in *The Good Terrorist*

Questions of voice were even more to the fore in reactions to Lessing's 1985 novel, *The Good Terrorist*. The novel is told from the perspective of Alice Mellings, a member of a Communist splinter group known as the Communist Centre Union (CCU). At the beginning of the novel she and other group members and hangers-on occupy a house that has been scheduled for demolition and Alice gradually makes it habitable. She negotiates with the authorities to restore the utilities, clears rubbish from the garden and cement from the toilets, and buries pails of excrement that have been left upstairs. The first half of the novel is an oddly pleasurable account of her slow renovation of the house and her role as quasi-mother to its 'family' of occupants. With the focus on restoring order and cleanliness from chaos and filth, the book makes many of the same points as *The Diaries* about the invisibility of women's domestic and emotional labour. However, the flip side of Alice's personality is capable of rage and violence against her mother and father (she steals from both and commits destructive acts against their homes); as the novel draws towards its ending the group to which she belongs, having previously been involved in nothing more disturbing than demonstrations, protests and spray-painting slogans, builds a bomb and explodes it outside a hotel in central London, as an act of solidarity with the IRA.

Lessing said that the novel grew out of listening to reporting of the bombing of Harrods in December 1983:

> Here the media reported it to sound as if it was the work of amateurs. I started to think, what kind of amateurs could they be? I got completely fascinated by this line of thought. Also, I happened to be in Ireland when they bumped off Mountbatten. I was just across the water from where it happened, and all the little boys, aged about 10 to 15, were rushing about, delighted, because of course they admire the I. R. A. I thought how easy it would be for a kid, not really knowing what he or she was doing, to drift into a terrorist group.[71]

The CCU's relations with the IRA are shady throughout the text. Two of the characters travel to Dublin and make overtures, offering their services to the Republican cause, but are rebuffed. It is implied that the CCU is viewed as jejune by a highly professionalised network of IRA and Russian operatives dealing in guns and drugs, who are themselves the subjects of surveillance by the British secret service. When the bomb explodes, the IRA repudiates the act supposedly committed in their name.

Undoubtedly relations between Britain and Northern Ireland around the time of the novel's publication were poor.[72] The Prevention of Terrorism Act of 1974 proscribed the IRA in Britain, allowed the exclusion from Britain of those suspected of involvement in terrorism and permitted arrest without warrant for seven days with the agreement of the Secretary of State. The Act was renewed each year and made permanent in 1988. The hunger strike of 1981 in the Maze prison aimed to reintroduce the 'political' status of Republican prisoners and generated increased publicity and sympathy for the Republican cause. The ill-fated Northern Ireland Assembly of 1982–86 attempted to introduce 'rolling devolution' to replace British direct rule of Northern Ireland. In 1985, the year *The Good Terrorist* was published, the Anglo-Irish Agreement introduced a role for the Republic of Ireland in Northern Irish affairs.[73] Memories of the Troubles are clearly still of significance to Lessing. In October 2007 she was quoted around the world after an interview in the Spanish newspaper, *El Pais*, in which she remarked:

> September 11 was terrible, but if one goes back over the history of the IRA, what happened to the Americans wasn't that terrible. Some Americans will think I'm crazy. Many people died, two prominent buildings fell, but it was neither as terrible nor as extraordinary as they think. They're a very naive people, or they pretend to be. Do you know what people forget? That the IRA attacked with bombs against our Government. It killed several people while a Conservative [party conference] was being held and in which the prime minister, Margaret Thatcher, was attending. People forget.[74]

However, it is certainly the case that these political contexts are merely implicit, if not invisible in the novel. Indeed some critics felt that the novel demonstrated a tendency to explain political activism and the move towards terrorist activity in primarily psychological terms. Alice is in a close relationship with Jaspar that is characterised by a cycle of bullying, dependency and intermittent threats of violence. The relationship is not sexual – Jaspar is homosexual – and Alice denies her own sexual needs; is Lessing making a crude link between sexual frustration and its expression in violent direct action? Could such a creative decision on Lessing's part constitute a denial of history? Margaret Scanlan argues that Lessing makes 'a political subject very nearly apolitical' and continues: 'Lessing inserts her novel into a contemporary discourse about terrorism that Edward Said has analyzed perceptively ... If we are terrified enough, the argument goes, we do not ask questions about the public causes of terrorism or about the measures our government adopts for stamping it out.'[75]

Other responses to the novel at the time it appeared were mixed, with many reviewers disturbed by Lessing's apparent drift towards conservatism and her repudiation of the Left. Walter Goodman, writing in *The New York Times*, felt that the book 'sounds like an old radical's revenge on the new radicals'.[76] Denis Donoghue remarked that the novel was 'bound to give comfort to the middle classes ... bourgeois liberalism is safe if these are the only opponents it has to face'.[77] In a review in *The Globe and Mail* Carole Corbeil claimed that Lessing was 'belatedly scrambling to get into the neo-con pantheon'.[78] Deirdre Levinson, writing in *The Nation*, was one of the most negative, commenting that 'this book may come as a shock to those who remember Lessing as a champion of the radical young' and concluding that 'while her animus against the left is now so well established, no work of hers to date so exclusively proclaims it'.[79] As Clare Hanson suggests, the reviews seem to believe that 'in this novel Lessing has given up: the ex-radical has sunk into the clichés of suburban fascism ... Such critics view Lessing's presentation of cliché-ridden (and driven) Alice Mellings ... as by definition an *attack* on Alice, and see Lessing as endorsing the opinions of Alice's mother.'[80] The apparent shift in Lessing's political sympathies was not the only problem, however. Many reviewers found Alice difficult to care about or like[81] and, of more (but related) importance for my argument here, found the style and voice of the novel difficult to take.

The review in *The Nation* identified a 'pervasive contempt in the narrative voice [which] makes it plain that Lessing is angry too' and continues, 'such authorial anger holds no brief for a complicated point of view, nor for painstaking, not to say complex, characterisation'.[82] Walter Goodman concluded his review with the comment: 'it is easy to understand that today's aspiring terrorists might win the attention of a writer who has been fascinated with radical politics for so much of her career. But Miss Lessing hasn't found the form or the voice for the task.'[83] At greater length, Denis Donoghue argues as follows:

> Mrs. Lessing is not a stylist. Perhaps because she hasn't decided whether words can be trusted or not she is sullen in their company ... Sometimes Mrs. Lessing treats words as servants, and finds that servants so treated respond with ill will. Sometimes she writes as if to imply that reality best inscribes itself by remaining indifferent to the blandishments of eloquence. Mostly, her style is a prose without qualities, as if it refused to consort with the corrupt glory of Shakespeare's tongue. The words on the page are there to be seen through, not regarded. They seem to want to be rid of themselves even before their sentences come to the ordinary gratification of ending. In 'The Good Terrorist' the pervading style is insistently drab, presumably in keeping with the dreariness of the life it depicts.[84]

Yet rather than merely making use of the supposedly transparent qualities of the realist mode, the text is extremely self-conscious about different styles and voices, as Margaret Scanlan notes. At one level, this is a simple matter of Alice being alert to the assumed accents of many of her fellow group members and conspirators. While some of them acquire middle-class accents that are clearly too perfect to be original, others self-consciously assume working-class regional accents, whether 'pretty Cockney' or 'modelled on Coronation Street'.[85] Alice judges that she is the only person to speak in her 'own voice, unmodified' (30). The power of voice as part of a panoply of rhetorical strategies to achieve certain political aims is also acknowledged. When addressing meetings, Jasper has a voice of 'desperate, ecstatic seriousness' (236), which contrasts with Pat's 'low-key, humorous, informative' style (238). Scanlan argues that the deliberate reference to speech differences in the novel is part of its attempt to ask questions about freedom, speech and power. She claims that the novel is 'an object lesson in the problematic relation between novelists and terrorists, a relationship grounded in a shared anxiety about the efficacy, the power and clarity, of language'.[86] What makes people move from what she calls 'verbal activism' to the belief that only violent action is effective? What generates the sense of 'absolute disillusion [sic.] with language that terrorists embody'?[87]

Despite noting Alice's concern with voice throughout the novel, Scanlan does not extend this analysis to the voice of the narrator and concludes that the text is 'reactionary in its implied politics of quietism and complicity with power'.[88] In fact, the flat, sometimes apparently condemnatory voice of the narrator (in the final paragraph the narrator famously refers to Alice as a 'poor baby' (397)), with its supposedly clear rejection of Left activism as childish, pointless and potentially dangerous, is not as straightforward as it seems. More recently, in the context of the rise of 'Islamic terrorism' and 'the War on Terror', the novel (and its voices) have been receiving more attention and reactions have been more positive. Writing in 2005 after the 7/7 bombings in London, Jane Rogers writes:

> The media image of a terrorist is shark-like in its simplicity – which is why it's terrifying ... yet such shark-people are rare, as Lessing shows us; her terrorists are contaminated by the muddle of being human ... this is not to suggest for a moment that Lessing demands sympathy for her characters ... it is a witty and furious book, angry at human stupidity and destructiveness, both within the system and without. It shows us people who commit an evil act and it shows how that evil springs out of our own society. It connects us to it, while condemning it. It makes any kind of complacency impossible.[89]

According to Rogers, the novel's strength is that it refuses to construct easy distinctions between the reader and narrator on the one side and the terrorist 'other' on the other; I would argue that by occupying the strange 'no man's land' of free-indirect discourse, which hovers between the voice of the protagonist and the voice of an omniscient narrator, Lessing implicates us in Alice's thought processes. While she is at times the 'poor baby' we can view from the outside, we are also intimately caught up in her experience and her way of thinking. Jeannette King comments as follows: 'the reader is thus interpellated into a reading position in which he or she cannot help share Alice's desires for change and improvement … is the reader then expected to share her desires for political change, drawn inexorably along the path of anticipation which climaxes in the bombing, so that we become in a sense co-conspirators?' She continues: 'There is no easy, comfortable position for the reader to adopt, either of detachment or of close identification.'[90]

As David Punter remarks when discussing *The Good Terrorist*: 'What is not shirked … is that parts of ourselves, as readers, as social beings, as terrorists, may be bound up in these liminal depictions. It is this admission of involvement which saves Lessing's text from … the inevitability of complicity, the feeling of voyeurism, the colouring of the salacious.' He continues: 'It is, seemingly paradoxically, the case that while we continue to depict the terrorist as uncompromisingly "out there" … we remain at the mercy of our own projections, always running the risk of revelling in a fear which we can justify as representative of a State legal system "in terror".'[91] The refusal to view terrorism as 'other' is central to much recent work on postcoloniality and terrorism. In 'Postcolonial Writing and Terror', Elleke Boehmer argues that 'the modern and imperialist state in fact solicits the terror through which it constitutes its authority'; she continues: 'in as much as terror has been the medium of the modern state and the modern imperium, terror has equally been the site for the critique of the modern state and imperium. To an extent it has *had to be* the site of the critique of the modern state. Under prevailing conditions of sovereignty other sites and other techniques have been rendered either unavailable or ineffective.'[92] Modernity, empire and terrorism are, according to this logic, mutually implicated. *The Good Terrorist*'s oxymoronic title is pertinent: it encapsulates the ways in which the book makes it difficult to view Alice's implication in terrorist activity as something alien from the modern, supposedly civilised state. That state has its casualties, but they are not people like Alice (who are in fact sustained by their ability to manipulate civil society and sources of welfare support). The real victims are characters like Jim, Philip, Faye and Monica, who, for a variety of reasons – racism, poor education, mental illness, homelessness – are the detritus of modern civic society. These individuals are all ignored, destroyed or killed during the novel: Jim disappears after being accused of robbing Alice's father when she was, in fact, responsible; Philip is involved in a fatal accident on a building site; Faye attempts suicide once and then deliberately times the car bomb wrongly, so that she is killed in the blast; Monica disappears from the text after failing to find a home. Their fate is hardly mourned and apparently adjacent to the main concerns of the novel when it is actually central. Rather than suggesting that terrorism represents disillusionment with language, Lessing's analysis of the voices and actions of terrorism in this novel suggests that terror in *The Good Terrorist* becomes, as Boehmer puts it, 'the site for the critique of the modern state and imperium'.[93]

In her essay on *The Good Terrorist* Scanlan returns to one of Lessing's earliest statements about the importance of the authorial voice – published in 1957 – and argues that in her later work, Lessing loses trust in what she had called the 'small personal voice' of the novelist talking as one individual to another. She suggests that in the *Canopus* series Lessing's style becomes increasingly 'anonymous … colourless, abstract, pompous'.[94] Like Scanlan, Clare Hanson also refers to a 'loss of faith … in voice'; she argues that 'it is, surely, quite missing the point to see the drabness as the symptom of authorial laziness' and views it, instead, as symptomatic of a postmodernist challenge to the 'authority of identity and the identity of the author'.[95] It is certainly the case that in her work in this period, Lessing tests out in various different ways the status, legitimacy and effects of different kinds of narrative and authorial voices. Her postcolonial feminist SF constructs a 'creolised' (to borrow from

Brah) parody of colonial rhetoric in order to defamiliarise the familiar imperialist narratives of science fiction and suggest alternative ways of voicing new worlds. The Jane Somers hoax allowed Lessing to cross the borders of the authorial persona and voice; in doing so she was at the forefront of an increasing body of work by both writers and critics that examines the relationship between race, nation, gender, authorship and commercial literary culture. In *The Good Terrorist* Lessing provides the most searching examination of the implication of modern society in the terrorist voice. In 'The Small Personal Voice', Lessing claimed that 'words, it seems, can no longer be used simply and naturally. All the great words like love, hate; life, death; loyalty, treachery; contain their opposite meanings and half a dozen shades of dubious implication.'[96] Her work in the early to mid 1980s, despite its apparently vast differences in mode, genre and subject, can be viewed as a self-conscious experimentation with the authority of voice.

5

Writing in a minor key: Doris Lessing's late-twentieth-century fiction

Doris Lessing's late-twentieth-century fiction has often provoked and discomfited. Some readers of *The Fifth Child* (1988), its sequel *Ben, in the World* (2000) and Lessing's 1999 novel *Mara and Dann* were disturbed by her appropriation of racially marked stereotypes of the animal, the primitive and the atavistic. Such imagery has controversial implications in relation to ideas about 'race' and nation. A secondary and related concern for readers surrounds the success or otherwise of Lessing's choices of genre and narrative technique; Lessing deploys what might be termed the 'minor' genres of urban gothic, picaresque and disaster narrative in her late-twentieth-century work in unfamiliar and disturbing ways. Certainly, genre and 'race' are connected issues in Lessing's work, and it is only when those connections are understood that we can make an assessment of this fiction and understand Lessing's attack on dominant cultural and ideological formations in the late twentieth century. This attack is a clear response to the cultural climate of the period in which the novels were written, a climate in which 'race' issues were of increasing concern.

The Story of General Dann (2005) is a sequel to *Mara and Dann*. Both novels revise our conception of world geography or cartography in their founding premise, which is that an ice-age has reshaped the map of the globe by obscuring the 'first' world. Moreover, the idea of the sequel suggests a particular kind of interest in repetition and revision. Lessing again plays with our expectations about genre, transforming the conventions of speculative fiction and, more particularly, post-apocalyptic writing, which Rosenfeld states is 'one of the four main categories of future history' and defines as 'a tale of the struggle to return to civilisation'.[1] *General Dann* suggests the radical implications of climate change for human social, cultural and personal identities. It draws on the idea of the acquisition of knowledge through palimpsestic accretion rather than the preservation of logos and points towards Lessing's growing interest in memory, life writing and history in her work since 2000, which will be discussed in chapter 6.

In analysing Lessing's late-twentieth-century 'fabular' fictions in relation to ideas about genre and 'race', Gilles Deleuze and Felix Guattari's discussion of 'minor' literature proves instructive. Deleuze and Guattari define minor literature as exhibiting three main characteristics: 'the deterritorialization of language, the connection of the individual to a political immediacy, and the collective assemblage of enunciation'.[2] Thus, minor literature has a partial relation to nationality both linguistically and, I will argue, generically. The 'social milieu'[3] is not merely background or context for the individual protagonist or author; rather, her relation to that context is directly, explicitly political. The concept of the author as 'master' of the text or gifted individual is replaced by a 'collective, and even revolutionary, enunciation'.[4] Of particular relevance to Lessing's late-twentieth-century fiction is the conception of 'becoming animal', which constitutes an '*absolute deterritorialization* ... an immobile voyage'.[5] Deleuze and Guattari suggest that in Kafka's work the 'becoming-human of the animal and the becoming-animal of the human' are part of a 'single circuit'[6] that deliberately resists metaphoricity, symbolism and allegory. This attempt to block the impulse to read the human/animal metaphorically is clearly related to the resistance of the territoriality of genre in Lessing's late-twentieth-century fiction. When reading this work, we are unable to secure or anchor our response to identity in terms of the well-worn distinction between the animal and the human; we are equally unable to find a safe home in familiar genres.

Lessing's resistance to territoriality is the overriding concern of her 1987 collection of four short essays, *Prisons we Choose to Live Inside*. In this volume Lessing writes about the relationship between the individual and the group. Despite the emphasis in Western culture on the idea of 'the lonesome individualist who overturns conformity',[7] the individual's need to feel part of a group is extremely powerful and the different ways in which group identity and psychology work are well understood by those in power. If, as she suggests, the establishment continually makes use of such knowledge (for example, that the majority of individuals will eventually give in to group pressure and form consensus) for its own ends, then ordinary individuals have the right to be made aware of how the dynamics of group interaction function: this is the aim of the book. Lessing defines the group not merely in terms of politics or religion, but focuses (not surprisingly) on more nebulous groups such as the literary establishment. Here she refers back to the Jane Somers hoax and the notion of literary culture as a kind of 'prison' which, as we saw in the last chapter, packages and consumes authorial identity. She also (crucially for my argument here) relates the idea of the group to nationalism: 'Nearly all the pressures from outside are in terms of group beliefs, group needs, national needs, patriotism and the demands of local loyalties, such as to your city and to local groups of all kinds' (55). To make individuals aware of the influence of group pressure is antithetically opposed to celebration of national identity and culture because, as Lessing puts it, 'passionate loyalty and subjection to group pressure is what every state relies on' (60). Lessing's attempt to make her readers aware of the prison, or group mind, inside which they live can be mapped onto Deleuze and Guattari's stress on deterritorialisation, or escape from boundaries, whether territorial, national or generic.

Although its disturbing qualities were often noted, *The Fifth Child* was generally well received. Lessing's blend of elements of fantasy, horror, fable and fairy-tale within the realist fabric and framework of the text was generally seen as successful and as an explanation for 'the visceral response the novel has engendered'.[8] Those who admired the play with generic convention also appreciated the text's ambiguous treatment of Ben's 'difference'. Throughout the text, Harriet, Ben's mother, seeks to explain his behaviour in terms of the animal, the primitive and the atavistic, suggesting that he may be an alien, goblin, troll or monstrous changeling. Most significantly, Harriet repeatedly returns to the interpretation of Ben as a Neanderthal genetic throwback.

Despite praise for the novel, many critics saw its message as profoundly conservative and potentially racist. Louise Yelin, for example, argues that in representing Ben as a throwback Lessing evokes the threat of the 'enemy within' or racial 'other'. She links this process of racial 'othering' to contemporary British politics, particularly to the increasingly racist elements of British Conservative Party ideology during Margaret Thatcher's governments of the 1980s, which made use, she suggests, of the figure of 'the enemy within'.[9] Yelin concludes that Ben's attacks on Harriet represent an alien invasion of the white British motherland by black people: 'In the national narrative that unfolds in *The Fifth Child*, the alien invader, a version of the enemy within, is Ben – that is, the discursive construction of Ben's difference reproduces the discursive construction of racial difference common to Powellite "new racism" and Thatcherite ideology'.[10] Enoch Powell was a Conservative Member of Parliament famous for his 'rivers of blood' speech of 1968, in which he argued that infiltration of white British culture by non-white peoples in the post-Second World War period would inevitably produce social tension and ultimately violence. Enoch Powell gave his speech on 20 April 1968 to the Annual General Meeting of the West Midlands Area Conservative Association. He spoke of the future of 'race-relations' in Britain thus: 'As I look ahead, I am filled with foreboding; like the Roman, I seem to see "the River Tiber foaming with much blood".' The speech was substantially quoted in the *Birmingham Post* on 22 April 1968. Powell subsequently lost his position as shadow cabinet minister under the leadership of Edward Heath.[11] Although Yelin conflates two very different periods in Conservative Party politics and ideology (the 1960s and the 1980s), it is the case that in the 1980s many commentators saw rioting and social unrest in inner-city areas of London, Bristol, Liverpool and Birmingham as evidence of the accuracy of Powell's prophecy rather than a legitimate response to deindustrialisation, escalating unemployment and social deprivation.

Yelin's argument constructs *The Fifth Child* as one of a number of texts that establish Lessing's 'exclusionary concept of national identity'.[12] (See also her discussion of *In Pursuit of the English*, discussed in chapter 1.) Yet this reading of the novel as profoundly racist is possible only because she downplays the generic complexity and ambivalence of narrative perspective in the text. In this respect, Yelin's negative assessment of *The Fifth Child* more closely resembles critical opinion about Lessing's sequel, *Ben, in the World*, which is more often seen as inferior. Michiko Kakutani argues that whereas the first novel worked because it 'created a perfect balance between naturalistic detail and fablelike allegory' the sequel is an artistic failure because it 'reads entirely like a fairy-tale, and a not very compelling one at that'.[13] Other reviewers have commented negatively on the novel's fabular, allegorical and picaresque qualities and have doubted the wisdom of switching the point of view to Ben himself.[14] Kakutani describes the novel as exhibiting a 'primitive, knee-jerk brand of story-telling'.[15]

The negative response to Lessing's choices of genre, style and narrative technique in *Ben, In the World* corresponds with judgements about the novel's treatment of issues of 'race'. Alex Clark writes: 'We are given to understand, over and over again, that Ben does in fact belong to a branch of the species that has long since died out'.[16] Kakutani suggests that the novel's animalistic descriptions of Ben 'make him out to be some sort of generic creature, endowed with only the most instinctual reactions and responses, and Ms. [sic.] Lessing does nothing to give him a discernible personality'.[17] The concern here is that Lessing's style, technique and generic choices encourage readers to objectify Ben and position him as animal, non-human and unfathomably 'other' in ways that are subtly and disturbingly racially coded.

Responses to *Mara and Dann*, published the year before *Ben, In the World*, suggest similar anxieties about both form and content. Many reviewers note the fairy-tale or fabular plot of orphaned siblings who make a long journey to safety through trials and tribulations.[18] The consensus seems to be that the novel is a failure as science fiction, either because of its 'iffy technology',[19] or the 'clichéd' message about twentieth-century industrialised culture's reliance on technology and indifference to the environment and global warming.[20] The suggestion persists that Lessing never quite manages to jettison her realist roots, which remain as unhappy traces of unrealised characters and unfortunately clumsy style. She would have been better off sticking to 'her greatest strength as a writer: her ability to dissect the vacillations and delusions of 20th-century people living in a 20th-century world'.[21]

The 'tribal' treatment of character in the novel and its implicit racial marking of physical difference also provoke comment. Kakutani points out that 'virtually all the bad people Mara and Dann meet are short, thick and ugly; virtually all the good people they meet are tall, thin and gracious ... the minor characters in the novels are crude types, not individuals'.[22] Wagner also remarks on the 'tribal' nature of difference in the world of Ifrik: 'Mara and Dann, dark-haired, brown-skinned Mahondis, move northwards, encountering different tribes along the way; the controlling, sybaritic Hadrons; the clone-like, sinister Hennes; the pale-skinned Albs, who claim their origin in the frozen continent of Yerrup'.[23] At its most extreme, a tribe of look-alikes represents, according to Upchurch, one of a number of 'menacing racial varieties'.[24] This apparently 'lazy' characterisation is most apparent in what is believed to be the swift recourse to the idea of the tribe as a way of grouping and naming people in the novel.

The ease with which some readers have made these three texts occupy racist positions results from a misreading of what Lessing has attempted in each case in terms of genre and narrative perspective. These novels make much more sense if they are seen as 'minor' genres which ultimately critique racist narrative. As Deleuze and Guattari suggest: 'A minor literature doesn't come from a minor language; it is rather that which a minority constructs within a major language',[25] or to rephrase, 'what a minor genre constructs within the territory of a major one'. Lessing utilises characteristics of urban gothic in *The Fifth Child*; she uses the picaresque tradition in *Ben, In the World*; and she works in the sub-genre of the disaster narrative in *Mara and Dann*.

The representation of Ben in *The Fifth Child* is, as Yelin suggests, intimately related to the decade of the 1980s and what that signified in British culture. However, rather than evoking a white British motherland threatened by 'the enemy within' in order to construct an 'exclusionary concept of national identity',[26] Lessing attempts something rather different: something that closely resembles what has come to be known as the urban gothic. According to Roger Luckhurst, in his account of 'London gothic', British gothic fiction in the late 1980s and 1990s began to respond in new ways to ideas of the metropolitan and the urban, creating 'a newly Gothicized apprehension of London'.[27] Gothic fiction of the last two decades of the twentieth century, he argues, responds to debates over how to govern London that occurred in this period. During the 1980s the abolition of ILEA (the Inner London Education Authority) and the GLC (Greater London Council), the principal local authority for London, was a key part of a Conservative ideological agenda that sought to remove conflict with central government and eradicate challenges from implicitly subversive (and Left-leaning) local government. Luckhurst claims that we can witness the 'deliberate evisceration of London's democratic public sphere marked out on the physical landscape of the city' and also read it in the period's gothic fiction.[28] Placing *The Fifth Child* in this context allows us to interpret it as a family 'romance' where the gothic convention of the return of the repressed is deliberately deployed in order to generate a critique of 1980s Conservative Britain and its defensive focus on family values and fear of inner-city social unrest. Margaret Thatcher famously denied the existence of such a thing as 'society', suggesting that there were no larger social groups than the family.[29] In this way, she rejected any larger-scale explanation for social problems that sought to find answers in the consequences of unemployment and inner-city deprivation rather than in individual and family breakdown.

At the opening of the novel we are told that when Harriet and David met, they both recognised something familiar in the other: 'conservative, old-fashioned, not to say obsolescent; timid, hard to please … they defended a stubbornly held view of themselves, which was that they were ordinary and in the right of it, should not be criticised for emotional fastidiousness, abstemiousness, just because these were unfashionable qualities'.[30] The use of the word 'conservative' here primarily suggests a fundamental timidity and traditionalism rather than any specific political position, but the core values of the couple are, more importantly, positioned as *defensive*. Specifically, they are defensive of their normality and typicality in their adherence to family values and traditional sexual propriety during the 1960s (when the novel opens), a decade where such values were being challenged. The couple feel similarly 'abstemious' about establishing their home in London: 'Not possible to find the kind of house they wanted, for the life they wanted, in London. Anyway, they were not sure London was what they needed – no, it wasn't, they would prefer a smallish town with an atmosphere of its own' (13). Given that the couple represent family and suburban commuter values it is not surprising (given that this is a gothic novel) that their fifth child is born with the opposite inclinations: he has an aggressively animalistic, violent and physical nature, coupled with, as he gets older, an affiliation to youthful gang or street culture that represents an anti-family and stereotypically urban stance: 'These days the local newspapers were full of news of muggings, hold-ups, break-ins. Sometimes this gang, Ben among them, did not come into the Lovatts' house for a whole day, two days, three' (147). Ben represents everything the couple repudiate in their rejection of the urban: sexuality, violence, the city, the gang and the animal.

The reader necessarily shares Harriet's fear of Ben and her near inability to define him as human, but identification with Harriet is only ever partial. The text encourages readers to reach beyond surface meanings and construct allegorical ones, but it then deconstructs those allegories so that, as Collins and Wilson suggest, 'the novella actually undermines its own legitimizing allegorical dimension and that of other legitimizing narratives'.[31] This happens partly as a consequence of what Collins and Wilson term 'genre-boundary trespass'[32] and partly through the clever use of narrative perspective. In other words, if readers are encouraged by Harriet to interpret Ben as a genetic throwback to a more 'primitive race', they are also encouraged to question this interpretation by the novel's textual and generic strategies of 'deterritorialisation' of genre. Although the narration is in the third person the point of view is closely but not exclusively aligned with Harriet's; this shifting focalisation both encourages and resists the complete identification of the reader with Harriet. Throughout the text we see the explanations that various characters offer for Ben's 'difference' as powerful but ultimately insufficient. This involvement of our most as well as our least reactionary responses is, I believe, one of the strengths of Lessing's use of genre and one of the ways in which the novel makes very uncomfortable reading. Luckhurst argues that the fiction he terms London or urban gothic cannot be described as a 'coherent political analysis of London ills'; it can just as easily create 'nostalgia for those very spaces of unregulated violence or disorderly conduct'.[33] In other words, we might feel an almost pleasurable revulsion when Ben is found eating raw meat because we feel (temporarily at least) able to position him as securely 'other' and animal. The serious engagement with deeply disturbing beliefs is characteristic of the gothic genre and explains why critics such as Yelin can interpret *The Fifth Child* as endorsing a racist agenda. As David Punter remarked when discussing *The Good Terrorist*: 'What is not shirked … is that parts of ourselves, as readers, as social beings, as terrorists, may be bound up in these liminal depictions. It is this admission of involvement which saves Lessing's text from … the inevitability of complicity, the feeling of voyeurism, the colouring of the salacious'.[34] In other words, because we have been forced to share Harriet's response to Ben we are unable to repudiate it prematurely. We have to acknowledge how we are implicated in fear of difference and thus come to understand this fear and question it.

Harriet's decision to rescue Ben from the institution where he has been incarcerated (after an unspoken family agreement made without her knowledge) demonstrates that she is unable literally to expel Ben from the family, the human and the suburban: she is unable to make him 'become animal'. At the point where she decides to take him home, she thinks that 'he looked more ordinary [read 'human'] than she had ever seen him' (100). Becoming human – becoming animal is, as Deleuze and Guattari suggest, a 'single circuit'.[35] In returning him to the family she takes his place as scapegoat and endures the resentment and blame (but also the pity) of her husband and children (and the reader). This mobility in the figure of the 'other' within the family unit is more disturbing than the simple fear of Ben. Who might be rejected next? The text's strategies thus involve a more complex critique of family values and the place of the mother within them than is acknowledged if we interpret it as simply racist in its depiction of Ben.

The unpopularity of *Ben, In the World* when compared with *The Fifth Child* is partly a result of the fact that contemporary readers did not recognise Lessing's intentions in deploying elements of the picaresque in the text. Like many writers before her, she uses Ben, her picaro figure, as a way to comment on a society experiencing intense social upheaval. As Angela Hague remarks, the critical consensus is that: 'picaresque literature flourishes when a society is in a state of flux'.[36] Her article analyses a number of 1950s' novelists who have been retrospectively grouped with the 'angry young men' movement and notes that their use of features of the picaresque novel is important in establishing their critical, 'outsider' stance on 1950s Britain. According to Hague, the typical hero of these novels and those of the picaresque tradition is a marginal figure, critical of society but unable to find a space outside it. Other important features are the emphasis on 'the material level of existence … where existence and subsistence are discussed in terms of "sordid facts, hunger, money" and a profusion of objects and details' and contemptuous attitudes towards art.[37] In the 1950s Lessing was aligned with many of the writers Hague discusses; as we saw in chapter 1, she contributed her well-known essay 'A Small Personal Voice' to the 1957 volume *Declaration*, which was associated with the 'angry' stance,[38] so perhaps it is not surprising that she might exhibit an interest in the possibilities of the picaresque, even if decades later.

If we examine how Lessing has deployed the features of the picaresque mentioned above in *Ben, In the World* we can see that her intention is to exaggerate them to the point where we are forced to ask a series of questions about the meaning of the distinction between the animal and the human. The picaro is a semi-outsider figure, but Ben's isolation is far more severe and his ability to survive by his wits and turn a series of exploitative situations to his advantage (another feature of the genre) far more in doubt. The emphasis on the material becomes, in this novel, a frequent detailing of Ben's animalistic urges for meat, violence and sex. Contempt for elite artforms and the idea that the picaro's own life *is* his artform is pushed to extremes when Ben is taken up by a film director, Alex, who imagines making a film about a Neanderthal in which Ben will star as himself: 'Alex was saying quietly to himself that Ben was not human, even if most of the time he behaved like one. And he was not animal. He was a throwback of some kind. If the company of ancient men were only a kind of animal how was it that Ben could live the life of human beings – well, for most of the time?'[39] The aim of *Ben, In the World* is satirical. Lessing uses Ben as a device to question how we define humanity and how we separate ourselves from the animal and the atavistic. Some, like Alex or the director of the research institute where Ben is imprisoned for the purpose of scientific experiment with other animals, attempt to quantify the difference between themselves and Ben as that between the primitive and the cultured or the animal and the human. This taxonomic attitude, Lessing implies, intensifies the racist attitudes that lie not far beneath the lip-service paid to diversity in contemporary Western industrialised cultures. The distinction between animal and human makes use of pseudo-Darwinian hierarchies or distinctions that position white masculinity at the apex of an evolutionary chain ascending from the apes to Africans (often figured as 'gorillas' and 'apes' or with ancient human ancestors, particularly Neanderthals) and finally to white European peoples. In collapsing such distinctions, Lessing also challenges the late-nineteenth-century positivist narrative that sanctioned colonisation. As Brickman suggests: 'the idea of "the primitive" and its network of associated meanings played a critical role as a central trope of colonialist discourse and its evolutionary approach to racial and cultural difference. The colonialist designation of conquered peoples as "primitive" was an attempt to cloak as scientifically respectable the domination of human beings considered as Europe's racial others'.[40]

If it is a feature of the picaresque novel to negotiate the opposition between nature and civilisation, *Ben, In the World* resembles other contemporary 'neo-picaresque' texts by women which exaggerate and parody the nature: culture opposition in order to demonstrate the fully cultural, indeed linguistic, construction of ideas of the natural, the animal and the freakish.[41] It is for this reason that, though often aligned with Ben's, the point of view in *Ben, In the World* is not confined to him as first-person narration as in many early picaresque texts. The narrator is thus able to demonstrate how those around Ben develop their perceptions of him and show how Ben acquires an understanding of himself through the responses of others. Indeed, the questionable reliability of perception in the novel extends to the 'objectivity' of the narrator's own voice, which is parodied through the humorous device of prolepsis.[42] To take just one example, we are told that Alfredo and Teresa had a strong understanding which 'ended in their marrying, some months in the future. So their story at least has a happy ending: things turned out well for them' (134). Lessing is here exaggerating to the point of ridicule the device of omniscience, associating our naïve belief in what the narrator tells us with the acceptance of 'common sense' judgements about Ben's difference from others and questioning both.

In *Mara and Dann,* Lessing returns to science fiction, a genre that Luckhurst argues underwent resurgence in the late 1990s. At this specific historical moment, he suggests, government rhetoric was focused on incorporating previously oppositional cultural industries such as avant-garde fine art and popular music into the work of the New Labour government. SF was one of the few genres (others are gothic and fantasy) that 'could still find spaces outside the general de-differentiation or "mainstreaming" effect sought by the strategy of cultural governance'.[43] One specific SF sub-genre he considers is the disaster narrative, which has always formed a significant part of the British SF tradition. Fredric Jameson argues that such narratives are often concerned with 'the canceled future of a vanished colonial and imperial destiny'.[44] What is striking about *Mara and Dann* is the way it attempts to rewrite the construction of an embattled but surviving England that is key to such classic English SF texts as *The Day of the Triffids* (1951) and *The Midwich Cuckoos* (1957). In this novel the ice-age that has completely redrawn the map of the world has obscured Europe, or 'Yerrup' (and presumably the rest of the industrialised West). The action takes place in 'Ifrik' (Africa), where drought is threatening all but the northern parts of the continent. In many disaster narratives there is a reversion to a folkloric, pastoral idyll associated by implication with reactionary class and race formations, or as Luckhurst suggests, a return to 'conservative narratives of belonging to some ancient tradition inhering in the land'.[45] Lessing alludes to this tradition at the novel's opening, where Mara and Dann are forced, as children, hurriedly to leave home with changed identities, for their own (and, it is strongly implied, their tribe's) protection. At this time Mara's main sense of the world around her is tribal: of her (superior) Mahondi People as opposed to the (inferior) Rock People. We are encouraged to believe throughout the novel that Mara and Dann are special, 'chosen' and being watched and kept for a unique destiny. Towards the end Mara and Dann's 'true' identities as Mahondi royalty are revealed. However, when urged to marry her brother Dann and form a new dynasty capable of ruling Ifrik when the ice finally retreats, Mara responds: '"I don't know why you are so anxious to rule Ifrik … It is a desert of dust and death below the River Towns"'.[46] Instead of gracefully and gratefully accepting their future, she and Dann run away and continue their journey north. The novel ends with them forming a small self-sufficient farm on the temperate northern coast, joined by several others from a number of different tribes or 'races'. Suggestively, Dann asks Mara a question that concludes the novel: '"Mara, tell me honestly, no truthfully, the real truth: when you wake up in the morning, isn't it the first thing you think of – how far you're going to go up today, one foot after another, another little bit of the way up Ifrik?"' (407). Mara admits that this is true. The novel's final emphasis on process rather than conclusions refuses a mythic narrative trajectory that should conclude with racial and class difference confirmed as absolute, hierarchical and bound up with a notion of nation and land.

Writing a sequel to *Mara and Dann*, as with *Ben, In the World*, allows Lessing to revise many of the expectations created by the first novel as well as to expose further some of the former text's (and the genre's) implications. The novel received mixed reviews. Some found it 'rambling and clumsy', the plot cumbersome and complicated and the style 'perfunctory'.[47] More favourable reviews noted the apocalyptic, fabular qualities of the book.[48] Geraldine Bedell, writing in *The Observer*, described the novel's 'unwieldy, apparently naïve' title as providing 'quite a lot of clues to what follows'. She continues: 'this is a meandering, episodic book, peopled by disconnected characters, told in pared-down, at times, almost perfunctory prose'. However, Bedell concludes that 'I think we have to assume that this is deliberate: the apparently uncrafted quality of the novel is crafted to mimic an oral storytelling tradition, reminiscent of ancient epics in which characters had more role than psychology … the book is a puzzle and a palimpsest.'[49] Bedell's insight into the palimpsestic quality of the novel is, I will argue, extremely important.

The novel is most obviously, like *Mara and Dann*, a disquisition on the effects of extreme climate change on human identity. Fiona Becket positions both books as 'postnatural fables' but argues that they fail to live up to their promise of deconstructing human involvement in environmental catastrophe:

> As we know, the postmodern (posthuman) fable decentres, therefore, displaces the human subject from the narrative of the familiar. Lessing's environmental fables (the Dann novels), while they foreground contingency and purposelessness are, however, or so it is argued here, strangely incapable of properly seeing through, properly completing, the (necessary) interrogation of human centrality. In a way which is determined by the form (even, the formula) of the Dann novels, there is the irresistible draw of the 'happily ever after' which everywhere undermines the radical potential of the Ifrik novels (as postnatural) in as much as they are poised to offer a critique of the complexities of human authority in relation to environmental catastrophe.[50]

In fact, *General Dann* precisely continues and expands on the first novel's 'interrogation of human centrality'. The very idea of sequel is bound up with the pleasures of repetition, but Lessing begins her novel with Mara's death, Dann's return to the Centre and a new landscape of water and humidity rather than drought and ice. The loss of Mara is important for the reader. Despite the title, the point of view of *Mara and Dann* is exclusively hers, focusing particularly on the intimate details of sexuality and reproduction that she contends with during her journey, as well as her relationship with her brother. This certainly serves to challenge the conservative and patriarchal focus of much speculative fiction and post-apocalyptic narrative in particular, addressing female rather than male experience and avoiding the clichéd focus on father–son relationships. More importantly, however, the 'sacrifice' of Mara in the sequel reinforces the first novel's focus on women's difference by having Mara die in childbirth. It also, at a stroke, attacks the reader's investment in the notion that the sequel particularly confirms the continuity of identity. Given her literal absence from the text, the reader is urged to look for Mara in her daughter, Tamar, who is 'like Mara, and like Dann too',[51] but this search for an inter-generational repetition of personality, or a notion of character as lineage, is also complicated and refused by the painful intensity with which Dann experiences it. Haunted by grief at Mara's death and obsessed with her memory, as a result Dann is almost unable to connect with Tamar and becomes completely dysfunctional for much of the text, existing in a drug-induced stupor.

The narrative 'arc' of the novel is dominated by return rather than departure and arrival. *Mara and Dann* ended with the rejection of the Centre and the establishment of the utopian community at the farm, but when *The Story of General Dann* begins Dann has returned to the Centre because the farm community has begun to fragment as a result of internal power struggles. Dann then makes a journey to see the ice cliffs of Yerrup, but returns once again. The ironically named 'Centre' is a magnet for refugees, who camp outside its walls and join the army that 'General' Dann is supposedly forming. In effect, the army's *raison d'etre* seems merely to be to give a purpose to those who join it. Not only is the Centre being overtaken by refugees, it is also slowly being flooded by melting ice so that much of it is under water. The novel concludes with the community leaving the Centre for the country of Tundra and with Tamar's vision of her life as '"moving from one bad dark place to a better – from the Farm to the Centre, and then to a good place … this is living happily ever after"' (281). This idealistic vision is challenged by the 'stupid' but ever-increasing threat of invasion and warfare that Griot and Dann discuss immediately after she has spoken.

During the course of the novel a discovery is made which offers the possibility of accessing all the lost knowledge of earlier civilisations. Griot finds a secret room in the Centre that contains a transparent capsule. In the capsule is a selection of literature from before the catastrophe. Scribes begin work on the process of translation and interpretation. This is the most important of a number of key images that Lessing uses in the novel to suggest to the reader that the palimpsestic text rather than the logos or myth of origin provides the key to interpretation. The concept of the palimpsest balances the idea of absence with presence, erasure with revelation. Literally, a manuscript that has been erased and written over again, the palimpsest bears textual traces of its history as visible evidence of change. In poststructuralist criticism the palimpsest is a marker of scepticism about the notion of origin and suggests the endless deferral of final and fixed meaning that lies at the heart of language.[52] Postcolonial critics find the concept 'a useful way of understanding the developing complexity of culture, as previous "inscriptions" are erased and overwritten, yet remain as traces within present consciousness. This confirms the dynamic, contestatory and dialogic nature of linguistic, geographic, and cultural space as it emerges in post-colonial experience'.[53] As was suggested in chapter 1, in relation to *In Pursuit of the English*, the palimpsest is undoubtedly an important motif in Lessing's work, not merely in relation to how she perceives the city, but also for identity and writing more widely.

Where many post-apocalyptic texts would conclude with the recovery and reinscription of past texts and the culture they evidence, Lessing allows the words in the Centre to be (apparently) lost. The capsule is shattered by the rising waters and the ancient texts are destroyed by exposure to the air. This could be a moment of intense nostalgia and is for Dann, but Lessing also gives us the rather different reaction of Griot, whose name in West African culture means a 'wise storyteller entrusted with relaying the history and genealogy of the tribe':[54]

> 'Damn, sir, what has been made can be made again', said Griot.
>
> 'And again, and again, and again', said Dann.
>
> He sat down at his table and Ali's, and watched the people all down the hall scurrying and scrabbling over the bits of browning paper.
>
> 'It's the again and again, Griot. I can never understand why you don't see it'.
>
> Griot sat down near Dann. 'Sir, you make things so hard for yourself'. (251)

Griot's determination to remake could imply a naïve faith in the human capacity to create anew, but it also questions whether anything is original enough to be genuinely lost, thus challenging

Dann's nostalgia for the past and respect for authenticity (or logos). In Tundra a College of Learning is established where the work of recovery of the past takes place. At the entrance there is a large wall on which is written:

> This great white expanse represents the area of knowledge of the Ancient World. The small black square in the lower right-hand corner represents the amount of knowledge we have. All visitors are asked to reflect for a few moments, asking themselves if they perhaps have information or learning which is not general, and which could be added to our common store. There was once, long ago, a shared culture covering the whole world: remember, we have only fragments of it. (272)

The idea of culture as the work of preservation, recovery and homogeneity ('a shared culture covering the whole world') is juxtaposed at the novel's end with an understanding of it as provisional, oral and local. Griot sings songs about Mara and Dann's adventures and Tamar's friends sing teasing songs about her inability to dance. In these songs, Lessing suggests, inevitably lie traces of the words and cultures that have gone before. It is impossible to reconstruct a complete version of the past because texts are fluid and interpretation is endless, but this also means that it is impossible to erase the influences and memories of pre-apocalyptic civilisations.

This is nowhere more apparent than in two quite different images of revision that dominate the novel: the map and the underwater city. When Dann travels to see the ice cliffs of Yerrup he finds two maps on an inn wall – one showing the Middle Sea when it was full of water and one showing how it is now. He finds the experience of 'reading' the maps difficult; it creates a sense of confusion and self-loss: 'But now, standing on land protruding from the Bottom sea that had once been deep under it, when the seabirds cried over the waves, and disappeared, that was how he felt: who was Dann? – standing here where ... [ellipsis original]' (58). The sensation of geological fluidity in this sentence enacts a process of subjective violation that Dann finds painful but also important. In allowing him to understand the haphazard creativity of millennia of climate change he is also made aware of the provisional, approximate nature of interpretation and of identity. Both the map and the self as palimpsest are forever unfinished, in process, marked by what went before but never static.

The second image, of the underwater city, is more negatively charged. Throughout the novel Dann is preoccupied by the fact that before the ice-age destroyed Europe the decision was taken to copy some of the most admired European cities in North Africa in order to preserve their architecture and culture. However, once the permafrost on which they were built began to melt they were all left deep under water. This attempt at preservation is riven by power struggles: '*each city wanted to be rebuilt in North Afrique … Some were richer than others. The rich ones succeeded*' (188). The image operates to suggest the futility of human ambition in the face of the forces of nature. It also, like the image of the texts in the Centre's shattered capsule, which were destroyed by contact with the air, suggests that nostalgic attempts at preservation and reconstruction are flawed by their failure to recognise that culture is never static and that the official rhetoric of what we might now call 'heritage management' is inevitably skewed in favour of those with the power to insist on their own preservation. Lessing's preference for the idea of reading and interpretation as palimpsestic accretion rather than the 'preservation of heritage' suggests a sceptical stance towards those narratives of national origin that are often implied in the genre of post-apocalyptic or disaster narrative. The recovery or preservation of a particular tribal, national or imperial myth becomes impossible in the world that Dann, Griot and Tamar inhabit. The novel ends with the threat of a pointless war in order to make clear Lessing's distrust of such myths and the harm they can do.

In deploying and disrupting the features of a number of what Deleuze and Guattari might term 'minor' literary genres, Lessing aimed to challenge the implicitly racist cultural constructs of the animal, the primitive and the tribe that were becoming significant in late-twentieth-century Britain. Her growing awareness that writers and readers can become imprisoned in the territory of particular genres is closely connected to her understanding in *Prisons* that dominant ideas (such as those of 'race' and 'nation') can also imprison those without the knowledge or power to challenge them. In the late twentieth century her writing offers a progressive challenge to realism as the 'majority' mode. As Gasiorek suggests: 'Lessing disrupts realist narrative modes from within and turns to other genres in her search for ways to mediate contemporary social life'.[55] In its rough, unresolved style, what Deleuze and Guattari term 'sobriety of language' rather than 'intensities, reversals and thickenings of it',[56] Hanson sees her work as typically postmodernist.[57] Lessing's periodic and deliberate choice of minor genres suggests a growing awareness that the formal strategies of 'expressive realism' can be aligned with reactionary positions that have attempted to silence and exclude the feminine and minority ethnic voices. (We can see this suspicion of realism in feminist and postcolonial challenges to conventional accounts of the 'rise of the novel'.) Lessing's movement in and out of realism (what Gasiorek terms an experimental realism rather than an outright rejection of it[58]) is an attempt not merely to raise issues about form, style and technique, but also to explore the political implications of certain generic and stylistic choices, particularly in relation to those issues that have dominated the late twentieth century and continue to dominate the twenty-first: 'race', nation and ethnicity.

As Lessing suggests in *Prisons*:

> I see writers, generally, in every country, as a unity, almost like an organism, which has been evolved by society as a means of examining itself. This 'organism' is different in different epochs and always changing … The organism must be expected to develop, to change, as society does. The organism is not conscious of itself as an organism, a whole, though I think it will soon be. The world is becoming one, and this enables us all to see our many different societies as aspects of a whole, and the parts of those societies shared by them all … I think that writers everywhere are aspects

> of each other, aspects of a function that has been evolved by society. (7–8)

Lessing's conception of the writer as part of a trans-national, evolving organism, whose function is to examine and criticise the world, reminds us of Deleuze and Guattari's conception of the author of minor literature as speaking in a 'collective, and even revolutionary, enunciation'.[59] As she continues writing in the twenty-first century, Lessing becomes fascinated with different ways of writing the past. In *General Dann* she moves away from the idea of the accurate preservation of history and culture towards a collective notion of cultures as composed, like the palimpsest, of traces of all that has gone before. In her work in the first decade of the twenty-first century, Lessing further refines and develops her thinking about the relationships between memory, history, narrative and identity.

6

Sweet dreams and rememories: narrating nation and identity

In her work since 2000, Doris Lessing is concerned with different ways of writing both personal and political histories. Although this is a preoccupation that goes back at least as far as *The Golden Notebook*, working on the two volumes of her autobiography, *Under My Skin* (published in 1994) and *Walking in the Shade* (1997), must have heightened her interest in the question of how to narrate the past. This question is also addressed in her 1995 novel *Love, Again*, in which Sarah Durham, a theatre producer, writes and produces a play based on the journals of a nineteenth-century mixed race Martiniquan musician and artist, Julie Vairon, who was a 'fallen woman' and social outcast. In 1992 Lessing had also published *African Laughter*, an account of four visits made to the new nation state of Zimbabwe. The situation there in the decades post-independence continued to concern her in 'The Jewel of Africa' (2003), an article for the *New York Review of Books* that was republished as 'The Tragedy of Zimbabwe' (2004).

In the author's note to her 2001 novel, *The Sweetest Dream*, she explained that she was not writing a third volume of her autobiography 'because of possible hurt to vulnerable people'. With these words she seemed to offer this novel as a substitute autobiography while simultaneously refusing that interpretation (she also stated that she had not 'novelised autobiography'). The novel was widely read as an attack on the political idealism of the 1960s that attempted to revise or rewrite the radicalism of the period. In 2007, Lessing published *The Cleft*, an account of a Roman senator's attempt to grapple with the unpleasant pre-history of humanity. Lessing's vision of the Clefts, a tribe who resemble women physiologically and reproduce parthenogenetically, who are disturbed by the sudden birth of 'monsters' or Squirts (physiologically male babies) makes for disturbing reading. However, the focus is again on how the Senator makes sense of and narrates human history in the context of the Roman empire.

Lessing's work in this period strongly suggests, as we saw in the last chapter in the discussion of *General Dann*, that official histories are flawed and imperfect. Apparently 'fictional' writings, Lessing implies, may be more fruitful than ostensibly factual ones in allowing both individuals and nations to make sense of their immediate and distant pasts. In her last work, *Alfred and Emily* (2008), Lessing embodies this idea in the very structure of the work. The book is divided into two halves. The first is speculative, imagining her parents' lives as if the First World War never happened; the second half is a memoir. In much of her work in this period Lessing returns to important preoccupations that are central in her writing: the Great War, her African childhood and girlhood, the impact of colonialism in Southern Africa and the emergence of African nation states after decolonisation.

In her writing in this period Lessing makes use of notions of city, home and memory that can be instructively compared with some of Toni Morrison's ideas in her novel *Beloved* (1987) and the essays 'Home' (1998) and 'The Site of Memory' (1990). Lessing revises the notion of 'home' so that it becomes capable of both recognising racial and national differences and moving outside them. She also interprets memory as productive for the individual and the nation only when it becomes, as Morrison would say, 'rememory': when it can acknowledge the importance of imagination in dealing with trauma and thus suggest the fluctuating, mobile status of identity. Similar ideas about home and memory are present in Lessing's fiction, essays and autobiography, indicating that her intention is to explore generic classification and blur the boundaries between different methods of writing personal and political history. In doing so she is attempting a manipulation of genre, one which challenges the way both individuals and nations narrate their pasts.

I want to begin by discussing Lessing's use of particular conceptions of the city and the home as a means of exploring connections between race, nation and identity. In her introductory essay, 'Home', in the collection *The House that Race Built,* Toni Morrison remarks:

> I have never lived, nor has any of us, in a world in which race did not matter. Such a world, one free of racial hierarchy, is usually imagined or described as dreamscape – Edenesque, utopian, so remote are the possibilities of its achievement. From Martin Luther King's hopeful language, to Doris Lessing's four-gated city, to Jean Toomer's 'American,' the race-free world has been posited as ideal, millennial, a condition possible only if accompanied by the Messiah or situated in a protected preserve – a wilderness park.
>
> But for the purposes of this talk and because of certain projects I am engaged in, I prefer to think of a-world-in-which-race-does-*not*-matter as something other than a theme park, or a failed and always-failing dream, or as the father's house of many rooms. I am thinking of it as home.[1]

In a series of metaphors, a world in which race does not matter becomes a gated city, a wilderness park, theme park or protected preserve with attendant implications of the fortress mentality. The fortress excludes precisely that (race) which is said 'not to matter', which of course means that race, despite its denial, is intrinsically part of the structure. Later in the essay, Morrison elucidates key questions that have dominated her work: 'How to be both free and situated; how to convert a racist house into a race-specific yet nonracist home. How to enunciate race while depriving it of its lethal cling.'[2] Her choice of Lessing's image of the four-gated city as a 'race-less' utopian dreamscape, which unknowingly contains precisely what it attempts to exclude, is interesting for a number of reasons. Lessing first uses this image of the city in her 1952 novel *Martha Quest*. In *Martha Quest* the four-gated city is clearly positioned as a naïve, idealistic day-dream. Martha repudiates race prejudice and recognises how she has been formed by it, yet ironically is unable to make significant moves outside it. The fact that the 'race-free' city is gated to exclude all those Martha dislikes is ruefully acknowledged by the narrator to be a problematic element in the fantasy:

> Outside one of the gates stood her parents, the Van Rensbergs, in fact most of the people of the district, forever excluded from the golden city because of their pettiness of vision and small understanding: they stood grieving, longing to enter, but barred by a stern and remorseless Martha – for unfortunately one gets nothing, not even a dream, without paying heavily for it, and in Martha's version of the golden age there must always be at least one person standing at the gate to exclude the unworthy.[3]

In the last novel in the 1952–69 *Children of Violence* sequence, the title of which is *The Four-Gated City*, Martha still has utopian day-dreams about such a city, but cannot avoid imagining it surrounded 'just like all the cities we know, like Johannesburg for instance' by 'a shadow city of poverty and beastliness. A shanty town. Around that marvellously ordered city another one of hungry and dirty and short-lived people. And one day the people of the outer city overran the inner one and destroyed it.'[4] The novel ends with a series of small-scale nuclear and chemical accidents that devastate European and North American civilisation and redraw the map of global power. Lessing's work does, therefore, as Morrison and others recognise, make frequent use of the image of the city.[5] However, the utopian ideals of 'post-racial' integration or assimilation as 'dreamscape' that this might imply are always critiqued, deconstructed or ironised. Lessing shares Morrison's concern that nonracist should not mean not race specific.

The image of 'home', which Morrison suggests as an alternative to the city or the house, is also present in Lessing's fiction of this period and in her essays and autobiography. For Lessing the concept of 'home' is always bound up with its other, exile. Home is not always a place of safety and familiarity but necessarily includes within it differences, resistances and dependencies that must be acknowledged and that cannot be excluded and positioned as exterior. Lessing writes home as a key concept for women, but also critiques it when proffered as a grand narrative that remains the same throughout twentieth-century political history. In one sense, then, Lessing always acknowledges, not merely what Freud refers to as the presence of *das Heimliche* (the homely) in its apparent opposite, *das Unheimliche* (the uncanny/unhomely) but also the necessity of admitting the presence of the uncanny or unhomely in the homely.[6]

The Sweetest Dream spends much of its time attacking the homes, or safe-houses, people find in utopian idealism in various different forms: in crude Marxism, in radical feminism and in certain types of nationalism. The dream of the title encompasses any metanarrative that suggests that 'they were all on an escalator of Progress, and that present ills would slowly dissolve away, and everyone in the world would find themselves in a happy healthy time'.[7] Key to the novel is the point that the idealism of 1960s' political radicalism was often at the expense of women's emotional and domestic labour and later generations' emotional development. The heroine of the novel, Frances Lennox, spends much of her time cooking and caring for her extended family, which consists, at different points, of her ex-mother-in-law, her ex-husband's child with his second wife, various friends and hangers-on of her own children and, finally, her ex-husband himself. Lessing did something similar herself, as she recounts in *Walking in the Shade*: 'For about six years in the sixties I proved my rapport with the times by becoming a housemother – now, that is a "sixties" word – for adolescents or young adults … All of them were in some kind of trouble.'[8] Many of the important scenes in the novel involve lengthy discussions about where different people will sleep and others focus on the preparation, serving and eating of huge meals around the kitchen table.

The image of the kitchen table as the focus for the home is one that Lessing has used elsewhere (notably in *The Fifth Child* (1988)) and here it generates an important debate in the reader about the virtues and vices of the nuclear family and its alternatives. It is possible to read the novel as conservative and reactionary (Lynne Segal terms it 'a truly reactionary work'[9]) as a critique of single parenting and the values that allow 'Comrade' Johnny (Frances's revolutionary Marxist ex-husband) to dismiss the role of father and the claims of his wife and children on his money and property. In some important ways *The Sweetest Dream* does imply that his children are damaged by his behaviour and the linked cycles of dependency and rebellion it generates. However, it is equally possible to see that the ways in which home and family life are represented are potentially productive in acknowledging difference. The novel implies that the family is certainly not about genetic or blood ties; neither is it about the economic ties that operate through the exchange of women in marriage: such relationships are the most flawed, painful and transient in the text. Instead, the family is a loose agglomeration of people who are connected emotionally in a variety of ways. Similarly, in *Love, Again* the narrator, Sarah Durham, finds that the company that is producing and acting her play, *Julie Vairon*, becomes a family of a kind. Not without its own emotional tensions and dependencies, her theatre family is still presented as superior to her 'genetic' family, which includes a thoughtless brother and a shiftless, emotionally damaged niece.

The dream of political idealism that *The Sweetest Dream* satirises is also connected with, indeed dependent on, the subordinated status of the once British colonies in Africa, which emerge during the novel as independent nation states. Throughout the novel Lessing explores interesting analogies between the Lennox family and the nation of 'Zimlia' (a thinly disguised Zimbabwe). Lessing interweaves Africa into the novel from the beginning, initially as an 'adjunct' to the revolutionary Marxist agenda of people like Johnny Lennox. Early in the novel he begins making all-expenses-paid trips to Africa funded by the Left to assist 'the comrades' in their struggle for independence. As time goes on Frances finds that she is cooking and caring for comrades from the African nationalist movements who become important political figures after independence. What therefore begins as 'incidental background' to the lives of the main characters is deliberately allowed to overtake and critique them.

The latter half of *The Sweetest Dream* is about Sylvia Lennox (Johnny's daughter with his second wife) and her work in a mission hospital in Kwadere, Zimlia. Sylvia's life in Zimlia includes encounters with corrupt officials in the new regime, attempts to educate her patients dying of AIDS, and fruitless negotiations with representatives of the various International Aid and Finance organisations. She is more successful in her efforts, with the help of priests and nuns who represent the local Catholic church and the local Nganga or witch-doctor, to establish a rudimentary hospital, school and library. Her story suggests how the 'dream' of the novel's title has impacted negatively on the cherished national identity of the newly independent Zimlia. The country, like the Lennox family, has been failed by grand narratives such as Marxism and functions most effectively at the local, not national level. As Chennells suggests: 'that global visions blind people to what has a significant existence only in the local is a seminal [sic.] idea in the novel'. He continues: 'Lessing knows Africa well enough to understand that "Africa" signifies a concept as much as a geographical location'.[10]

Lessing's analysis in *The Sweetest Dream*, then, accepts what Anderson terms the 'imagined' status of nations and seeks to examine the 'style in which they are imagined'.[11] Unlike Anderson, however, who sees 'race' as a remnant from traditional culture, Lessing sees the concept of 'race' as intrinsic in national identity: co-existent with the Enlightenment project of modernity as its unacknowledged but ever-present other. Like Bhabha, she suggests that 'racism' is not simply 'a hangover from archaic conceptions of the aristocracy, but a part of the historical traditions of "civic" and liberal humanism that create ideological matrices of "national" aspiration, together with their concepts of "a people" and its imagined community'.[12] Indeed, at its most negative, nationalism in *The Sweetest Dream* is a kind of 'derivative discourse', as Chatterjee describes it, which borrows its politics from the Marxism of privileged English Comrades like Johnny.[13] The impact of this dependency corrupts and nearly strangles both post-independence Zimlia and successive generations of the Lennox family.

The novel clearly suggests that there are similarities between the memorialising and narration of nations, individuals and families. However, it is also possible that the text offers the prospect, as Bhabha would put it, of establishing 'the cultural boundaries of the nation so that they may be acknowledged as "containing" thresholds of meaning that must be crossed, erased and translated in the process of cultural production'.[14] Chennells argues, for example, that the novel's conclusion, where Sylvia decides to return home with two Zimlian boys, undertakes just such a rewriting. It

> affronts the belief that identities derive from race and nation, a belief that is still enthusiastically promoted in parts of Africa. The children will die unless they are taken from Zimlia to England, and the novel implies that if to take them is cultural or racial murder then so be it. But it is not only the children who benefit from being taken away from their home. By their presence, the Kwadere children confirm, if further confirmation were needed, that the family is more than a genetic inheritance. The Lennox family has been, throughout the novel, a voluntary community. That is one of its strengths. As a trope, the Lennox family is placed in opposition to meta-narratives of social determinism, whether these are Marxism, Pan-Africanism or one or other of the many versions of globalization.[15]

Although the Lennoxes may have been more negatively marked by dependence on Utopian idealism than Chennells here admits, the family home contains the potential to become the kind of home Toni Morrison wants to find 'outside the raced house',[16] as she puts it: 'race-specific but nonracist',[17] acknowledging difference but capable of moving 'outside' it. As Franklin, one of the officials in the Zimlian government who first encountered the Lennoxes as a child who ate and slept in their family home remembers: 'A funny thing: he felt that that house in London had more in common with the ease and warmth of his grandparents' huts in the village ... than anything since' (435).

Franklin's remark suggests that something akin to Toni Morrison's concept of rememory is also apparent in *The Sweetest Dream* and is linked in the novel, as it is in Morrison's work, with ideas about home, nation and identity. In *Beloved* (1987), memory is an important way of accessing the inner life of those who have been excluded from official history, a way of challenging the forgetting of the traumatic and violent experiences of slavery. For Toni Morrison, memory is creatively linked with imagination to form rememory:

> The absence of the interior life, the deliberate excising of it from the records that the slaves themselves told – is precisely the problem in the discourse that proceeded without us. How I gain access to that interior life is what drives me and is the part of this talk which both distinguishes my fiction from autobiographical strategies and which also embraces certain autobiographical strategies. It's a kind of literary archeology: on the basis of some information and a little bit of guesswork you journey to a site to see what remains were left behind and to reconstruct the world that these remains imply. What makes it fiction is the nature of the imaginative act: my reliance on the image – on the remains – in addition to recollection, to yield up a kind of truth.[18]

The 'literary archeology' that Morrison describes here also involves the writing of trauma on the female body, which 'create[s] a close affinity between corporeality and textuality'.[19] Such rituals 'mobilize the collective force of the community and through the power of sympathy free traumatized characters from layers of repressed memories and further empower them to battle against imposed racial, sexual and class oppressions'.[20] All the characters in *The Sweetest Dream* engage in continual negotiation with memory and the past, although some do so more successfully than others. Obviously Lessing's white European characters enter this process from a considerably more privileged starting point than Morrison's, victims of slavery and white supremacy who bear the traces of their history on the body in different ways (which will be discussed in more detail later).

In *Love, Again* the process of engaging with the past is extremely ambivalent and can often be compromised. Julie Vairon herself produced journals, paintings and music as an attempt to negotiate and memorialise her life as an outsider. Sarah writes a play based on her translation of the journals, accompanied by selections of the music. She has to deal with patrons, all of whom have particular investments in Julie's story; these are sometimes personal (the wealthy Stephen Ellington-Smith, for example, is in love with Julie) and sometimes not (the French sponsor and civic official, Jean-Pierre le Brun, wants the play to be performed in the French town of Belles Rivieres, at the site where Julie lived, as part of a heritage tourism agenda). A number of different productions of the play are performed in different places during the course of the novel and a musical based on the play is also developed. Context, audience and environment can change the story substantially. In England,

> it was not that the tale became bathos, though these sad loves had to balance on that edge, it was rather that the English setting itself became a criticism of the girl. In the south of France, Martinique was only a thought or a sea's breath away, but here it was a tropical island, with associations of Captain Cook and South Sea hedonism (never mind that it was the wrong ocean), and Julie and her mother could only have the look of misplaced Victorians.[21]

At times, Julie's story *can* seem trite and sentimental: Sarah and her colleagues summarise this version of her life with joky allusions to the music hall song 'She was poor but she was honest', a traditional 'fallen woman' narrative. It is clear that Lessing is still interested in the consumption, promotion and packaging of life narratives in the arts and culture industries, an issue she explored earlier in the 'Jane Somers' hoax (see chapter 4). There is one occasion, however, when the production of the play is perfect. Afterwards, Sarah thinks:

> *Julie Vairon* would never take shape in this way again, in this setting, with these people. Well, it was not the first time – rather perhaps the hundredth – that she had been part of some play or piece, and it had always been sad to see the end

> of something that could never happen again. The theatre, in short, was just like life (but in a condensed and brightly illuminated form, forcing one into the comparison), always whirling people and events into improbable associations and then – that's it. The end. *Basta!* But this event, Julie's, was not anything she had known before. (191)

In *Love, Again* recreating the past in art can be contradictory and partial and when it works it is difficult to know precisely why.

Much of Lessing's work since 2000 is concerned with how art can negotiate the legacy of two world wars and their connection with the violence of the colonial encounter. As we saw in chapter 2, Lessing characterises the twentieth century as a begetter of 'children of violence'. As she puts it in *Under My Skin*, 'we are all of us made by war, twisted and warped by war, but we seem to forget it'.[22] Her parents met as a consequence of the First World War and in the speculative half of *Alfred and Emily* she imagines that without it, they would have married other people and she would not have been born. This is an idea that clearly began to preoccupy her when writing *Under My Skin*, where she writes:

> These two people, these sick and half-crazy people, my parents – it was the War, it was the First World War, that was what had done them in. For years I kept bright in my mind, like scenes from a film, what they would have been without that war. She, a jolly, efficient English-woman, probably running the Women's Institute for the whole of Britain, or some nursing service … And I only had to look at pictures of my father, before the war – these idealizations refused any of the other chances and choices life comes up with, but I was sure about one thing: my father had been strong, vigorous, in command of himself, this is how he would have gone on [… .][23]

In *The Sweetest Dream*, Johnny Lennox's parents meet on the eve of the First World War. His English father Philip, a secretary in the Berlin embassy, carries the memory of Johnny's German mother Julia, whom he meets when she is fourteen years old, throughout the painful experiences of the trenches. Julia represented for Philip the exotic and foreign other when contrasted with his sisters' typically 'English' middle-class friends: 'jolly tomboys enjoying the exemplary summer that has been celebrated in so many memoirs and novels' (26). His parents' preference is for 'Betty … teased because she came to supper with solid brown arms where white scratches showed how she had been playing in the hay with the dogs' (26). After the war the two lovers 'have to decide whether their dreams of each other for all those terrible years were strong enough to carry them through into marriage. Nothing was left of the enchanting prim little girl, nor of the sentimental man who had, until it crumbled away, carried a dead red rose next to his heart' (26). Philip's marriage has consequences for his career: 'certain posts would be barred to him … and he might find himself in places like South Africa or Argentina' (27). The narrator concludes: 'these two people, who had been so fatally in love, had lived always in patient tenderness, as if they had decided to protect their memories, like a bruise, from any harsh touch, refusing ever to look too closely at them' (37).

Repressing memory is shown to have negative effects, however, for both the individual and the nation. The revolutionary circles in which Johnny and for a time Frances move continually deal with eruptions of unpleasant memories that run counter to their adherence to the Communist dream. As information about Stalin's atrocities and the labour camps filters into public consciousness through the publicised memories of gulag interns, Johnny refuses to abandon his strict attachment to 'the Dream'. The novel ends with him still drinking to Stalin in his 80s. Lessing discusses this stubbornness and the reasons for it in *Walking in the Shade*, where she writes that 'some of the most socially concerned, hopeful-for-the-future, dedicated souls connived at the crimes in the communist world, by refusing to recognize them and, then, by refusing to acknowledge them openly'.[24] Lessing concludes that the loss of respect for government caused by the First World War led to a 'feeling of being participants in an understanding denied to an unheeding, ignorant majority'.[25] This in turn led to the idea that 'truth was the preserve of a knowledgeable and experienced minority. Initiates. Identification with pain, with suffering.'[26] From this followed the idea that 'unspeakable suffering is the price exacted by "life itself" in its tortuous progress upwards'.[27]

Like the dream of a Socialist revolution, the dreams of education and land for all that are offered to the people by the Nationalist leaders who come to power in Zimlia prove after independence to be dangerous memories, swallowed by the inefficiency and corruption of officialdom. It is only those individuals and, by implication, nations that can productively engage in the rewriting and revising of memory to include the repressed, the unpleasant and the inferior or subordinated that can succeed. As Feng claims:

> To make a traumatic experience into a narrative memory, in Toni Morrison's terms, is to make something 'unspeakable spoken.' Providing a narrative form for an unspeakable memory helps the victim go beyond the dis-ease of individual suffering and reach the reality of a history, in this case, the history of physical and mental colonisation.[28]

One good example of successful 're-remembering' in *The Sweetest Dream* is the case of Sylvia, who finds that her hybrid existence between London and Zimlia is 'like the equivalent of a decompression chamber' (327). In London discussing Frances's latest trials with her lover's teenaged children, Sylvia is haunted by the memory of Rebecca, a woman from Kwadere who works an eighteen-hour day and has lost two children to AIDS, from which she later begins to suffer herself. In comparison with this woman's existence, Frances's problems seem insignificant. The harsh intrusion of memories of Zimlia when Sylvia returns to London forces a revision of her own belief systems and concepts of self: 'her own real self, her substance, the stuff of belief, was leaking away as she stood there' (367). During a serious bout of malaria, Sylvia reflects that her role as do-gooder has less to do with her attachment to Catholicism than 'something in her nature that had seen to it that she was in as poor a place as possible' (445). Sylvia abandons Catholicism, the 'dream' or metanarrative that she lived by, and dies unexpectedly towards the end of the novel, leaving Frances to care for the two children from Kwadere.

In its final scene the loose-knit family group looks on as the children from Zimlia play with Frances's grand-daughter, who moves from person to person, creating a magic circle out of the diverse people in the room. This open ending is not without its ironies. The legacy of dependency we have seen in both family and nation state may be recurring yet again. However, it is also possible that Sylvia's memory and the presence of the two Zimlian boys in the family group may have the potential to inspire a new sense of community, family and home. This potential rewriting of the concept of home necessitates the inclusion and revision, rather than repression, of memory (or rememory) and the modification of the 'Englishness' of the family group by the Zimlian children in the next generation.

Love, Again is preoccupied with examples of less successful 're-remembering'. The novel is, as its title suggests, about being overwhelmed by 'inappropriate' love – inappropriate for Sarah because of her age and the fact that she falls in love with two younger men; inappropriate for Stephen because he is in love with Julie Vairon: a long-dead woman whom he never met. Stephen's experience recalls Lessing's interest in mourning and melancholia in *The Golden Notebook*. Here, however, melancholia is not rewritten as a creative strategy for dealing with past loss, but completely overtakes Stephen, resulting in depression and his suicide. The conclusion of the novel has Sarah speculate that the pain and anguish she has endured as part of loving again can be related to her childhood experience of being ousted from her mother's affections by her younger brother and transferring her affections to that brother. She asks: 'am I really to believe that the awful, crushing anguish, the longing so terrible it seems one's heart is being squeezed by cruel fingers – all that is only what a baby feels when it is hungry and wants its mother?' (338). Uncertain about this thought, Sarah concludes that 'to fall in love is to remember one is an exile, and that is why the sufferer does not want to be cured' (338).

The interest in memory, home and identity dominates Lessing's fiction but is also present in her essays and autobiographical writing in this period. Most of the reviews of *The Sweetest Dream*, for example, comment on the Author's Note to the novel, in which Lessing hints at the autobiographical aspects of the book. Reviewers generally felt that the novel 'lacks the acuity, accountability and density of her own autobiographical writings'[29] and that 'the autobiography would have had a sharper focus'.[30] Alternatively, the blend of autobiography and fiction is seen as confusing: 'an awkward melange lacking both the realism of great fiction and the truthfulness of history'.[31] Equally, reviewers want to believe that the novel is part *roman a clef*; after all, when questioned about the 'real' identities of the characters, Lessing teased: 'these people are middle-aged, and some of them are very well-known … I just wouldn't want to embarrass them.'[32]

Lessing's suggestive preface can be interpreted as part of her interest in the possibilities that are occasioned by experimenting with genre in her recent work: in that which is ostensibly fictional and that which is purportedly non-fiction. Lessing's collection of essays, *African Laughter: Four Visits to Zimbabwe*, contains, in its account of visits made in 1982, 1988, 1989 and 1992, remarkable similarities to the Zimlia sections of *The Sweetest Dream*. These include discussions of non-governmental organisations, the new black bureaucracy, the lives of white farmers, teachers in mission schools, experiences on Air Zimbabwe and at Customs, the work of the convents and local clinics, the AIDS epidemic, and disquisitions on Robert Mugabe and his wife (Matthew Mungozi in *The Sweetest Dream*). The essays also cover much more explicitly Zimbabwean history, the Bush War and Land Reapportionment. Like *The Sweetest Dream* the essays are dominated by ideas about memory, home and identity. John McCallister argues that their 'concern with memory, and particularly with the relationship between memory and the sense of belonging, is also part of a more radical project … its objects are to contest the dominant, colonialising mode of African travel writing and to propose a model of what a truly post-colonial travel literature might be like'.[33] Lessing spends a considerable amount of time plucking up the courage to return to the sites of her old family home on a farm and to a hotel where she spent many weekends with friends as a young woman (fictionalised as the Mashopi hotel in *The Golden Notebook*). The twists and turns of memory that these visits provoke occupy much of the text, and the same points about the fallibility (but therefore creative flexibility) of memory (or rememory) are generated by meeting up with her brother, a conservative white farmer who has very different childhood memories from Lessing.

Strikingly, Lessing uses the same image of the bruise that I have discussed earlier in relation to Julia and Philip in *The Sweetest Dream* to raise issues of memory and rememory in a variety of her work in this period. In the first volume of her autobiography, Lessing describes meeting a woman who introduced herself as the first girlfriend of Lessing's second husband, the German refugee Gottfried Lessing, at a book signing in Munich. She describes the meeting as awkward, because surrounded by lines of people waiting for signatures, but also because

> when a German and British person of the same age meet now, between us is the memory of the two wars, the thought we were enemies, and that our parents were enemies – a heavy, weary, painful incredulity – *how could it have happened?* – like a bruise that is invisible but which both know is there.[34]

The image of the invisible bruise is also present in *Love, Again*, where it is used to describe a 'weight of longing, usually, thank heavens, well out of sight and "latent" – like an internal bruise? – and then, for no obvious reason, just like that, there he was (who?), and onto him is projected this longing, with love. If the patterns don't match, don't fit, they slide apart, and the burden finds its way to someone else' (206).

The bruises here are hidden, latent, to be avoided. Touching the bruise or examining memories too closely is avoided. However, interestingly, in *African Laughter*, Lessing revises this image to suggest an alternative way of 're-remembering' trauma:

> Suppose one was able to keep in one's mind those childhood miseries, the homesickness like a bruise on one's heart, the betrayals – if they were allowed to lie in the mind always exposed, a cursed country one has climbed out of and left behind for ever, but visible, not hidden … would then that landscape of pain have less power than I'm sure it has?[35]

The simile of the bruise works here less on the body than 'on the heart', which is one way in which Lessing's use of rememory differs from Morrison's, where the physical traces of trauma are also literal. However, the choice of bruising as an analogy is interesting, as bruising is more visible on white than on black skin. It is as if in choosing this simile Lessing encourages the reader to examine how bodies 'wear' different histories of oppression because of skin colour.[36] The simile of the bruise also includes notions of home, landscape and country that are integral to the narrator's sense of identity. As a prohibited immigrant for the twenty-five years of white rule preceding the visits detailed in *African Laughter*, Lessing was directly forced to confront her own conceptions of home, nation and identity:

> I dreamed the same dream night after night. I was in the bush, or in Salisbury, but I was there illegally, without papers. 'My' people, that is, the whites, with whom after all I had grown up, were coming to escort me out of the country, while to 'my' people, the blacks, amiable multitudes, I was invisible. This went on for months. To most people it comes home that inside our skins we are not made of a uniform and evenly distributed substance, like a cake-mix or mashed potato, or even sadza, but rather accommodate several mutually unfriendly entities. It took me much longer to ask myself the real question: what effect on our behaviour, our decisions, may these subterranean enemies have? That lake of tears, did it slop about, or seep, or leak, secretly making moist what I thought I kept dry?[37]

The domestic image of typically English mashed potato is juxtaposed here with sadza (staple Zimbabwean food of maize porridge) to form a mixed diet that echoes Lessing's fragmented and multiple subjectivity and suggests the importance of her own (and Zimbabwe's) hybrid historical location. As Bhabha suggests:

> hybrid hyphenations emphasise the incommensurable elements – the stubborn chunks – as the basis for cultural identifications. What is at issue is the performative nature of differential identities: the regulation and negotiation of those spaces that are continually, *contingently*, 'opening out', remaking the boundaries, exposing the limits of any claim to a singular or autonomous sign of difference – be it class, gender or race.[38]

The metaphors of occupying spaces and 'opening out' of boundaries have interesting parallels with Lessing's image of identity as a leaky lake of tears which makes moist everything she thought was dry. In 'The Site of Memory' Toni Morrison also connects memory with flooding:

> All water has a perfect memory and is forever trying to get back to where it was. Writers are like that: remembering where we were, what valley we ran through, what the banks were like, the light that was there and the route back to our original place. It is emotional memory – what the nerves and the skin remember as well as how it appeared. And a rush of imagination is our 'flooding'.[39]

Rememory forces the acknowledgement of the 'truth' about the past by recognising memory's creative fallibility and identity's fluctuating, mobile status. Lessing comments:

> In any case it [memory] is such a flickering, fleeting record. Sometimes I feel I could wipe it all away with one sweep of my hand, like brushing away a kind of highly coloured veil or thin rainbow … and there still sits the autobiographer, uneasy about her memories, about the truth, and the book is not being written. Why a book at all? Why do we have this need to bear witness? We could dance our stories, couldn't we?[40] (Ellipsis in original)

In 'The Tragedy of Zimbabwe' Lessing discusses the worsening crisis in Zimbabwe generated by Robert Mugabe's policy of compulsory land reapportionment. The essay begins with the words of President Samora Michel of Mozambique and President Julius Nyerere of Tanzania to Robert Mugabe at Independence in 1980: 'You have the jewel of Africa in your hands … Now look after it.'[41] Lessing writes: 'Twenty-three years later, the "jewel" is ruined, dishonoured, disgraced.'[42] This metaphor of the corruption of innocence provides the framework for the essay and suggests that one of its key strategies will be to make use of others' memories, sayings and stories (as well as Lessing's own) to argue her case. Although the seriousness of the situation in Zimbabwe and the comparative brevity of the piece generate a more polemical and less discursive tone than in *African Laughter*, the content is similar to both the earlier essays and *The Sweetest Dream*. In addition, the narrative has a personal quality and directness that associates it with storytelling. The narrator considers interpretations and rejects them: it is too simple, for example, to see Mugabe as a 'tragic' figure. She uses her own memories of what people were saying at different points in Zimbabwe's history: 'when you travelled around the villages in the early Eighties you heard from everyone, "Mugabe will do this … Comrade Mugabe will do that …"';[43] 'This week (January 2003) I heard from one of the Book Team. "I was out this week. I was talking about books to people who haven't eaten for three days".'[44] She constructs the essay around a series of episodic memories: 'Another little scene: it is 1982, two years after Independence, and there is still a sullen, raw, bitter, postwar mood.'[45] Lessing criticises the official history of the situation in Zimbabwe, as it forms before her eyes, for emphasising the experience of white farmers who have lost land at the expense of the stories of those black farm-workers who have also lost homes and livelihoods.

In a letter to the *New York Review of Books* in a subsequent issue, Janet Jagan argues that Lessing ignores the role of opposition leader Joshua Nkomo in the history of Zimbabwe. She concludes: 'the whole episode of Mugabe's treacherous behaviour in relation to Nkomo needs to be woven into her article if we are to have a balanced view of the situation in Zimbabwe'.[46] Lessing's reply, whilst acknowledging that she should have 'said something about' Nkomo, is interesting in that it again returns to memory as a privileged site for 'historical' reconstruction; implicitly she rejects the idea that an essay should provide the 'balanced view of the situation' Jagan requires. She states that she knew Nkomo in London before the Lancaster House agreement (which ended white rule in what was then Southern Rhodesia) and remembers him as 'a pretty stupid man, but on a public platform a spell-binder'. She concludes: 'I do not think Joshua Nkomo's entry in the history book can add much luster to Zimbabwe's story.'[47] Lessing's return to the image of Zimbabwe as a jewel that has now lost its lustre is a final way of suggesting that the country's situation is better told as a 'story' rather than a 'history'. The problem of history is that it fails to acknowledge its inevitable exclusions or biases; the story, however, can offer its own kind of truth through what Toni Morrison termed 'literary archeology', which moves from the image to the text through memory.[48] Lessing operates in a similar way, delving episodically into her own and others' memories and sayings to creatively explore Zimbabwe's past. As Lessing wrote when preparing the first volume of her autobiography, 'I have to conclude that fiction is better at "the truth" than a factual record. Why this should be so is a very large subject and one I don't begin to understand.'[49]

Both volumes of Lessing's autobiography share *The Sweetest Dream*'s suspicion of naïve utopianism. In *Under My Skin* Lessing writes:

> Millions of people in our time behave as if they have been made a promise – by whom? – when? – that life must get freer, more honest, more comfortable, always better … Yet nothing in history suggests that we may expect anything but wars, tyrants, sickness, bad times, calamities, while good times are always temporary. Above all, history tells us that nothing stays the same for long. We expect gold at the foot of always renewable rainbows.[50]

At the conclusion of *Walking in the Shade*, in the year 1962, Lessing writes:

> We were all still on the escalator Progress, the whole world ascending towards prosperity. Did anyone challenge this happy optimism? I don't remember it. At the end of a century of grand revolutionary romanticism; frightful sacrifices for the sake of paradises and heavens on earth and the withering away of the state; passionate dreams of utopias and wonderlands and perfect cities; attempts at communes and commonwealths, at co-operatives and kibbutzes and kolkhozes – after all this, would any of us have believed that most people in the world would have settled gratefully for a little honesty, a little competence in government?[51]

The ironic distancing from utopian images of 'perfect cities' returns us to where this chapter started, to the distrust Lessing shares with Morrison of the sweetest dream and her attempt to create an alternative. Lessing makes use of what have previously been termed narrative strategies of doubling and repetition[52] in order to make readers question distinctions between genres and revise the relative status of fiction, essay and autobiography. In addition, doubling functions to deconstruct binary oppositions such as truth and fiction, centre and periphery, and feminine and masculine. Since the work of De Man critics have questioned the assumptions of authenticity invoked in autobiographical forms and have demonstrated how these are strategic linguistic constructions.[53] Feminist critics have also argued that women writers in particular have found the narrative devices of autobiography appealing for a number of reasons. Autobiography is challenging precisely because it disrupts generic and disciplinary boundaries and allows performative play with notions of self and authenticity. It encourages an 'intersubjective' conception of the self, narrative and memory.[54] There is also an important body of work in autobiographical forms by those of subordinated races and cultures, for example the slave narratives that Morrison discusses in 'The Site of Memory'. Writers of 'intercultural' autobiographies[55] construct a self in the space between different languages and cultures. What has also been termed 'the life writing of otherness' necessarily modulates between strategies that dislocate the universal subject and strategies that acknowledge its appeal to the disenfranchised.[56] Lauren Rusk's first chapter in *The Life Writing of Otherness* discusses *A Room of One's Own* under this rubric, demonstrating that, before Lessing, women writers like Virginia Woolf found the autobiographical essay a flexible way of insinuating feminist ideas into the heart of patriarchal forms.

Lessing's work in this period argues for a revision of the conventions we use to prioritise autobiography as truth, the novel as fiction and the essay as opinion. Her work parallels all three forms, with the intention of making serious points about the narration and memory of personal and political history. Even in the case of *The Cleft* this was a preoccupation, although this was not considered important in many of the reviews of the novel, which focused on its apparently stereotypical, essentialist, even misogynist accounts of gender difference. Ursula Le Guin's review in *The Guardian* was fairly typical:

> Anatomy is destiny. Gender is an absolute binary. Women are passive, incurious, timid and instinctively nurturant; without men, they scarcely rise above animal mindlessness. Men are intellectual, inventive, daring, rash, independent, and need women only to relieve libido and breed more men. Men achieve; women nag. Much of the presentation of this is familiar from the literature of misogyny.[57]

In fact, Transit's role as narrator is, as Phyllis Perrakis suggests, 'crucial to the metafictional layering of the novel' and allows him to reassess the colonial project of the Roman empire; she argues that:

> Transit's narrative, itself a genre crossing combination of fact and fiction, history and literature, fits what Linda Hutcheon calls 'historiographic metafiction' – postmodern novels that 'are intensely self-reflexive but that also both re-introduce historical context into metafiction and problematize the entire question of historical knowledge' (285–6). Transit's narrative raises the very questions about the history/literature divide and the borders of truth/fact/fiction that Hutcheon addresses in her discussion of the status of historiographic metafiction.[58]

In many ways, Lessing's final work, *Alfred and Emily*, represents the culmination of her thinking about life writing. In the foreword, she describes the Great War as something that 'squatted all over my childhood … And here I still am, trying to get out from under that monstrous legacy, trying to get free.' She expresses the hope that her parents would 'approve the lives I have given them'.[59] One question suggested by these remarks is whether Lessing would consider the speculative half of the text or the memoir as the liberating element. Is the 'fictionalised' part of the book liberating because it moves away from the restrictions of fact, allowing her to play fast and loose with the truth? Or is the memoir liberating because it generates a 'talking/writing cure' for the author, confronting the truth directly? In fact, it is the creative interplay between both parts of the book – its generic indeterminacy – and the fact that both and neither represent the 'truth', that allows Lessing to negotiate her 'monstrous legacy'. In *Alfred and Emily* Lessing does not so much 'get out from under' her own history as enter into it: the book is about her as much as it is about her parents.

To accept the fragility of categories such as genre and work against generic classification acknowledges the possibility that apparently 'fictional' writings, rememories rather than official Memory, may be more fruitful than ostensibly factual ones in allowing individuals and nations to make sense of their immediate pasts. As Morrison writes:

> My inclusion in a series of talks on autobiography and memoir is not entirely a misalliance. Although it's probably true that a fiction writer thinks of his or her work as alien in that company, what I have to say may suggest why I'm not completely out of place here. For one thing, I might throw into relief the differences between self-recollection (memoir) and fiction, and also some of the similarities – the places where those two crafts embrace and where that embrace is symbiotic.[60]

Or, as Lessing herself writes: 'if the novel is not the literal truth, then it is true in atmosphere, feeling, more "true" than this record [*Under My Skin*] which is trying to be factual'.[61] When reflecting later on the experience of writing her autobiography, Lessing concluded:

> So, when you are shaping an autobiography, just as when you shape a novel, you have to decide what to leave out. Novels are given shape by leaving out. Autobiographies have to have a shape, and they can't be too long. Just as with a novel, you have choice: you have to choose. Things have to be left out. I had far too much material for the autobiography. Yet it should be like life, sprawling, big, baggy, full of false starts, loose ends, people you meet once and never think of again, groups of people you meet for an evening or a week and never see again. And so as you write your autobiography it has to have a good deal in common with a novel. It has a shape: the need to make choices dictates that. In short, we have a story. What doesn't fit into the story, the theme, gets cut out.[62]

Lessing's work in this period, all in its way a form of life writing, offers a scathing critique of the political idealism of the second half of the twentieth century that demonstrates its problems dealing with the impact of war and its unacknowledged dependence on the invisible labour of women and those struggling to emerge from British colonial rule. One review of *The Sweetest Dream* refers to the text as a 'kitchen-sink novel'[63] which seems nothing more than sexist and ageist. Yet of course in one sense, Lessing's work *is* about the kitchen-sink in its 're-remembering' of home, nation and identity.

7

Critical overview and conclusion

Before the award of the Nobel in 2007, Doris Lessing's reputation (in the UK at least) was looking rather shaky. Her best work behind her, she seemed to express increasingly reactionary and hectoring views and her recent writing (with some exceptions) tended to the loose, baggy and monstrous (to borrow from Henry James).[1] She appeared to be more and more distant from the cosmopolitan feel of contemporary fiction: some kind of relic from the colonial past, the Communist past, even the feminist past. Reviewers felt the need to acknowledge the weight of this past with mostly respectful nods, often positioning her as the 'grande dame' figure, but her work seemed to have fallen out of favour. The idea of Lessing as the 'grande dame of literary fiction'[2] is in itself an extremely ambiguous one, as I have previously suggested.[3] The title of 'Dame' is that conferred on women members of the Order of the British Empire, carrying with it ideas about seniority and public recognition. Lessing's difficulty with the prospect of becoming a part of the establishment is apparent in the fact that she actually refused the title when it was offered her, remarking: 'I spent a good part of my youth trying to undo the British Empire. And there are very few more unimpressive sights than some old person licking the hand that it used to bite.'[4] The notion of seniority is itself ambivalent, implying both the capacity to reflect on history but at the same time the possibility of being 'past it'. The dame in the pantomime, of course, is a comic figure associated with licensed misrule, cross-dressing and the grotesque performance of a militant feminism. The grande dame is therefore prized, feted but also potentially difficult (and always feminine). The Lessing we encounter in the figure of the grande dame is a figure from the past.

In many ways the award of the Nobel did not really alter this assessment. Lessing herself remarked: 'I'm 88 years old and they can't give the Nobel to someone who's dead, so I think they were probably thinking they'd probably better give it to me now before I've popped off.'[5] In her case, the Nobel seemed to be a kind of 'lifetime achievement' award, but at the same time (as with so many attempts to recognise a whole life's cultural production) to refer back to early successes rather than discuss recent work. Many commentaries on the award focused on *The Golden Notebook* as Lessing's most important book and included comparatively little about the rest of her literary output in the latter half of the twentieth century and into the twenty-first. Harold Bloom called the award 'pure political correctness', acknowledging the 'few admirable qualities' in Lessing's early work, but concluded that he believed her writing for the past fifteen years to be 'quite unreadable'.[6] Bloom's grudging respect for the early fiction fits with the tendency to look backwards to find Lessing's 'finest hour' as a writer; his judgement that the Nobel committee's decision was a 'politically correct' one brings into play a number of contradictory ideas. We sense a suspicion that the prize is a respectful nod to Lessing's early attachment to radical causes such as Communism, feminism and the fight against colonial oppression and racial segregation, rather than an acknowledgement of supposedly 'pure' literary merit. By implication, Bloom also asks us to consider exactly what literary prizes such as the Nobel are rewarding.

The Nobel foundation website states in response to the question 'Why do you use the word Nobel Laureate and not Nobel Prize Winner?' that '[t]he awarding of the Nobel Prizes is not a competition or lottery, and therefore there are no winners or losers. Nobel Laureates receive the Nobel Prize in recognition of their achievements in physics, chemistry, physiology or medicine, literature, or peace.'[7] There do not appear to be any criteria for nomination. The issue of literary prizes and their relation to different kinds of cultural capital is a complex one that is attracting increasing critical interest, as was discussed in chapter 4. What is clear is that Bloom's opinion that Lessing became Nobel Laureate for reasons other than merit (and his contention that those reasons may be political ones) is less an apposite comment about Lessing's particular case than (in the broadest sense) a truism about prizes and awards in general. No literary prize can be divorced from the cultural, social and historical contexts of which it is a part. Prizes and awards can generate cultural capital, in Bourdieu's terms, but different prizes generate different *kinds* of cultural capital. Making the Granta 'Best of Young British Novelists' list, or winning the Orange prize, creates quite specific kinds of authority for the writers concerned. Lessing has never won the Booker prize, for example, although she has been nominated twice (see chapter 4).

The Nobel was, then, a marker of Lessing's cultural significance, but that significance was, for the most part, located in the past. However, Lessing has continued writing, right up until the announcement in 2008 that *Alfred and Emily* would be her final book. As we move further into the twenty-first century we need an assessment of Lessing's oeuvre that avoids concentration on the early works at the expense of the later and that acknowledges her status as a contemporary world writer. As this book has argued, Lessing's work engages with colonialism, decolonisation, race, nation and empire and connects these ideas with concepts of gender, class and age. Her non-fiction writing has been an important part of her corpus and her use of autobiographical forms throughout her work (whether ostensibly novel, memoir or official autobiography) can be viewed as a creative engagement in forms of life writing. In terms of genre, Lessing has refused to fit into the niches that academics, publishers and booksellers use to classify fiction: this resistance to categorisation is undoubtedly connected to her suspicion of other attempts to categorise, whether in terms of gender, race, nation or age. Throughout her writing life there have been many processes of revision at work in constructing Lessing's public and academic persona: different critical trends have affected the ways in which we have read and interpreted her work. It is no coincidence that just as her own reputation has been subject to alteration, creative changes and transformations have been crucial in her own writing.

In the sub-title of her ground-breaking 1977 book, *A Literature of their Own*, Elaine Showalter framed her study of British women novelists by referring to two figures: Charlotte Brontë and Doris Lessing. Showalter constructed a narrative about the maturation of women's writing from the Victorian period to the twentieth century, proposing that:

> First there is a prolonged phase of *imitation* of the prevailing modes of the dominant tradition, and *internalization* of its standards of art and its views on social roles. Second, there is a phase of *protest* against these standards and values, and *advocacy* of minority rights and values, including a demand for autonomy. Finally, there is a phase of *self-discovery*, a turning inward from some of the dependency of opposition, a search for identity. An appropriate terminology for women writers is to call these stages, *Feminine*, *Feminist*, and *Female*.[8]

Concluding the transition from feminine to feminist to female writing with a reference to Doris Lessing is a marker of the importance of her work for feminist critics; yet for Showalter Lessing makes an equivocal figure. She suggests that:

> The change in Lessing's fiction from the individual to the collective, from the personal to the communal, from the female to the global, consciousness seems at first like an abrupt transformation. It has, however, been a systematic, willed process of escape from a very painful encounter with the self, with the anguish of feminine fragmentation.[9]

What Showalter sees as Lessing's reluctance to confront her femininity directly connects her work with Virginia Woolf's: 'the feminine ego is merged for Woolf into a passive vulnerable receptivity; for Lessing, into a transmitter for the collective consciousness'.[10] Showalter's 'problem' with Lessing's writing resembles her problem with Woolf's attraction to ideas of androgyny in her work. Her claim that androgyny represents an 'escape from the confrontation with femaleness'[11] was famously contested by Toril Moi in *Sexual/Textual Politics*, in which she argues that Woolf's androgynous aesthetic becomes part of a deconstructive strategy designed to challenge stereotypical binary formulations of gender.[12]

Moi's rebuttal of Showalter's argument about Woolf's writing is also helpful, I think, in relation to her comments on Lessing. Moi notes Showalter's dislike of Woolf's playful style, commenting that her particular impatience with the voice and narrative strategies of *A Room of One's Own* is 'motivated much more by its formal and stylistic features than by the ideas she extrapolates as its content'.[13] Moi rescues Woolf's style as a 'conscious exploitation of the sportive, sensual nature of language, [which] rejects the metaphysical essentialism underlying patriarchal ideology, which hails God, the father or the phallus as its transcendental signified'.[14] Therefore her interest in androgyny becomes more than 'a flight from fixed gender identities': instead it entails 'recognition of their falsifying metaphysical nature'.[15] Moi's defence of Woolf's feminist writing strategy allows us to reconsider Lessing's purported 'escape' from the fragmented feminine self as a deconstructive technique that demands a reconsideration of fixed gender categories; it also encourages us to pay more attention to the relation between form and gender in her work.[16]

In fact, feminist criticism of Lessing's work has, to some extent, followed this trajectory between what we might call *gynocriticism* and *gynesis*,[17] even if many critics (feminist and otherwise) still fail to acknowledge the formal innovations of Lessing's writing. Initially, many North American women academics were attracted by Lessing's work precisely because of what Gayle Greene has called its 'centering on women's consciousness and concerns'.[18] Greene's 1994 book, *Doris Lessing: The Poetics of Change* was written some time after the second wave of feminism in the 1960s and 1970s but she begins by noting that Lessing's work presented 'the malaise that produced the second wave of feminism ... in political terms'.[19] She notes that Lessing's novels played a 'crucial role in the consolidation of the movement that took place in the course of the decade' (the 1960s) and 'helped make the second wave of feminism'.[20] Greene points out that *The Golden Notebook* was published 'within a year of Betty Friedan's *Feminine Mystique*, Plath's *Bell Jar*, and *The Report of the Commission on American Women* – all appeared in 1962–3'[21] and Lessing herself remarks that it was written 'as if the attitudes that have been created by Women's Liberation movements already existed'.[22] Greene quotes other women academics and novelists who have acknowledged their debt to Lessing. The academic names she mentions read like a roll-call of well-known North American feminist critics, including (by way of example) Elizabeth Abel, Annette Kolodny, Tania Modleski and Molly Hite. In her own book Greene focuses on the idea of change as a central poetics in Lessing's work that is itself consistent with a genuinely transformative feminist project.

Greene recognises that Lessing's engagement with feminism spoke directly to some women's experience. She stresses, however, that her writing involves more than providing strong women role models, detailing women's oppression, reversing current gender stereotypes (or binary oppositions) or merely including women in patriarchal structures without questioning them. These have been (and continue to be) important strategic feminist goals, but Greene's discussion of what she calls 'textual feminism' in *The Golden Notebook* seeks (like Moi writing on Woolf) to connect form, language and politics. Other feminist analyses of the novel have also moved away from its content to discuss the way that the form itself comments on gender, responding to Lessing's own hope that the novel would 'talk through the way it was shaped'.[23] Near the beginning of 'For the Etruscans', Rachel Blau DuPlessis's 'feeling-rich essay',[24] she writes: 'Frankly, it was *The Golden Notebook*. Which pierced my heart with its two-headed arrow.'[25] Asked about her interest in avant-garde practices she mentions *The Golden Notebook* as an example of 'non-conformist fictional forms'; for her the novel was 'extremely inspiring … for its dynamic depiction of female lives and choices, and for the dimensionality – psychic life, sexual life, and political life all addressed'.[26] In 'For the Etruscans' the novel is cited as an example of 'antiphonal many-voiced works, beguilingly, passionately subjective, seeing emotional commitment as an adventure'.[27] It is an example of DuPlessis's 'both/and'; 'insider/outsider' female aesthetic and allusions to it run throughout the essay. She famously describes the novel as 'the first tampax in world literature'[28] and is also preoccupied by the image of 'a room where clippings paper the walls'.[29]

The intimate connection that DuPlessis makes in these images between the book, the female body and feminist politics is also central in the more conventionally academic register of Elizabeth Abel's important essay '*The Golden Notebook*, Female Writing and the Great Tradition', which explicitly makes use of French feminist ideas of *écriture feminine*. Abel argues that: 'contemporary French definitions of *écriture feminine*, of female writing as heterogenous and disruptive, as a radical tool for exploding symbolic structures, describe a potential always available to the woman writer'.[30] She concludes by suggesting that the novel 'suggests the prospect of a different tradition, explicitly radical, implicitly female, a tradition moulded less by moral concern than by the disruption of moral and aesthetic categories. It is the woman writer, Lessing implies, who can initiate this new tradition.'[31] Although troubled (as one might argue French feminism itself has been) by the spectre of essentialism (Abel suggests that 'the novel shares with the French perspective the belief that female biology shapes female experience in ways that are resistant to male codes of liberation and that serve as a touchstone of female authenticity'[32]), the essay is an important attempt to link Lessing's treatment of gender with her formal choices and with a feminist politics. Molly Hite's *The Other Side of the Story: Structures and Strategies of Contemporary Feminist Narratives* makes a similar point when she argues that the text is one of a number of 'experimental fictions by women' that 'seem to share the decentering and disseminating strategies of postmodernist narratives, but they also seem to arrive at these strategies by an entirely different route, which involves emphasizing conventionally marginal characters and themes, in this way *re*-centering the value structure of the narrative'.[33]

Feminist readings of Lessing's work exemplify transitions that have been important in feminist criticism and theory more widely. We can note the move away from a concern with images of women and with fairly straightforward ideas of representation and oppression towards a concern with the gendered body, gendered form and feminist politics as more slippery, difficult and challenging concepts. These transitions are important to any understanding of the second wave of feminism and the place of Lessing's writing in that narrative is central. What is more difficult, perhaps, is to assess the relation between Lessing's work and what has variously been described as third wave or post-feminism. As was suggested in chapter 1, this is a difficulty partly occasioned by Lessing's own increasingly articulate distancing of herself from feminism and partly by the elusiveness of the terms 'third wave' and 'post-feminism' themselves, an elusiveness undoubtedly connected with the supposed disappearance of feminism from Western politics, culture and the academy.[34] In fact, like third wave feminism, Lessing's recent writing has clearly concerned itself with the interesting intersections and overlaps between gender and class, sexuality, 'race', nation and age.

Criticism of Lessing's work that considers the relationship between gender and age is an important area of this work, given the West's increasingly aging population. Chapter 4 discussed some of this material, but of particular note are the following. In 2004 a special issue of the journal *Doris Lessing Studies*[35] entitled 'Coming to Age' was published. In the editorial, Josna Rege suggested that Lessing's writing on age allows younger readers to anticipate, imaginatively, their own aging process. Her work, according to Rege, is 'pioneering' in that it 'prepar[es] her readers to welcome "the old man or woman waiting to emerge" from within each one of us'.[36] Diana Wallace's 2006 essay '"Women's Time": Women, Age and Inter-Generational Relations in Doris Lessing's *The Diaries of Jane Somers*' also notes that 'old age is Other – but it is also that which we must become. In this it differs radically from gender, race, and even class as categories of otherness.'[37] She argues that 'Lessing's text ... offers a highly suggestive exploration of the aging process and its complex relations with identity, femininity, the body and decay, and abjection'.[38] She also suggests that a key (if submerged) aspect of the text is the relation between aging and imaginative relationships with 'the aging maternal body'.[39] In the introduction to the edited collection *Adventures of the Spirit: The Older Woman in the Works of Doris Lessing, Margaret Atwood, and Other Contemporary Women Writers*, Phyllis Perrakis considers 'diverse kinds of introspective women's journeys at various stages on the developmental spiral'.[40] Perrakis argues that in different ways a number of contemporary women writers imagine 'the spiritual development of the midlife and older woman ... as a dynamic spiral of consciousness – a movement back that facilitates the move forward, a revisiting of the past enriched by the perspective of the present that leads to a transformative future'.[41] The connections these critics make between gender, age, narrative patterns and the reader's perspective and position are indicative of a third-wave feminist focus on the complex relation in different cultural forms between gender and other power structures.

Despite Lessing's personal history and her continued imaginative interest in Southern Africa, as well as in issues of 'race' and nation, it is only relatively recently that her work has been studied in relation to postcolonial theory and criticism, something this book has attempted to rectify. There are a number of reasons for the tendency to ignore Lessing amongst postcolonial critics and a number of notable exceptions. As was suggested in chapter 1, unease at categorising white settler or second-world literatures as 'postcolonial' is part of this tendency: as a member of the colonising class who shares the privileges of white skin Lessing cannot be *uncomplicatedly* separated from the structures and cultures of empire. However, postcolonial theory has increasingly recognised the multiple and complex ways in which colonial structures and cultures interpenetrate with forms of resistance, often finding such intersections fascinating and particularly productive to analyse.[42] In relation to Lessing, some of the most interesting work in this area has examined the surprising connections and disparities between gender and colonial identities. Victoria Rosner's essay, 'Home Fires: Doris Lessing, Colonial Architecture, and the Reproduction of Mothering', is a case in point. Rosner claims that the figure of the mother in white colonial society is key to the inculcation and maintenance of colonial attitudes to space, as it is constructed in gendered and raced terms. She argues that the 'ideology of motherhood serves to ground white separatism, providing a rationale for the racist divisions of colonialism ... domestic space in the colonies was inexorably linked to the maternal body, creating the grounds for the psychological and territorial contest of a daughter's separation from her mother'.[43] Her method in the essay is to read 'the form, construction and use of Lessing's childhood home as an architectural representation of colonial subjectivity in order to discuss the cross-hatched operations in the colonies of gender, race, and class'.[44] The metaphor of 'cross-hatching', an artistic method which involves drawing two layers of fine parallel lines at right angles to create illusions of depth and shade, is not only a description of how gender, race and class intersect in the white settler society she examines, but also emblematic of what we might think of as a postcolonial feminist critical practice. Louise Yelin's *From the Margins of Empire: Christina Stead, Doris Lessing, Nadine Gordimer*, which was discussed in detail in relation to *In Pursuit of the English* in chapter 1 and also in chapter 5, embodies this approach. Yelin's book describes her own 'eclectic critical perspective' as necessary, given the fact that the novels she considers are 'products of the multiple positioning and complex and shifting national affiliations of their authors and ... explorations of the question of national identity'.[45] Like Rosner, Yelin seeks to 'put a feminist critique of gender in conversation with theories of nationalism and national identity'.[46] Yelin sees Lessing as a more conservative writer than either Stead or Gordimer, who attempts in her writing to 'become English'.

Two other critics who have worked extensively on Lessing's connections to Southern Africa and postcolonial theory are Eve Bertelsen and Anthony Chennells. Bertelsen's 1985 edited collection, *Doris Lessing,* in the Southern African Literature series published by the South African publisher McGraw-Hill, contains an extremely useful section on 'literary background', an interview with Lessing and a section with 'contemporaneous' reviews (many of which first appeared in Southern African newspapers, some of which were written by other African writers and journalists, for example Nadine Gordimer) as well as a symposium on particular texts. Bertelsen makes many important points about Lessing's relationship to Southern Rhodesia and Africa as a whole. She points out that 'what strikes a Southern African reader of Lessing most forcibly is less the universal element than the fact that the fiction offers a very exact scrutiny of a particular society with working details that are fiercely local'.[47] She argues that 'unless Lessing criticism is going to be doomed endlessly to repeat itself, we must begin to address ourselves to the relationship of the fiction to history, to the informing contexts of Lessing's life and times, and to the cultural discourses of which it is a function'. She also suggests, presciently for this book, that 'it is her Rhodesian experience that has made her a perpetual outsider … her colonial experience [that] appears to have cast her forever in a marginal role' and that 'one could justifiably claim [as this book does] that her African background writes the whole Lessing oeuvre'.[48] However, Bertelsen has also provided one of the most trenchant and influential criticisms of Lessing's *The Grass is Singing* from a postcolonial perspective in her 1991 essay in *Modern Fiction Studies,* 'Veldtanshauung: Doris Lessing's Savage Africa' (see discussion in chapter 2).[49]

Anthony Chennells, whose work was also discussed in chapter 1, considers the issue of what he terms the 'near-total silence'[50] of black Africans in Lessing's writing as particularly problematic for postcolonial criticism. In 'Postcolonialism and Doris Lessing's Empires' he suggests that questions of 'race', voice and silence in Lessing's work are more complex than has been assumed and that her writing demonstrates a particular, self-conscious suspicion of 'white advocacy' as 'irrelevan[t] … to the political aspirations of blacks'.[51] Chennells also considers

Lessing's critical attitude to African nationalism as another reason for her neglect by certain postcolonial critics. She refuses, according to Chennells, the appeal of cultural nationalism and Pan-Africanism. Instead, Chennells claims that Lessing 'identified one aspect of the post-colonial condition before it became a foundational idea in post-colonial theory';[52] she 'is at one with post-colonial theorists who proclaim cultural hybridity as the irretrievable condition of post-colonial modernity'.[53]

Claiming Lessing as an example of cultural hybridity might seem to sit uneasily with the image of her as the venerated 'grande dame' that began this chapter. Yet this curious mixture of authority, distinction and what Chennells calls 'the diverse, the varied, the hybrid'[54] may go some way towards explaining her popularity across the globe and in parts of the postcolonial world particularly. Graham Huggan argues that what he terms the 'alterity industry' tends to commodify and market the 'postcolonial exotic' to Western readerships (see chapter 4);[55] yet Lessing lacks the obvious markers of 'otherness' that would make this easily achievable. However, she is widely read in South and East Asia and in the Far East as well as in Europe, North America and Australia.[56] Lessing is very popular in India: the recent publication in 2008 of a special section of the Indian journal *Re-Markings* on her work was planned by the journal editor before the award of the Nobel on the grounds that '"some people obtain fame, others deserve it"' and that 'we needed no apology to record our deep appreciation' for Lessing's work.[57]

This international, even cosmopolitan, readership has interested a number of critics. In 1990, Claire Sprague's *In Pursuit of Doris Lessing: Nine Nations Reading* specifically focused on the many Lessings that emerge from readings in different historical and cultural contexts. The collection is dominated by 'first world' perspectives (the essays focus on Zimbabwe, South Africa, the UK, the US, Canada, France, Germany, Spain and the USSR) but provides a fascinating snap-shot in time. Written before the fall of the Berlin wall, the first free elections in South Africa and the break-up of the Soviet Union, the collection reminds us of the volatility of history and its impact on reading practices; as

Sprague suggests: 'Lessing's international, transcultural qualities are differently situated'.[58] Whether or not they are, as Sprague continues, 'too deeply imbedded to fluctuate with any market or fashion' is more doubtful.[59] In fact, for Nibir K. Ghosh, the editor of *Re-Markings*, it is precisely Lessing's paradoxical endorsement of the marginal *everywhere* that explains her work's appeal: 'What can be a more perfect illustration of globalization and multiculturalism than this collaborative venture wherein avid lovers of Lessing from three continents, separated by cultures and vast geographical space, have come together to offer such a grand tribute to the Persian-born, Rhodesian-raised and London-residing novelist who has taught the world to value the inner lives of those who live life on the margins.'[60]

Few critics have made connections between what Chennells terms Lessing's postcolonial 'cultural hybridity' and her work's generic and formal innovations; however, many critics have been preoccupied with these innovations as worthy of study in themselves. At the micro level, Lessing is generally believed not to be a stylist. Gayle Greene claims that 'one often encounters' terms such as '*turgid, prolix, polemical, preachy,* and *flat-footed*' in assessments of Lessing's style.[61] Other critics have acknowledged that Lessing's experimentalism tends to operate at the level of genre, mode and narrative perspective. Elizabeth Abel makes this clear when she suggests that 'disruptions occur not at the level of syntax … but at the level of narrative structure'.[62] Jeannette King's 1989 book on Lessing in the Edward Arnold Modern Fiction series is centrally concerned with her 'adventurousness, her readiness to experiment with the novel form' and aims to demonstrate 'the variety of formal experiments Lessing has undertaken'.[63] King claims that Lessing occupies a marginal position that allows her to 'explore and analyse the "centres" of our culture'.[64] One of this book's great strengths is its analysis of Lessing's self-conscious, awkward and provisional use of realism as an open and critical mode with its own tensions and contradictions. Both Betsy Draine, in *Substance Under Pressure: Artistic Coherence and Evolving Form in the Novels of Doris Lessing* and Claire Sprague, in *Rereading Doris*

Lessing: Narrative Patterns of Doubling and Repetition focus on formal innovations of various kinds in Lessing's fiction as central to her oeuvre. Draine argues that

> [I]n the universe of Lessing's fiction, there is a central abiding thematic substance, but it is constantly under the pressure of artistic evolution. A single theme persists throughout her work, but the 'forms and shapes' of her novels are 'subject to sudden reversals, upheavals, changes, cataclysms,' under the pressure of her drive towards self-transcendence in the realm of fictional technique.[65]

Quoting from *Shikasta* in her assessment of the importance of change and reversal in Lessing's form, Draine stresses, however, the need to find coherence in her work. In 1987, Claire Sprague was also interested in the 'complicated and unexpected' ways in which 'pattern and meaning in Lessing's fiction interpenetrate'. She continues:

> Lessing's 'profoundly dialectical consciousness' sees double and multiple forms in constant interaction. It is a consciousness that displays itself in the way characters and narrative patterns are deployed. It is not limited to political or thematic statement. It has a formal component … the term 'doubling' can be used for both kinds of dialectic if its use assumes multiplication beyond twoness, for Lessing multiplies as frequently as she doubles characters, naming and numerological patterns, environments … and narrative forms.[66]

There is a noticeable shift in critical assessments of the relation between form and meaning in Lessing's work from the desire to impose coherence on her varied work to an increased willingness to acknowledge the value of formal diversity in itself. As Sprague remarked in 1987 of Lessing studies: 'a few years ago we were all talking … about splits and divisions and fragmentation … Now I'm hearing about diversity, about multiplicity, about protean selves, about incoherence as a potentially positive thing.'[67]

Critical assessment of Lessing's relation to both realism and postmodernism has tended, understandably if not entirely, to focus on *The Golden Notebook*. One exception is Clare Hanson's

'Doris Lessing in Pursuit of the English, or, No Small, Personal Voice'. In this essay, Hanson argues that a number of Lessing's novels exhibit the strains of realism and argues that 'in contradiction to the prevailing English view, Doris Lessing is not a realist novelist who, after some aberration and dallying with "science fiction", is returning to the realist fold'. She continues: 'Lessing is a far, far more radical writer than this, one whose work reflects almost every possible stage and process in the "dehumanisation of art" and of the individual in the post-humanist world. Her work should be seen as post-modern and post-humanist.'[68] Appearing in Sprague's 1990 collection (discussed earlier) where nine nations read Lessing's work, Hanson's argument (as was suggested in chapter 5) is also about national identity and a particularly English reluctance to allow Lessing to move outside the valued category of realism.[69]

For Patricia Waugh, writing in *Metafiction* (1984), the novel's 'parody of realism, its revelation of the extent of the inadequacy of realist writing ... represents the ironic end of self-discovery for Doris Lessing the novelist'.[70] Despite this rather bleak remark, Waugh also claims that in exposing the inadequacies of the traditional novel, *The Golden Notebook* generates the release function that is typical of parody and metafiction.[71] Some critics, including Waugh herself in *Feminine Fictions: Revisiting the Postmodern*, have argued that this release function is capable of serving political ends, particularly feminist ones. According to Magali Cornier Michael, the novel 'co-opts a number of postmodern aesthetic strategies' and 'blends together and attempts to negotiate between a variety of aesthetic and conceptual modes to fulfill aims that are feminist in impulse'.[72] Waugh's argument about *The Golden Notebook, The Four-Gated City* and *Memoirs* is that they represent a move towards a utopian vision 'of a collective mode of existence which ... projects the possibility of a community founded on the sort of relational identity which has been associated with women and devalued by the present society'.[73]

If critics have recognised that Lessing's innovations occur at generic, modal and structural level, fewer have closely studied her complex use of narrative perspective. One exception is Virginia Tiger, whose detailed analysis of the two short stories 'To Room Nineteen' and 'A Room' makes it abundantly clear that it is always a mistake to assume that the voice of the narrator in a Lessing novel is identical with that of Lessing herself. Tiger carefully analyses the multiple ways in which Lessing manipulates free-indirect discourse and plays with the idea of narrative 'omniscience'.[74] In fact Lessing's use of 'point of view' is a far more interesting aspect of her work than it may at first appear to be. Nicole Ward-Jouve's 'Of Mud and Other Matter: *The Children of Violence*', is another excellent, thought-provoking and difficult-to-categorise essay. It addresses narrative perspective and the relation between narrator and character as part of a consideration of larger issues to do with Lessing's style, voice and relation to traditions of classic realism and modernism. Ward-Jouve finds the way Lessing writes *Children of Violence* a failure in fundamental ways: for her '[t]he novels as they proceed become aware of something false, a vacuity, which is the falsity of their own fictional mode'.[75]

In more recent years, echoing developments in her own writing, critical attention has focused more closely on the relation between Lessing's work and ideas of the mind, mysticism and spirituality. One of the earliest books in this area is Roberta Rubenstein's *The Novelistic Vision of Doris Lessing: Breaking the Forms of Consciousness*, which appeared in 1979. Even at this point in time, before the publication of *Canopus in Argos: Archives* (*Shikasta* appeared in the same year), Rubenstein's argument is that Lessing's central concern throughout her work is consciousness itself, or 'the mind discovering, interpreting, and ultimately shaping, its own reality'.[76] The fiction, according to Rubenstein, demonstrates a development of consciousness from 'passive to active, from negative to positive, from recorder of a reality initially perceived outside the self to creator of a reality ultimately construed as a function of the mind as it transcends the labels of "subjective" or "objective"'. As a result of this process, she continues, a 'transpersonal, mystic' vision replaces a 'depersonalised, psychotic' one.[77] Rubenstein's articulation of the increasing capaciousness of consciousness in Lessing's fiction is certainly persuasive: a number of critics have gone on to study the relation between Lessing's work and theories of the mind of various kinds. There has been more focus on psychology rather than psychoanalysis in the majority of this work. A good example is Judith Kegan Gardiner's *Rhys, Stead, Lessing and the Politics of Empathy,* which borrows from mothering theory to develop a new understanding of how empathy, as a woman-centred experience, can be used to describe the manifold relationships between authors, readers and characters. According to Kegan Gardiner, Lessing's most well-known novel, *The Golden Notebook,* adopts the strategy of the 'self-originating child' in relation to literary traditions, as opposed to the position of 'mother's daughter' and 'father's son' associated with Rhys and Stead respectively.[78]

The impact of Sufism on Lessing's writing has also focused on questions of consciousness. Shadia Fahim's 1994 book, *Doris Lessing: Sufi Equilibrium and the Form of the Novel* argues that it is a mistake to identify 'phases' in Lessing's writing career and isolate the 'Marxist phase, her psychological novels or her Sufi-influenced fiction'. Instead, she claims that the 'common denominator in Lessing's fictional world is the question of finding "the right path for moral equilibrium" within the novel – through motifs of descent and ascent – and between the individual and society – through motifs of return'.[79] It is the 'balance between outward and inner modes of perception which attracts Doris Lessing to Sufism'.[80] Whereas Fahim's focus is on how the idea of equilibrium affects the content and form of the fiction, Müge Galin's *Between East and West: Sufism in the Novels of Doris Lessing* provides a more detailed discussion of Sufi thinking and its place in Islam, in Western Sufism, in Orientalist scholarship and in relation to postcolonial theory, particularly the work of Edward Said. Galin discusses 'not only how Lessing's novels are affected by Sufism but how Sufism itself is altered and adapted in Lessing's Western context'.[81] By contrast, in *Spiritual Exploration in the Works of Doris Lessing,* edited by Phyllis Perrakis, the focus is on 'one of the most elusive issues in Lessing's canon – her spirituality' much more broadly defined.[82]

Lessing's relationship to Communism and the British Left has attracted far less critical commentary. Jenny Taylor's excellent introduction to her edited collection: *Notebooks/Memoirs/Archives: Reading and Rereading Doris Lessing* is an exception. Taylor makes clear the extent to which Lessing was embedded in a range of specific political and cultural activities associated with the Left-leaning intelligentsia in the 1950s and early 1960s. Taylor focuses on three 'broad axes: the move from region to metropolis, the crisis of Stalinism and, the least visible, the position of the isolated woman intellectual' in explaining her position in this field.[83] She argues that 'Lessing's relation to the Left during the 1950s arose in part from her own very specific position and history as a successful colonial woman writer interested in psychoanalysis and subjectivity. But her situation was also bound up with the more general position of the committed writer within the relation of cultural production in the 1950s.'[84] Taylor argues that Lessing's concerns with commitment, with the relationship between literary form and political aims, and with the renewal of realism as a mode need to be placed in relation to the work of other writers and activists in this period, for example Raymond Williams's *The Long Revolution,* which first appeared in 1961.

Another area of Lessing's work that has received comparatively little critical attention is the relation between her science fiction work and the wider tradition of SF, utopian and dystopian writing. This may well be because, as was discussed in chapter 4, Lessing is arguably a somewhat untypical SF writer, but it is also undoubtedly because many critics and reviewers have found her work in this genre less successful. One of the few critics to have written extensively about the science fiction is Katherine Fishburn in *The Unexpected Universe of Doris Lessing*. Fishburn argues that 'it is in her science fiction that Lessing sets out most clearly to critique modern social and political stuctures' and 'transcend the limitations of known reality'.[85] She also sees narrative technique as key to the science fiction novels:

> To tell their story successfully, Lessing's narrators try to engage our imaginative complicity in their tale. They want us to believe what they are reporting ... Because she is primarily intent upon shattering our paradigms, it is not the story itself but the telling of the story that she [Lessing] values. Unlike her narrators, Lessing is less concerned with convincing us of an alien reality than she is in subverting our current reality.[86]

Fishburn's sense of the importance of narrative technique and voice in the science fiction is extremely helpful. In Lucie Armitt's edited collection *Where No Man Has Gone Before: Essays on Women and Science Fiction* there are two essays on Lessing. Armitt's own piece on Lessing's *The Marriages Between Zones Three, Four, and Five* (which also discusses the writer Suzette Elgin) also sees SF's self-reflexiveness as key. She focuses on the way in which 'contemporary science fiction by women has made a by no means insignificant contribution to the current theoretical debate on women's relationship to language – and thus power'.[87] In the interview with Bertelsen Lessing remarked on the importance of metaphor and language in her SF work and expressed surprise at the way different readerships have responded:

> I always found that the younger people have always read my new books, and the older people didn't like them. And the younger people didn't like the old books. Both sides are very intolerant. And I think that the younger people who read a great deal of space fiction and science fiction and non-realistic books don't have to be told why I'm writing these books, it's their language anyway, you see. They understand perfectly well that you use metaphors. They're not looking for systems or some kind of dogmatism, they understand it. It's a form of narrow-mindedness you know, and also an ignorance of our tradition which has always included the fantastic and the imaginative alongside realism.[88]

Lessing makes an appeal here for the diversity and range of her work to be appreciated, yet she dislikes critical strategies that attempt to impose uniformity on her writing, or that view it as expressing clearly defined developmental stages in her thinking. The reaction in the Western media to the award of the Nobel prize was, in places, somewhat grudging, focusing on the early fiction at the expense of more recent work. However, Lessing's world-wide reputation, particularly in parts of the postcolonial world, suggests that readers do respond to the interesting mixture of distinction and marginality in her image and in her writing. Just as Lessing's own writing has undergone substantial creative change and transformation, so have critical approaches to her work. Rather than abandoning earlier interpretative frameworks, this book argues the need to engage with the diversity of Doris Lessing's oeuvre and make visible the range of readings it can produce. At the same time, however, it is undoubtedly the case that what Lorna Sage called 'the colonial metaphor' is a key to her work. In 1983 Sage suggested of Lessing that

> She is, after all, an expert in unsettlement. The colonial experience – the colonial metaphor – is central to her identity as a writer. Her earliest African writing and her most recent space fiction alike are preoccupied with the transience of our world-pictures – with ways, that is, of analyzing and heightening their transience, of decentering imaginative life. So long as we behave imaginatively like colonists (for her the archetypal enemies of change), we are doomed to repeat ourselves wherever we turn – doomed to cast ourselves in dubious character parts, and to impose dead patterns on the worlds we inhabit.[89]

The colonial metaphor and its rewriting continue to provide an important imaginative locus in Lessing's writing. As a contemporary world writer Lessing engages imaginatively with colonialism, decolonisation, race, nation and empire, and demonstrates in her work how these ideas connect with concepts of gender, class and age. Her suspicion of such categories is echoed in her attempts to challenge generic and formal classification. Asked how she felt about being regarded as an African or Southern African writer, Lessing answered:

> Well, I think it's perfectly right that I should be, because

> I did after all spend twenty five years growing up there and that's what makes people – this is what forms people. Certainly everything that's made me a writer happened to me growing up in Southern Rhodesia, the old Rhodesia.[90]

However, when she was then asked if she objected to the label 'African' or 'Southern African' writer as 'limiting', Lessing replied:

> Well, recently in Germany they gave me the Austrian State Prize for Literature for European Writing, because they regard me as a European writer, and that's fine too. The whole of Europe has been involved in the colonial influence for two or three hundred years. You can't separate Europe from what is now called the Third World.[91]

Notes

Chapter 1

1 Doris Lessing, *Under My Skin: Volume One of my Autobiography, to 1949*, London: Harper Collins, 1994, 407.

2 Doris Lessing, *Walking in the Shade: Volume Two of my Autobiography, 1949–1962*, London: Flamingo, 1998, 4.

3 *Ibid.*

4 Louise Yelin, *From the Margins of Empire: Christina Stead, Doris Lessing, Nadine Gordimer*, Ithaca: Cornell University Press, 1998, 63–5.

5 The phrase comes from David Kynaston's *Austerity Britain 1945–1951*, London: Bloomsbury, 2007.

6 Doris Lessing, *In Pursuit of the English*, London: Flamingo, 1993, 212. Further page references are to this edition and will be given in the text.

7 Yelin, 59.

8 *Ibid.*, 60.

9 John McLeod, *Postcolonial London: Rewriting the Metropolis*, London: Routledge, 2004, 78.

10 Yelin, 60, 69.

11 McLeod, 75, 81.

12 Yelin, 61–2.

13 *Ibid.*, 64.

14 McLeod, 78.

15 *Ibid.*, 78–9.

16 *Ibid.*, 80. Rosario Arias also argues that Lessing uses the image of

the city as palimpsest in her work in order to suggest that the city is a multi-layered text capable of being rebuilt, re-read, revised and interpreted in manifold ways. See Rosario Arias, '"All the World's a Stage": Theatricality, Spectacle and the *Flaneuse* in Doris Lessing's Vision of London', *Journal of Gender Studies*, 14, 2005, 3–11 (4). Christine Sizemore was one of the first critics to note Lessing's use of the city as palimpsest as a feminist writing strategy. See Christine Wick Sizemore, *A Female Vision of the City: London in the Novels of Five British Women*, Knoxville: The University of Tennessee Press, 1989, 29–64. I would like to thank Christine for sending me a copy of her book.

17 Dennis Walder, '"Alone in a Landscape": Lessing's African Stories Remembered', *Journal of Commonwealth Literature*, 43, 2, 2008, 99–115 (103).

18 Doris Lessing, 'The Jewel of Africa', *New York Review of Books*, 50, 6, 10 April 2003. Available at <http://www.nybooks.com/articles/16170> (accessed 4 September 2009). The essay was re-titled 'The Tragedy of Zimbabwe' in her 2004 collection of essays, *Time Bites*. See Doris Lessing, 'The Tragedy of Zimbabwe', in *Time Bites: Views and Reviews*, London: Fourth Estate, 2004, 231–46.

19 Doris Lessing's Nobel lecture, then entitled 'A Hunger for Books', was delivered on Friday 7 December at the Swedish Academy, Stockholm, by Nicholas Pearson, Doris Lessing's publisher in the UK. It was published in *The Guardian*, in the Review section on Saturday 8 December 2007. See Doris Lessing, 'A Hunger for Books', *The Guardian*, 8 December 2007, <http://www.guardian.co.uk/books/2007/dec/08/nobelprize.classics> (accessed 4 September 2009). The text of the lecture can also be read on the Nobel Prize website, although the lecture has been re-titled 'On Not Winning the Nobel Prize'. The website states that 'the Nobel lecture has been changed according to the wish of the author'. See <http://nobelprize.org/nobel_prizes/literature/laureates/2007/lessing-lecture.html> (accessed 4 September 2009).

20 Barbara Probst Solomon, 'The Lady Laureate', *The New York Sun*, 12 October 2007, <http://www.nysun.com/article/64471> (accessed 4 September 2009).

21 Lessing, *Under My Skin*, 16–17.

22 Stephen Slemon, 'Unsettling the Empire: Resistance Theory for the Second World', *World Literature Written in English*, 30, 2, 1990, 30–41 (38).

23 Doris Lessing, *Martha Quest*, London: Paladin, 1990, 63.

24 *Ibid.*, 67.

25 *Ibid.*, 67–8, 67.

26 *Ibid.*, 68.

27 Slemon, 147, 38.

28 Helen Tiffin, 'The Body in the Library: Identity, Opposition and the Settler-Invader Woman', in *Postcolonial Discourses: An Anthology*, ed. Gregory Castle, Oxford: Blackwell, 2001, 374–88 (377).

29 Doris Lessing, 'Afterword to *The Story of an African Farm* by Olive Schreiner', in *A Small, Personal Voice: Essays, Reviews, Interviews*, ed. Paul Schlueter, London: Flamingo, 1994, 161–84 (162).

30 Anthony Chennells, 'Doris Lessing and the Rhodesian Settler Novel', in *Doris Lessing*, ed. Eve Bertelsen, Johannesburg: McGraw-Hill, 1985, 31–43 (31).

31 *Ibid.*, 32.

32 *Ibid.*, 32–3.

33 Anthony Chennells, 'Reading Doris Lessing's Rhodesian Stories in Zimbabwe', in *In Pursuit of Doris Lessing: Nine Nations Reading*, ed. Claire Sprague, Basingstoke: Macmillan, 1990, 17–40 (18).

34 *Ibid.*, 17.

35 *Ibid.*, 25.

36 *Ibid.*, 25, 27.

37 *Ibid.*, 39.

38 Robin Visel, '"Then Spoke the Thunder": *The Grass is Singing* as a Zimbabwean Novel', *Journal of Commonwealth Literature*, 43, 2, 2008, 157–66 (160).

39 *Ibid.*, 157.

40 *Ibid.*, 159.

41 *Ibid.*, 160.

42 Doris Lessing, *Going Home*, New York: Harper Collins, 1996, 248.

43 Doris Lessing, 'The Small Personal Voice', in *A Small Personal Voice: Essays, Reviews, Interviews*, ed. Paul Schlueter, London: Flamingo, 1994, 7–26 (23).

44 Doris Lessing, Preface to *The Golden Notebook*, London: Flamingo, 1993, 14.

45 *Ibid.*

46 Lessing, *Walking in the Shade*, 203–14.

47 Lessing's essay 'The Small Personal Voice' appeared first in the collection. See Tom Maschler (ed.), *Declaration*, London: MacGibbon and Kee, 1957, 11–28.

48 Lessing, 'The Small Personal Voice', 18.

49 Lessing, *Walking in the Shade*, 213.

50 See her comments in an interview with Eve Bertelsen in Eve Bertelsen (ed.), *Doris Lessing*, Johannesburg: McGraw-Hill, 1985, 93–120 (116).

51 Lessing, *Under My Skin*, 275.

52 Lisa Appignanesi, 'Interview: Doris Lessing', *Bookforum*, Spring 2002, <http://www.bookforum.com/archive/spr_02/interview_lessing.html> (accessed 4 September 2009).

53 See for example Arthur Koestler's *Darkness at Noon*, originally published in 1941, London: Vintage Classics, 1994 and *The God that Failed* (first published in 1950), revised, ed. Richard H. Crossman, New York: Columbia University Press, 2001.

54 Paul Foot, 'The Lessing Legend', *Socialist Review*, 216, February 1998, 26–7, <http://pubs.socialistreviewindex.org.uk/sr216/foot.htm> (accessed 4 September 2009).

55 Nick Bentley, 'Doris Lessing's *The Golden Notebook*: An Experiment in Critical Fiction', in *Doris Lessing: Border Crossings*, eds Alice Ridout and Susan Watkins, London: Continuum, 2009, 44–60.

56 Svenska Academien, 'The Nobel Prize in Literature 2007: Bio-Bibliography', <http://nobelprize.org/nobel_prizes/literature/laureates/2007/bio-bibl.html> (accessed 4 September 2009).

57 The Permanent Secretary, 'The Nobel Prize in Literature 2007: Doris Lessing', Press Release, 11 October 2007, <http://nobelprize.org/nobel_prizes/literature/laureates/2007/press.html> (accessed 4 September 2009).

58 Robert McCrum, 'Writing is Something I Have to Do', Review Section, *The Observer*, 14 October 2007, 8.

59 Motoko Rich and Sarah Lyall, 'Doris Lessing Wins Nobel Prize in Literature', *The New York Times*, 11 October 2007, <http://www.nytimes.com/2007/10/11/world/11cnd-Nobel.html?_r=4&hp&oref=slogin&oref=slogin&oref=slogin&oref=slogin> (accessed 13 September 2009).

60 Lisa Allardyce, 'Saturday Interview', *The Guardian*, 13 October 2007, 33.

61 Fiachr Gibbons, 'Lay off Men, Lessing Tells Feminists', *The Guardian*, 14 August 2001, <http://www.guardian.co.uk/Archive/

Article/0,4273,4238674,00.html> (accessed 4 September 2009).

62 For a discussion of the neo-con anti-feminist 'pro-family' agenda see Susan Faludi, *Backlash: The Undeclared War Against American Women*, New York: Crown, 1991. Chapter 9, 'The Politics of Resentment: The New Right's War on Women', 259–89 covers the neo-con agenda, and the 'pro-family' stance is discussed on pp. 269–70 and 312.

63 Stacey Gillis, Gillian Howie and Rebecca Munford (eds), *Third Wave Feminism: A Critical Exploration*, second edition, Basingstoke: Palgrave, 2007, xxx.

64 Alice Ridout, 'Review of *Third Wave Feminism: A Critical Exploration*', *Contemporary Women's Writing*, 1, 1–2, 2007, 208–9 (209).

65 The term 'overloaded' comes from Imelda Whelehan's *Overloaded: Popular Culture and the Future of Feminism*, London: The Women's Press, 2000.

66 See Virginia Woolf's comments in *Three Guineas*, London: The Hogarth Press, 1947, 184–5.

67 Gayle Greene, *Doris Lessing: The Poetics of Change*, Ann Arbor, MI: The University of Michigan Press, 1994, 28.

68 *Ibid.*

69 Lessing, Preface to *The Golden Notebook*, 20.

70 Bentley, 44.

71 Christine Sizemore discusses this 'local cosmopolitanism' in '*In Pursuit of the English*: Hybridity and the Local in Doris Lessing's First Urban Text', *Journal of Commonwealth Literature*, 43, 2, 2008, 133–44. She notes Lessing's tendency to 'overlay[s] London geography with African images both visual and aural' (140). McLeod in *Postcolonial London* remarks of one such image that it 'underwrites the inseparability of the imperial centre and its periphery. What is "foreign" can manifest itself at the heart of the Empire, in London: the division cannot hold' (80–1).

72 See for example Elizabeth Maslen, *Doris Lessing*, Plymouth: Northcote House, 1994, 22, 29, where she makes the comparison with Foucault's work on madness and civilisation. See also Marion Vlastos, 'Doris Lessing and R. D. Laing: Psychopolitics and Prophecy', *PMLA*, 91, 2, 1976, 245–58 and Roberta Rubenstein, 'Briefing on Inner Space: Doris Lessing and R. D. Laing', *The Psychoanalytic Review*, 63, 1976, 83–93 for discussion of the similarities between Lessing's and Laing's ideas.

73 Vlastos, 246.

74 Ann Scott, 'The More Recent Writings: Sufism, Mysticism and Politics', in *Notebooks/Memoirs/Archives: Reading and Rereading Doris Lessing*, ed. Jenny Taylor, London: Routledge and Kegan Paul, 1982, 164–90 (166).

75 Doris Lessing, 'In the World, Not Of It', in *A Small Personal Voice: Essays, Reviews, Interviews*, ed. Paul Schlueter, London: Flamingo, 1994, 193–202 (193).

76 Müge Galin, *Between East and West: Sufism in the Novels of Doris Lessing*, Albany, NY: State University of New York Press, 1997, xviii.

77 *Ibid.*

78 Scott, 167.

79 Lessing, Preface to *The Golden Notebook*, 10.

80 Lessing, 'The Small Personal Voice', 8.

81 Doris Lessing, 'What Novel or Novels Prompted Your Own Political Awakening?', *Time Bites: Views and Reviews*, London: Fourth Estate, 2004, 251–2 (252). Lessing's childhood reading is listed in *Alfred and Emily*, London: Fourth Estate, 2008, 165–9.

82 Lessing, 'The Small Personal Voice', 15, 18.

83 Doris Lessing, 'Between the Fax and the Fiction', *The Guardian*, 13 December 1991. This article can be accessed on the website, *Doris Lessing: A Retrospective*, an extremely useful site with details of all Lessing's works and other relevant material, at <http://lessing.redmood.com/between.html> (accessed 4 September 2009).

84 Clare Hanson, 'Reproduction, Genetics, and Eugenics in the Fiction of Doris Lessing', *Contemporary Women's Writing*, 1, 1–2, 2007, 171–84 (171).

85 Lessing, *Walking in the Shade*, 307.

86 Doris Lessing, 'A Reissue of *The Golden Notebook*', in *Time Bites: Views and Reviews*, London: Fourth Estate, 2004, 138–41 (141).

87 Lessing, *Under My Skin*, 28.

88 Doris Lessing, 'Preface', *The Sweetest Dream*, London: Flamingo, 2001.

Chapter 2

1 Doris Lessing, *A Proper Marriage*, London: Paladin, 1990, 159. Further references are to this edition and will be given as page numbers in the text.

2 Doris Lessing, *A Ripple from the Storm*, London: Grafton, 1966, 196. Further references are to this edition and will be given as page numbers in the text.

3 Dennis Walder, '"Alone in a Landscape": Lessing's African Stories Remembered', *Journal of Commonwealth Literature*, 43, 2, 2008, 99–115 (102).

4 Walder borrows this term from Svetlana Boym, in her book *The Future of Nostalgia*, New York: Basic Books, 2001. See Walder, 105.

5 Until 1923 Rhodesia (now Zimbabwe) was run by Cecil Rhodes's British South Africa Company. The white settler population then chose to become a 'self-governing colony' rather than become part of what was then the Union of South Africa. Ian Smith's government made a unilateral declaration of independence (UDI) from Britain in 1965 in order to avoid making concessions to black advancement. It would not be until the Lancaster House Agreement (1979) after more than a decade of armed struggle that the whites were forced to concede defeat. The Republic of Zimbabwe became independent in 1980 after the victory of ZANU-PF under Robert Mugabe.

6 Christine Sylvester, *Zimbabwe: The Terrain of Contradictory Development*, Boulder: Westview Press, 1991, 43.

7 Colin Stoneman (ed.), *Zimbabwe's Inheritance*, New York: St Martin's Press, 1981, 4.

8 Doris Lessing, 'The Wind Blows Away Our Words', in *The Wind Blows Away Our Words and other Documents Relating to the Afghan Resistance*, London: Picador, 1987, 33–141 (74).

9 Doris Lessing, *Going Home*, London: Harper Collins, 1996, 7. Further references are to this edition and will be given as page numbers in the text.

10 Doris Lessing, 'The Old Chief Mshlanga', in *This Was the Old Chief's Country: Collected African Stories, Volume One*, London: Flamingo, 1994, 13–25 (17).

11 *Ibid.*, 23.

12 Doris Lessing, *Martha Quest*, London: Paladin, 1990, 28. Further references are to this edition and will be given as page references in the text.

13 The practice of 'coming out' into society as a debutante ended in 1958, the year when the last debutantes were presented at court.

14 Victoria Rosner, 'Home Fires: Doris Lessing, Colonial Architecture, and the Reproduction of Mothering', *Tulsa Studies in Women's Literature*, 18, 1, 1999, 59–89 (60).

15 Pat Louw, 'Inside and Outside Colonial Spaces: Border Crossings in Doris Lessing's *African Stories*', in *Doris Lessing: Border Crossings*, eds Alice Ridout and Susan Watkins, London: Continuum, 2009, 26–43 (27).

16 Nicole Ward Jouve, 'Of Mud and Other Matter: *The Children of Violence*', in *Notebooks/Memoirs/Archives: Reading and Rereading Doris Lessing*, ed. Jenny Taylor, London: Routledge and Kegan Paul, 1982, 75–134 (78, 80).

17 *Ibid.*, 79.

18 Edward Said, *Reflections on Exile and Other Literary and Cultural Essays*, London: Granta Books, 2000, 186.

19 Robert J. C. Young, *Colonial Desire: Hybridity in Theory, Culture and Race*, London: Routledge, 1995, xii.

20 Homi K. Bhabha, *The Location of Culture*, London: Routledge, 1994, 112–16.

21 Young, 9.

22 *Ibid.*, 27.

23 Anthony Chennells, 'Doris Lessing and the Rhodesian Settler Novel', in *Doris Lessing*, ed. Eve Bertelsen, Johannesburg: McGraw-Hill, 1985, 31–43 (40).

24 *Ibid.*, 41.

25 Murray Steele, 'Doris Lessing's Rhodesia', in *Doris Lessing*, ed. Eve Bertelsen, Johannesburg: McGraw-Hill, 1985, 44–54 (46).

26 Chennells, 41.

27 Ann Stoler, *Carnal Knowledge and Imperial Power: Race and the Intimate in Colonial Rule*, Berkeley: University of California Press, 2002, 7. Julie Cairnie's essay on 'The Antheap' makes good use of the work of Ann Stoler. See Julie Cairnie, 'Rhodesian Children and the Lessons of White Supremacy', *Journal of Commonwealth Literature*, 43, 2, 2008, 145–56.

28 Doris Lessing, 'The Antheap', in *This Was the Old Chief's Country: Collected African Stories, Volume One*, London: Flamingo, 1994, 356–413 (371–2).

29 *Ibid.*, 413.

30 Cairnie, 153.

31 Lessing, 'The Antheap', 409.

32 *Ibid.*, 404.

33 *Ibid.*, 411.

34 See Sylvester, 43 and Ruth Weiss, *Zimbabwe and the New Elite*, London: British Academic Press, 1994, 29 for accounts of this.

35 Doris Lessing, *The Grass is Singing*, London: Michael Joseph, 1950, 21–2. Further references are to this edition and will be given as page numbers in the text.

36 Margaret Moan Rowe, *Doris Lessing*, Basingstoke: Macmillan, 1994, 17.

37 Lorna Sage, *Doris Lessing*, London: Methuen, 1983, 27, 28.

38 Eve Bertelsen,, 'Veldtanschauung: Doris Lessing's Savage Africa', *Modern Fiction Studies*, 37, 4, 1991, 647–58 (657).

39 *Ibid.*

40 Eve Bertelsen 'Interview with Doris Lessing' in *Doris Lessing*, ed. Eve Bertelsen, Johannesburg: McGraw-Hill, 1985, 93–120 (102).

41 Sage, 28.

42 *Ibid.*, 43.

43 Jenny Taylor, 'Situating Reading', in *Notebooks/Memoirs/Archives: Reading and Rereading Doris Lessing*, ed. Jenny Taylor, London: Routledge and Kegan Paul, 1982, 1–42 (18).

44 Georg Lukács, *Theory of the Novel: A Historico-Philosophical Essay on the Forms of Great Epic Literature*, trans. Anna Bostock, London: Merlin Press, 1971.

45 Elizabeth Maslen, *Doris Lessing*, Plymouth: Northcote House, 1994, 14.

46 Roberta Rubenstein, 'Fixing the Past: Yearning and Nostalgia in Woolf and Lessing', in *Woolf and Lessing: Breaking the Mold*, eds Ruth Saxton and Jean Tobin, New York: St Martin's Press, 1994, 15–38 (33).

47 *Ibid.*

48 *Ibid.*, 34.

49 See note 4.

Chapter 3

1 Doris Lessing, *The Golden Notebook*, London: Flamingo, 1993, 66. Further references are to this edition and will be given as page numbers in the text.

2 Doris Lessing, Preface to *The Golden Notebook*, London: Flamingo, 1993, 7–21 (10). Further references are to this edition and will be given in the text.

3 David L. Eng and David Kazanjian (eds), *Loss: The Politics of Mourning*, Berkeley: University of California Press, 2003, 5.

4 Dr Jennifer D. Williams's paper, entitled 'Motherless Girls: Melancholy Cosmopolitanism in Andrea Lee's *Sarah Phillips* and Jamaica Kincaid's *Lucy*', given at the 'Unsettling Women: Contemporary Women's Writing and Diaspora' conference at the University of Leicester, 11–13 July 2008, introduced me to the idea of melancholy cosmopolitanism and to Eng and Kazanjian's work on the politics of loss.

5 Doris Lessing, *The Memoirs of a Survivor*, London: Picador, 1976, 84. Further references are to this edition and will be given as page numbers in the text.

6 Gayle Greene, *Doris Lessing: The Poetics of Change*, Ann Arbor, MI: The University of Michigan Press, 1994, 15.

7 Doris Lessing, *Briefing for a Descent into Hell*, London: Granada, 1972, 240. Further references are to this edition and will be given as page numbers in the text.

8 Doris Lessing, *Walking in the Shade: Volume Two of my Autobiography, 1949–1962*, London: Flamingo, 1998, 242.

9 Victoria Bazin, 'Commodifying the Past: Doris Lessing's *The Golden Notebook* as Nostalgic Narrative', *Journal of Commonwealth Literature*, 43, 2, 2008, 117–31 (125).

10 The novel's status as metafiction and its relation to postmodernity and postmodernist fiction have dominated critical approaches to *The Golden Notebook* until comparatively recently. See for example Marguerite Alexander, *Flights from Realism: Themes and Strategies in Postmodernist British and American Fiction*, London: Edward Arnold, 1990; Marie A. Danziger, *Text/Countertext: Postmodern Paranoia in Samuel Beckett, Doris Lessing, and Philip Roth*, New York: Peter Lang, 1996; Betsy Draine, 'Nostalgia and Irony: The Postmodern Order of *The Golden Notebook*', *Modern Fiction Studies*, 26, 1980, 31–48; Suzette Henke, 'Doris Lessing's *The Golden Notebook*: A Paradox of Postmodern Play',

in *Rereading Modernism: New Directions in Feminist Criticism*, ed. Lisa Rado, New York: Garland, 1994, 157–87; Molly Hite, *The Other Side of the Story: Structures and Strategies of Contemporary Feminist Narratives*, Ithaca, NY: Cornell University Press, 1989; Magali Cornier Michael, *Feminism and the Postmodern Impulse: Post-World War II Fiction*, Albany: State University of New York Press, 1996; Patricia Waugh, *Metafiction: The Theory and Practice of Self-Conscious Fiction*, London: Methuen, 1984 and *Feminine Fictions: Revisiting the Postmodern*, London: Routledge, 1989.

11 Bazin, 127.

12 *Ibid.*, 124.

13 Aaron S. Rosenfeld, 'Re-membering the Future: Doris Lessing's "Experiment in Autobiography"', *Critical Survey*, 17, 1, 2005, 40–55 (48).

14 Sigmund Freud, 'Mourning and Melancholia', in *The Standard Edition of the Complete Psychological Works of Sigmund Freud*, vol. 14, trans. and ed. James Strachey, London: Hogarth Press, 1955, 1–59.

15 Eng and Kazanjian, 3.

16 *Ibid.*, 5.

17 *Ibid.*

18 *Ibid.*, 4.

19 *Ibid.*, 5.

20 Paul Gilroy, *Postcolonial Melancholia*, New York: Columbia University Press, 2005, 90.

21 *Ibid.*, 100.

22 *Ibid.*, xv.

23 *Ibid.*, 60.

24 Bruce Robbins, 'Introduction Part I: Actually Existing Cosmopolitanism', in *Cosmopolitics: Thinking and Feeling Beyond the Nation*, eds Pheng Cheah and Bruce Robbins, Minneapolis: University of Minnesota Press, 1998, 1–19 (2–3).

25 The term 'critical' cosmopolitanism is used by Paul Rabinow in his *Essays on the Anthropology of Reason*, Princeton, NJ: Princeton University Press, 1996, 56. The term 'discrepant' cosmopolitanism is used by James Clifford in his 'Traveling Cultures', in *Cultural Studies: Now and in the Future*, eds Larry Grossberg, Cary Nelson and Paula A. Treichler, New York: Routledge, 1992, 96–112.

26 Dominique Jullien, 'In Praise of Mistranslation: The Melancholy Cosmopolitanism of Jorge Luis Borges', *The Romantic Review*, 98, 2–3, 2007, 205–23 (206).

27 *Ibid.*, 222.

28 The transformative power of melancholia is also noted by Anne Anlin Cheng in *The Melancholy of Race: Psychoanalysis, Assimilation, and Hidden Grief*, Oxford: Oxford University Press, 2001, where she argues that 'the model of melancholia can help us comprehend grief and loss on the part of the aggrieved [which she earlier characterises as the 'racial other … the melancholic object'], not just as a symptom, but also as a dynamic process with both coercive and transformative potentials for political imagination' (xi).

29 The novel is discussed as part of 1950s New Left literary and political culture in Nick Bentley's 'Doris Lessing's *The Golden Notebook*: An Experiment in Critical Fiction', in *Doris Lessing: Border Crossings*, eds Alice Ridout and Susan Watkins, London: Continuum, 2009, 44–60. Sandra Henstra's 'Nuclear Cassandra: Prophecy in Doris Lessing's *The Golden Notebook*', *Papers on Language and Literature*, 43, 1, 2007, 3–23 relates the novel to Cold War anxiety about nuclear destruction. Henstra also makes use of ideas of mourning and melancholia, but argues that 'the kinds of losses suffered under nuclearism cannot be properly mourned … the dread of nuclear destruction generates a kind of collective melancholia' (4–5). Henstra is therefore maintaining Freud's distinction between healthy mourning and pathological melancholia.

30 Robbins, 4.

31 See Pheng Cheah, 'Introduction Part II: The Cosmopolitical Today', in *Cosmopolitics: Thinking and Feeling Beyond the Nation*, eds Pheng Cheah and Bruce Robbins, Minneapolis: University of Minnesota Press, 1998, 20–44 (26), for a discussion of Marx's view of cosmopolitanism.

32 Timothy Brennan, *At Home in the World: Cosmopolitanism Now*, Cambridge, MA: Harvard University Press, 1997, 144–5.

33 Bazin, 120.

34 *Ibid.*, 129.

35 *Ibid.*, 130.

36 Dennis Walder, '"Alone in a Landscape": Lessing's African Stories Remembered', *Journal of Commonwealth Literature*, 43, 2, 2008, 99–115 (105).

37 This point is also made in the work of a writer like Sylvia Plath, whose poetry is beginning to be analysed in relation to the Cold War and 1950s culture. See Robin Peel, *Writing Back: Sylvia Plath and Cold War Politics*, Madison, NJ: Fairleigh Dickinson University Press, 2002.

38 Julia Kristeva, *Strangers to Ourselves*, trans. Leon S. Roudiez, Hemel Hempstead: Harvester Wheatsheaf, 1991, 181.

39 Evy Varsamopoulou, 'The Idea of Europe and the Ideal of Cosmopolitanism in the Work of Julia Kristeva', *Theory, Culture and Society*, 26, 1, 2009, 24–44 (38).

40 Shameem Black, 'Cosmopolitanism at Home: Amitav Ghosh's *The Shadow Lines*', *Journal of Commonwealth Literature*, 41, 3, 2006, 45–65 (61).

41 Antoinette Burton, 'The Ugly Americans: Gender, Geopolitics and the Career of Postcolonial Cosmopolitanism in the Novels of Santha Rama Rau', *Journal of Commonwealth Literature*, 41, 2, 2006, 5–19 (7).

42 *Ibid.*, 17.

43 Eng and Kazanjian, 5.

44 Lessing's debate with realism in the novel is discussed by several critics. See for example Alexander, Anne Mulkeen, 'Twentieth-Century Realism: The "Grid" Structure of *The Golden Notebook*', *Studies in the Novel*, 4, 1972, 262–74; Draine, Jeannette King, *Doris Lessing*, London: Edward Arnold, 1989; Martha Lifson, 'Structural Patterns in *The Golden Notebook*', *Michigan Papers in Women's Studies*, 2, 1978, 95–108; Dennis Porter, 'Realism and Failure in *The Golden Notebook*', *Modern Language Quarterly*, 35, 1974, 56–65; Lorna Sage, *Doris Lessing*, London: Methuen, 1983; Ruth Whittaker, *Doris Lessing*, Basingstoke: Macmillan, 1988.

45 The 1970s have recently attracted considerable discussion among historians and cultural commentators. See for example Andy Beckett, *When the Lights Went Out: Britain in the Seventies*, London: Faber, 2009.

46 Marion Vlastos, 'Doris Lessing and R. D. Laing: Psychopolitics and Prophecy', *PMLA*, 91, 2, 1976, 245–58 (253–7). However, Roberta Rubenstein quotes a letter from Lessing in which she states that the identical last name was a coincidence. See Roberta Rubenstein, 'Briefing on Inner Space: Doris Lessing and R. D. Laing', *The Psychoanalytic Review*, 63, 1976, 83–93.

47 R. D. Laing, *The Divided Self: A Study of Sanity and Madness*, London: Tavistock, 1960, 34.

48 Vlastos, 256.

49 Doris Lessing, 'In the World Not Of It', in *A Small Personal Voice: Essays, Reviews, Interviews*, ed. Paul Schlueter, London: Flamingo, 1994, 193–202 (193).

50 See Brennan and Black.

51 The similarities with William Blake's poem 'Auguries of Innocence', with its well-known lines 'To see a world in a grain of sand,/ And a Heaven in a wild flower', are striking. See William Blake, 'Auguries of Innocence', in *Songs of Innocence and Experience and Other Works*, ed. R. B. Kennedy, Plymouth: Macdonald and Evans, 1970, 134.

52 Other writers who became interested in writing about extraordinary psychic phenomena in the science fiction genre include Isaac Asimov, Arthur C. Clarke, Robert A. Heinlein and Frank Herbert.

53 See Beckett, 125–56 for an account of the three-day week and 464–97 for an account of the Winter of Discontent.

54 Vlastos, 246.

55 Greg Garrard, *Ecocriticism*, Abingdon: Routledge, 2004, 2.

56 Fiona Becket, 'Environmental Fables?: The Eco-politics of Doris Lessing's "Ifrik" Novels', in *Doris Lessing: Border Crossings*, eds Alice Ridout and Susan Watkins, London: Continuum, 2009, 129–42 (132).

57 Eng and Kazanjian, 5.

58 Vlastos, 246.

59 Ann Scott, 'The More Recent Writings: Sufism, Mysticism and Politics', in *Notebooks/Memoirs/Archives: Reading and Rereading Doris Lessing*, ed. Jenny Taylor, London: Routledge and Kegan Paul, 1982, 164–90 (167).

60 Nancy Shields Hardin, 'The Sufi Teaching Story and Doris Lessing', *Twentieth-Century Literature*, 23, 3, 1977, 314–26 (314).

61 Rosenfeld, 43.

62 *Ibid.*, 47.

63 Eng and Kazanjian, 5.

Chapter 4

1 Eve Bertelsen, 'Interview with Doris Lessing', in *Doris Lessing*, ed. Eve Bertelsen, Johannesburg: McGraw-Hill, 1985, 93–120 (96).

2 *Ibid.*, 97.

3 Jeannette Winterson, *The Stone Gods*, London: Hamish Hamilton, 2007.

4 Virginia Tiger, '"The Words Had Been Right And Necessary": Doris Lessing's Transformations of Utopian and Dystopian Modalities in *The Marriages Between Zones Three, Four, and Five*', *Style*, 27, 1, 1993, 63–80, <http://web.ebscohost.com> (accessed 6 September 2009).

5 *Ibid.*

6 Lucie Armitt (ed.), *Where No Man Has Gone Before: Essays on Women and Science Fiction*, London: Routledge, 1990, 9.

7 Claire Chambers, 'Postcolonial Science Fiction: Amitav Ghosh's *The Calcutta Chromosome*', *Journal of Commonwealth Literature*, 38, 1, 2003, 57–72.

8 Michelle Reid, 'Postcolonial Science Fiction', *The Science Fiction Foundation*, 2005, <http://www.sf-foundation.org/publications/academictrack/reid.php> (accessed 6 September 2009).

9 Avtar Brah, *Cartographies of Diaspora: Contesting Identities*, London: Routledge, 1996, 208.

10 *Ibid.*, 209.

11 *Ibid.*, 210.

12 *Ibid.*, 183.

13 Marian Engel described *The Sirian Experiments* as 'social science fiction', in 'Lessing Still in Outer Space, But This Time Cataloguing a Myriad of Planets', *The Globe and Mail*, 21 February 1981, <http://www.lexisnexis.com/uk> (accessed 19 June 2008). Robert Alter used the term 'anatomy' in 'Doris Lessing in the Visionary Mode', *The New York Times*, 11 January 1981, <http://www.lexisnexis.com/uk> (accessed 19 June 2008).

14 Clare Hanson, 'Doris Lessing in Pursuit of the English, or, No Small, Personal Voice', in *In Pursuit of Doris Lessing: Nine Nations Reading*, ed. Claire Sprague, Basingstoke: Macmillan, 1990, 61–73 (62).

15 Bertelsen, 97.

16 Hanson, 62.

17 Harold Bloom, quoted in Sarah Crown. 'Doris Lessing Wins Nobel Prize', *The Guardian*, 11 October 2007, <http://www.guardian.co.uk/books/2007/oct/11/nobelprize.awardsandprizes> (accessed 6 September 2009).

18 Adam Roberts, 'Doris Lesfing' [sic.], *The Valve: A Literary Organ*, 12 October 2007 <http://www.thevalve.org/go/valve/article/doris_lessfing/> (accessed 6 September 2009).

19 See Rich Puchalsky's comment in response to Adam Roberts's posting, *ibid.*

20 Jayne Glover, 'The Metaphor of the Horse in Doris Lessing's *The Marriages Between Zones Three, Four and Five*: An Ecofeminist Question?', *Current Writing: Text and Reception in Southern Africa*, 18, 1, 2006, 119–33, <http://www.lexisnexis.com> (accessed 19 June 2008).

21 David Waterman, 'Who Am I When the Other Disappears?: Identity and Progress in Doris Lessing's *The Sirian Experiments*', *Journal of Evolutionary Psychology*, 29, 1–2, 2006, 74–86, <http://www.lexisnexis.com> (accessed 19 June 2008).

22 Doris Lessing, *The Sirian Experiments*, London: Grafton, 1982, 35. Further references are to this edition and will be given as page numbers in the text.

23 Waterman.

24 Glover.

25 Doris Lessing, *The Marriages Between Zones Three, Four, and Five*, London: Panther, 1981, 299.

26 Nisa Torrents, 'Testimony to Mysticism', Interview with Doris Lessing', in *Putting the Questions Differently: Interviews with Doris Lessing, 1964–1994*, ed. Earl Ingersoll, London: Flamingo, 1996, 64–9 (66).

27 See Shadia Fahim, *Doris Lessing: Sufi Equilibrium and the Form of the Novel*, Basingstoke: Macmillan, 1994.

28 Müge Galin, *Between East and West: Sufism in the Novels of Doris Lessing*, Albany, NY: State University of New York Press, 1997, 153.

29 Phyllis Sternberg Perrakis, 'Sufism, Jung and the Myth of Kore: Revisionist Politics in Lessing's *Marriages*', in *Doris Lessing*, Bloom's Modern Critical Views, ed. Harold Bloom, Broomall, PA: Chelsea House, 2003, 61–86 (83).

30 Roberts, 'Doris Lesfing'.

31 Adam Roberts, *The History of Science Fiction*, Basingstoke: Palgrave Macmillan, 2005, 344.

32 Doris Lessing, *The Making of the Representative for Planet 8*, St Albans: Granada, 1983, 113.

33 Perrakis, 74.

34 *Ibid.*

35 Bertelsen, 108.

36 *Ibid.*

37 Doris Lessing, Preface to *The Diaries of Jane Somers*, Harmondsworth: Penguin, 1985, 5–10 (7). Further references are to this edition and will be given as page numbers in the text.

38 See for example Cora Agatucci, 'Breaking from the Cage of Identity: Doris Lessing and *The Diaries of Jane Somers*', in *Redefining Autobiography in Twentieth-Century Women's Fiction: An Essay Collection*, eds Janice Morgan and Colette T. Hall, New York: Garland, 1991, 45–56.

39 See for example James Krasner, 'Accumulated Lives: Metaphor, Materiality, and the Homes of the Elderly', *Literature and Medicine*, 24, 2, 2005, 209–30, which relates the text to recent gerontological theories of spatialised memory. Mari-Ann Berg, 'Toward Creative Understanding: Bahktin and the Study of Old Age In Literature', *Journal of Aging Studies*, 10, 1, 1996, 15–26, reads *The Diaries* in relation to Mikhail Bakhtin's philosophy of dialogism and suggests that dialogism provides a fruitful contrast to ageism in the novel. A recent special issue of the journal *Doris Lessing Studies* entitled 'Coming to Age' also makes frequent reference to *The Diaries* (see *Doris Lessing Studies*, 24, 1–2, 2004).Other feminist readings situate the novel in relation to a number of important theoretical perspectives informed by ideas about mothering and maternity (see Gayle Greene, '*The Diaries of Jane Somers*: Doris Lessing, Feminism, and the Mother', in *Narrating Mothers: Theorizing Maternal Subjectivities*, eds Brenda O. Daly and Maureen T. Reddy, Knoxville: Tennessee University Press, 1991, 139–56); the double and the mirror (see Virginia Tiger, 'Ages of Anxiety: *The Diaries of Jane Somers*', in *Spiritual Exploration in the Works of Doris Lessing*, ed. Phyllis Sternberg Perrakis, Westport, CT: Greenwood Press, 1999, 1–16); the abject (see Diana Wallace, '"Women's Time": Women, Age and Inter-Generational Relations in Doris Lessing's *The Diaries of Jane Somers*', *Studies in the Literary Imagination*, 39, 2, 2006, 43–59), and empathy (see Judith Kegan Gardiner, *Rhys, Stead, Lessing, and the Politics of Empathy*, Bloomington: Indiana University Press, 1989).

40 Judith Butler, *Gender Trouble: Feminism and the Subversion of Identity*, London: Routledge, 1990.

41 Doris Lessing, *The Diaries of Jane Somers*, Harmondsworth: Penguin, 1985, 135. Further references are to this edition and will be given as page numbers in the text.

42 See Michel Foucault, 'What is an Author?', in *Modern Criticism and Theory: A Reader*, ed. David Lodge, London: Longman, 1988, 197–210 and Roland Barthes, 'The Death of the Author', in *Image-Music-Text*, ed. Stephen Heath, London: Fontana, 1977, 142–8.

43 Bertelsen, 113.

44 *Ibid.*

45 Foucault, 202.

46 John Mullan, *Anonymity: A Secret History of English Literature*, London: Faber and Faber, 2007, 7.

47 *Ibid.*, 297.

48 *Ibid.*, 286.

49 *Ibid.*, 287.

50 Claire Squires, *Marketing Literature: The Making of Contemporary Writing in Britain*, Basingstoke: Palgrave Macmillan, 2007, 6.

51 Pierre Bourdieu, 'The Field of Cultural Production; or, the Economic World Reversed', in *The Field of Cultural Production: Essays on Art and Literature*, ed. Randal Johnson, Cambridge: Polity Press, 1993, 29–73 (35).

52 *Ibid.*, 37.

53 *Ibid.*, 30.

54 *Ibid.*, 43.

55 Mary Eagleton, *Figuring the Woman Author in Contemporary Fiction*, Basingstoke: Palgrave Macmillan, 2005, 7.

56 Sinead McDermott, 'Notes on the Afterlife of Feminist Criticism', *PMLA*, 121, 5, 2006, 1729–34 (1732).

57 The collection is unique in that it includes not only literary criticism but also essays by the authors Margaret Drabble, Maggie Gee and Lisa Appignanesi and an interview with Carmen Callil, the founder of the Virago publishing house. See Judy Simons and Kate Fullbrook (eds.), *Writing: A Woman's Business. Women, Writing and the Marketplace*, Manchester: Manchester University Press, 1998, 1.

58 See Maggie Nolan and Carrie Dawson, 'Who's Who: Mapping

Hoaxes and Imposture in Australian Literary History', in 'Who's Who? Hoaxes, Imposture and Identity Crises in Australian Literature', eds Maggie Nolan and Carrie Dawson, special issue of *Australian Literary Studies*, 21, 3, 2004, v–xx (ix).

59 Maria Takolander and David McCooey, 'Fakes, Literary Identity and Public Culture', *Journal of the Association for the Study of Australian Literature*, 3, 2004, 57–66 (58).

60 Sue Vice, 'Helen Darville, *The Hand that Signed the Paper*: Who is "Helen Demidenko"', in *Scandalous Fictions: The Twentieth-Century Novel in the Public Sphere*, eds Jago Morrison and Susan Watkins, Basingstoke: Palgrave Macmillan, 2006, 172–86 (183).

61 Graham Huggan, *The Postcolonial Exotic: Marketing the Margins*, London: Routledge, 2001, vii.

62 Cynthia Port, '"None Of It Adds Up": Economies of Aging in *The Diary of a Good Neighbour*', *Doris Lessing Studies*, 24, 1–2, 2004, 30–5 (34).

63 Wallace, 57.

64 See for example Elizabeth Maslen, *Doris Lessing*, Plymouth: Northcote House, 1994 and Ruth Whittaker, *Doris Lessing*, Basingstoke: Macmillan, 1988.

65 Maggie Gee and Lisa Appignanesi, 'The Contemporary Writer: Gender and Genre', in *Writing: A Woman's Business. Women, Writing and the Marketplace*, eds Judy Simons and Kate Fullbrook, Manchester: Manchester University Press, 1998, 172–82 (173).

66 Pierre Bourdieu, *Distinction: A Social Critique of the Judgement of Taste*, trans. Richard Nice, London: Routledge and Kegan Paul, 1984, 3, 4.

67 Eagleton, 46–8.

68 Gee and Appignanesi, 173–4.

69 bell hooks, 'Postmodern Blackness', in *Yearning: Race, Gender and Cultural Politics*, Boston, MA: South End Press, 1990, 23–33.

70 Gee and Appignanesi, 182.

71 Denis Donoghue, 'Alice, the Radical Homemaker', *The New York Times*, 22 September 1985, <http://www.lexisnexis.com/uk> (accessed 3 July 2009).

72 In this period Lessing was also interested in the situation in Afghanistan, visiting Pakistan in 1986 to meet with refugees from the Russian invasion and leaders of the Muhjahidin. See her account in *The Wind Blows Away Our Words and other Documents Relating*

to the Afghan Resistance, London: Picador, 1987. Sandra Singer has written about *The Good Terrorist* in relation to this account in 'London and Kabul: Assessing the Politics of Terrorist Violence', in *Doris Lessing: Interrogating the Times*, ed. Phyllis Sternberg Perrakis, Debrah Raschke and Sandra Singer, Columbus: Ohio State University Press, forthcoming. I would like to thank Sandra for sending me a copy of her essay.

73 See the excellent website CAIN (Conflict Archive on the Internet - Conflict and Politics in Northern Ireland (1968 to the Present) for information about this period. <http://cain.ulst.ac.uk/index.html> (accessed 8 September 2009).

74 Anon., 'Lessing Says 9/11 "Not That Bad"', *BBC News Channel*, 24 October 2007, <http://news.bbc.co.uk/1/hi/entertainment/7057601.stm> (accessed 8 September 2009). The original article appeared in *El Pais* on 21 October 2007; Anon., 'La Guerra y la Memoria No Acaban Nunca', <http://www.elpais.com/articulo/reportajes/guerra/memoria/acaban/elpepusocdmg/20071021elpdmgrep_2/Tes> (accessed 13 September 2009). I would like to thank Katy Manns for finding and translating the original article for me.

75 Margaret Scanlan, 'Language and the Politics of Despair in Doris Lessing's *The Good Terrorist*', *Novel: A Forum on Fiction*, 23, 2, 1990, 182–98 (190–1).

76 Walter Goodman, 'Books of the Times', *The New York Times*, 17 September 1985, <http://www.lexisnexis.com/uk> (accessed 3 July 2009).

77 Donoghue.

78 Carole Corbeil, 'The Observer Author's Neo-Con Ideals Spawn a Loser of a Novel', *The Globe and Mail*, 19 December 1985, <http://www.lexisnexis.com/uk> (accessed 3 July 2009).

79 Deirdre Levinson, 'Future Shocked', *The Nation*, 23 November 1985, 557–9 (558).

80 Hanson, 70.

81 See both Carole Corbeil's and Denis Donoghue's reviews.

82 Levinson, 558.

83 Goodman.

84 Donoghue.

85 Doris Lessing, *The Good Terrorist*, London: Paladin, 1990, 28, 29. Further references are to this edition and will be given as page numbers in the text.

86 Scanlan, 183.

87 *Ibid.*

88 *Ibid.*, 196.

89 Jane Rogers, 'Saturday Rereadings: Dark Times: Jane Rogers Revisits a Novel She Was First Drawn To When She Was Living In A Squat', *The Guardian*, 3 December 2005, <http://www.lexis-nexis.com/uk> (accessed 3 July 2009).

90 Jeannette King, *Doris Lessing*, London: Edward Arnold, 1989, 103, 104.

91 David Punter, *Gothic Pathologies: The Text, the Body and the Law*, Basingstoke: Macmillan, 1998, 98–9.

92 Elleke Boehmer, 'Postcolonial Writing and Terror', *Wasafiri*, 22, 2, 2007, 4–7 (5, 6).

93 *Ibid.*

94 Scanlan, 186.

95 Hanson, 71.

96 Doris Lessing, 'The Small Personal Voice', in *A Small Personal Voice: Essays, Reviews, Interviews*, ed. Paul Schlueter, London: Flamingo, 1994, 7–26 (9).

Chapter 5

1 Aaron S. Rosenfeld, 'Re-membering the Future: Doris Lessing's "Experiment in Autobiography"', *Critical Survey*, 17, 1, 2005, 40–55 (40).

2 Gilles Deleuze and Felix Guattari, *Kafka: Toward a Minor Literature*, trans. Dana Polan, fwd. Reda Bensmaia, Minneapolis: University of Minnesota Press, 1986, 18.

3 *Ibid.*

4 *Ibid.*, 17.

5 *Ibid.*, 35.

6 *Ibid.*

7 Doris Lessing, *Prisons we Choose to Live Inside*, London: Perennial, 1987, 54. Further references are to this edition and will be given as page numbers in the text.

8 Sharon L. Dean, 'Lessing's *The Fifth Child*', *Explicator*, 50, 1992, 120–2 (122).

9 Louise Yelin, *From the Margins of Empire: Christina Stead, Doris Lessing, Nadine Gordimer*, Ithaca: Cornell University Press, 1998, 104.

10 *Ibid.*

11 The full text of the speech is available on several websites, including <http://www.sterlingtimes.org/powell_speech.doc> (accessed 8 September 2009).

12 Yelin, 106.

13 Michiko Kakutani, 'Books of the Times; His Weirdness Attracts Types Even More Weird', *The New York Times*, 8 August 2000, <http://query.nytimes.com/gst/fullpage.html?res=9A04E2DB103CF93BA3575BC0A9669C8B63> (accessed 8 September 2009).

14 See Alex Clark, 'Growing Pains: Alex Clark Finds Lessing's Sequel as Freakish as Its Hero',*The Guardian*, 17 June 2000, <http://books.guardian.co.uk/reviews/generalfiction/0,,332971,00.html> (accessed 8 September 2009) and M. Pye, 'The Creature Walks Among Us', *The New York Times*, 6 August 2000, <http://query.nytimes.com/gst/fullpage.html?res=9D06E4DE163DF935A3575BC0A9669C8B63> (accessed 8 September 2009).

15 Kakutani, 'Books of the Times; His Weirdness Attracts Types Even More Weird'.

16 Clark.

17 Kakutani, 'Books of the Times: His Weirdness Attracts Types Even More Weird'.

18 See for example H. Barnacle, 'On Thin Ice', *Sunday Times*, 4 April 1999, 9; Michiko Kakutani, 'Books of the Times; Where Millenniums are Treated Like Centuries', *The New York Times*, 26 January 1999, <http://query.nytimes.com/gst/fullpage.html?res=9D0DE2DD1539F935A15752C0A96F958260> (accessed 8 September 2009); and Michael Upchurch, 'Back to Ifrik', *The New York Times*, 10 January 1999, <http://query.nytimes.com/gst/fullpage.html?res=9C05E2DD1E3FF933A25752C0A96F958260> (accessed 8 September 2009).

19 Barnacle, 9.

20 Amongst those to use this term about the novel were Brian Aldiss, 'My Sort of Fairy Tale', *The Guardian*, 17 April 1999, 8 and Erica Wagner, 'Good on Science', *The Times*, 25 March 1999, 42.

21 Upchurch.

22 Kakutani, 'Books of the Times; Where Millenniums are Treated Like Centuries'.

23 Wagner, 42.

24 Upchurch.

25 Deleuze and Guattari, 16.

26 Yelin, 106.

27 Roger Luckhurst, 'The Contemporary London Gothic and the Limits of the "Spectral Turn"', *Textual Practice*, 16, 2002, 527–46 (527–8). I would like to thank Sue Chaplin for alerting me to this article.

28 *Ibid.*, 539.

29 D. Keay, 'Aids, Education and the Year 2000', Interview with Margaret Thatcher, *Woman's Own*, 31 October 1987, 8–10.

30 Doris Lessing, *The Fifth Child*, London: Flamingo, 1993, 7. Further references are to this edition and will appear as page numbers in the text.

31 J. Collins and R. Wilson, 'The Broken Allegory: Doris Lessing's *The Fifth Child* as Narrative Theodicy', *Analecta Husserliana: The Yearbook of Phenomenological Research*, 41, 1994, 277–91 (281).

32 *Ibid.*, 289.

33 Luckhurst, 540.

34 David Punter, *Gothic Pathologies: The Text, the Body and the Law*, Basingstoke: Macmillan, 1998, 98–9.

35 Deleuze and Guattari, 35.

36 Angela Hague, 'Picaresque Structure and the Angry Young Novel', *Twentieth Century Literature*, 32, 1986, 209–20 (211).

37 *Ibid.*, 213, 216.

38 See Tom Maschler (ed.), *Declaration*, London: MacGibbon and Kee, 1957.

39 Doris Lessing, *Ben, In the World*, London: Flamingo, 2000, 82. Further references are to this edition and will appear as page numbers in the text.

40 Celia Brickman, 'Primitivity, Race, and Religion in Psychoanalysis', *Journal of Religion*, 82, 1, 2002, 53–74 (55).

41 Thomas Pughe comes up with the term 'neo-picaresque' in 'Reading the Picaresque: Mark Twain's *The Adventures of Huckleberry Finn*, Saul Bellow's *The Adventures of Augie March*, and More Recent Adventures', *English Studies* 77, 1996, 59–70 (59).

42 This use of prolepsis was commented on negatively by many reviewers. See for example Kakutani, 'Books of the Times; His Weirdness Attracts Types Even More Weird' and Pye.

43 Roger Luckhurst, 'Cultural Governance, New Labour, and the British SF Boom', *Science Fiction Studies*, 30, 2003, 417–35 (425).

44 Fredric Jameson, *Archaeologies of the Future: The Desire Called Utopia and Other Science Fiction*, London: Verso, 2005, 288.

45 Luckhurst, 428.

46 Doris Lessing, *Mara and Dann*, London: Flamingo, 1999, 374. Further references are to this edition and appear as page numbers in the text.

47 Claire Messud, 'Future Imperfect', *New Statesman*, 13 June 2005, <http//www.lexisnexis.com> (accessed 27 July 2009), found the novel 'rambling', 'clumsy' and 'perfunctory'. Tom Adair also found the plot cumbersome. See 'Questing Again', *The Scotsman*, 18 June 2005, <http//www.lexisnexis.com> (accessed 27 July 2009).

48 See Michele Roberts, 'Chilling News from the Frozen Future', *The Independent*, 17 June 2005, <http//www.lexisnexis.com> (accessed 27 July 2009).

49 Geraldine Bedell, 'Ancestral Voices: Doris Lessing Evokes a Storytelling Tradition in her Haunting Novel', *The Observer*, 3 July 2005, <http//www.lexisnexis.com> (accessed 27 July 2009).

50 Fiona Becket, 'Environmental Fables?: The Eco-politics of Doris Lessing's "Ifrik" Novels', in *Doris Lessing: Border Crossings*, eds Alice Ridout and Susan Watkins, London: Continuum, 2009, 129–42 (135).

51 Doris Lessing, *The Story of General Dann and Mara's Daughter, Griot and the Snow Dog*, London: Harper Collins, 2005, 203. Further references are to this edition and will be given as page numbers in the text.

52 See for example Jacques Derrida, 'Freud and the Scene of Writing', in *Writing and Difference*, trans. Alan Bass, Chicago: University of Chicago Press, 1978, 196–231, where he uses the palimpsest as a model for language, writing and identity as inevitably intertextual and intersubjective.

53 Bill Ashcroft, Gareth Griffiths and Helen Tiffin, *Key Concepts in Post-Colonial Studies*, London: Routledge, 1998, 176. See also chapter 1, note 16 for other criticism on the city as palimpsest in Lessing's writing.

54 Bedell.

55 Andrzej Gasiorek, *Post-War British Fiction: Realism and After*, London: Edward Arnold, 1995, 93.

56 Deleuze and Guattari, 58.

57 Clare Hanson, 'Doris Lessing in Pursuit of the English; or, No Small, Personal Voice', in *In Pursuit of Doris Lessing: Nine Nations Reading*, ed. Claire Sprague, Basingstoke: Macmillan, 1990, 61–73 (57).

58 Gasiorek, 93.

59 Deleuze and Guattari, 17.

Chapter 6

1 Toni Morrison, 'Home', in *The House that Race Built*, ed. Wahneema Lubiano, New York: Vintage, 1998, 3–12 (3). I would like to thank Jago Morrison for alerting me to Toni Morrison's reference to Doris Lessing's use of the city in this essay.

2 *Ibid.*, 5.

3 Doris Lessing, *Martha Quest*, London: Paladin, 1990, 21–2.

4 Doris Lessing, *The Four-Gated City*, London: Grafton, 1972, 151.

5 See chapter 1, note 16.

6 See Sigmund Freud, 'The "Uncanny"', *Standard Edition of the Complete Psychological Works of Sigmund Freud*, vol. 17, trans. James Strachey, London: Hogarth Press, 1955, 217–56.

7 Doris Lessing, *The Sweetest Dream*, London: Flamingo, 2001, 54. Further references are to this edition and will be given as page numbers in the text.

8 Doris Lessing, *Walking in the Shade: Volume Two of my Autobiography, 1949–1962*, London: Flamingo, 1998, 368.

9 Lynne Segal, 'Formations of Feminism: Political Histories of the Left (II)', *Radical Philosophy* 123, 2004, 8–27 (15). I would like to thank Gordon Johnston for pointing out Segal's essay on memoirs of women on the Left.

10 Anthony Chennells, 'From Bildungsroman to Family Saga: *The Sweetest Dream*', *Partisan Review*, 69, 2002, 297–301 (300).

11 Benedict Anderson, *Imagined Communities: Reflections on the Origins and Spread of Nationalism*, London: Verso, 1991, 6.

12 Homi Bhabha, '"Race", Time and the Revision of Modernity', in *Postcolonial Criticism*, eds B. Moore Gilbert, G. Stanton and W. Maley, Harlow: Addison Wesley Longman, 1997, 166–90 (182).

13 Partha Chatterjee, *Nationalist Thought and the Colonial World: A Derivative Discourse*, London: Zed Books, 1986, 38.

14 Homi Bhabha, *Nation and Narration*, London: Routledge, 1990, 4.

15 Chennells, 301.

16 Morrison, 'Home', 8.

17 *Ibid.*, 5.

18 Toni Morrison, 'The Site of Memory', in *Out There: Marginalisation and Contemporary Cultures*, eds R. Ferguson, M. Gever, T. Minh-ha and C. West, The New Museum of Contemporary Art, New York: Documentary Sources in Contemporary Art Vol. 4, Cambridge, MA: MIT Press, 1990, 299–305 (302).

19 Pin-Chia Feng, 'Rituals of Rememory: Afro-Caribbean Religions in *Myal* and *It Begins with Tears*', *Melus*, 27, 2002, 149–75 (152).

20 *Ibid.*, 154.

21 Doris Lessing, *Love, Again*, London: Flamingo, 1996, 241. Further references are to this edition and will be given as page numbers in the text.

22 Doris Lessing, *Under My Skin: Volume One of my Autobiography, to 1949*, London: Harper Collins, 1994, 10.

23 *Ibid.*, 156.

24 Lessing, *Walking in the Shade*, 238.

25 *Ibid.*, 239.

26 *Ibid.*, 240.

27 *Ibid.*, 241.

28 Feng, 168.

29 See Bharati Mukherjee, 'Waiting for Lefties', *Bookforum*, Spring 2002, <http://www.bookforum.net/mukher.html> (accessed 6 November 2002).

30 Stephanie Merrill, '*The Sweetest Dream*', *New Statesman*, 130, 4557, 2001, 83.

31 Hywel Williams, 'The Dream is Over', *The Guardian*, 22 September, 2001, <http://books.guardian.co.uk/reviws/generalfiction/0,6121,555617,00.html> (accessed 6 November 2002).

32 Justine Ettler, 'Drunken Dinner Parties and a Quest for Truth', *The Observer*, 23 September 2001, <http://books.guardian.co.uk/reviews/generalfiction/0,6121,556330,00.html> (accessed 6 November 2002).

33 John McCallister, 'Knowing Native, Going Native: *African Laughter*, Colonial Epistemology, and Post-Colonial Homecoming', *Doris Lessing Studies*, 22, 2001, 12–15 (12).

34 Lessing, *Under My Skin*, 302.

35 Doris Lessing, *African Laughter: Four Visits to Zimbabwe*, London: Flamingo, 1993, 305.

36 Christina L. Bell suggested the different effects of bruising on black and white skin in her comments on an early version of this chapter that was presented as a conference paper at the 'Hystorical Fictions: Women, History and Authorship' conference at the University of Wales Swansea, 5–7 August 2003.

37 Lessing, *African Laughter*, 12–13.

38 Homi Bhabha, *The Location of Culture*, London: Routledge, 1994, 219.

39 Morrison, 'The Site of Memory', 305.

40 Doris Lessing, 'Writing Autobiography', in *Time Bites: Views and Reviews*, London: Fourth Estate, 2004, 90–103 (98).

41 Doris Lessing, 'The Tragedy of Zimbabwe', in *Time Bites: Views and Reviews*, London: Fourth Estate, 2004, 231–46 (231). This was first published, in slightly amended form, as 'The Jewel of Africa', *New York Review of Books*, 50, 6, 10 April 2003, <http://www.nybooks.com/articles/16170> (accessed 8 September 2009).

42 *Ibid.*, 231.

43 *Ibid.*, 233.

44 *Ibid.*, 235.

45 *Ibid.*, 239.

46 Janet Jagan, 'Letter in Response to "The Jewel Of Africa"', *New York Review of Books*, 50, 16, 23 October 2003, <http://www.nybooks.com/articles/16693> (accessed 8 September 2009).

47 *Ibid.*

48 Morrison, 'The Site of Memory', 302.

49 Doris Lessing, 'A Reissue of *The Golden Notebook*', in *Time Bites: Views and Reviews*, London: Fourth Estate, 2004, 138–41 (141).

50 Lessing, *Under My Skin*, 16.

51 Lessing, *Walking in the Shade*, 368.

52 Claire Sprague, *Rereading Doris Lessing: Narrative Patterns of Doubling and Repetition*, Chapel Hill: University of North Carolina Press, 1987.

53 Paul De Man, 'Autobiography as De-facement', *Modern Language Notes*, 94, 1979, 919–30.

54 Tess Cosslett, Celia Lury and Penny Summerfield (eds), *Feminism and Autobiography: Texts, Theories, Methods*, London: Routledge, 2000. See p. 1 for the argument about genre and discipline, p. 7 for the point about performative conceptions of subjectivity, and pp. 3 and 5 for the notion of intersubjectivity.

55 The term is Jan Hokensen's. See 'Intercultural Autobiography', *A/b: Auto/Biography Studies*, 10, 1995, 92–113.

56 Lauren Rusk, *The Life Writing of Otherness: Woolf, Baldwin, Kingston and Winterson*, London: Routledge, 2002.

57 Ursula Le Guin, 'Saved by a Squirt', *The Guardian*, 10 February 2007, <http://www.guardian.co.uk/books/2007/feb/10/fiction.dorislessing> (accessed 8 September 2009).

58 Phyllis Sternberg Perrakis, 'The Porous Border Between Fact and Fiction: Empathy and Identification in Doris Lessing's *The Cleft*', in *Doris Lessing: Border Crossings*, eds Alice Ridout and Susan Watkins, London: Continuum, 2009, 143–59 (143).

59 Lessing, *Alfred and Emily*, London: Fourth Estate, 2008, viii.

60 Morrison, 'The Site of Memory', 299.

61 Lessing, *Under My Skin*, 162.

62 Lessing, 'Writing Autobiography', 98–9.

63 Michiko Kakutani, 'Books of the Times: A Four-Decade Kitchen-Sink Tale (as in Everything But)', *The New York Times*, 1 February 2002, <http://query.nytimes.com/gst/fullpage.html?res=990CE2DE163DF932A35751C0A9649C8B63> (accessed 16 July 2003).

Chapter 7

1 See, for example, my discussion of reviews of *The Sweetest Dream* in chapter 6.

2 A review of her 2003 short story collection, *The Grandmothers*, claims that 'she more than deserves her reputation as the grande dame of literary fiction'. See Nadine O'Regan, 'Grande Dame Can Still Deliver', *The Sunday Business Post Online*, <http://archives.tcm.ie/businesspost/2003/10/26/story188365199.asp> (accessed 11 September 2009).

3 Susan Watkins, '"Grande Dame" or "New Woman"?: Doris Lessing and the Palimpsest', *LIT: Literature Interpretation Theory*,17, 3–4, 2006, 243–62.

4 Jennifer Byrne, 'Interview with Doris Lessing', *Foreign Correspondent*, 24 October 2001, <http://www.abc.net.au/foreign/stories/s390537.htm> (accessed 11 September 2009).

5 Motoko Rich and Sarah Lyall, 'Doris Lessing Wins Nobel Prize in Literature', *The New York Times*, 11 October 2007 <http://www.nytimes.com/2007/10/11/world/11cnd-nobel.html > (accessed 13 September 2009).

6 Bloom quoted in Anon., 'UK's Lessing Wins Nobel Prize in Literature', *Associated Press*, 11 October 2007, <http://www.msnbc.msn.com/id/12784353/> (accessed 11 September 2009).

7 See Anon., <http://nobelprize.org/nobel_prizes/faq.html> (accessed 11 September 2009).

8 Elaine Showalter, *A Literature of Their Own: British Women Novelists from Bronte to Lessing*, London: Virago, 1978, 13.

9 *Ibid.*, 309.

10 *Ibid.*, 311.

11 *Ibid.*, 289.

12 In the revised edition of *A Literature of Their Own*, published in 1999, Showalter argues that Moi 'missed the real theoretical assumptions' of her book, which were 'historical and cultural'. See Elaine Showalter, *A Literature of Their Own: British Women Novelists from Bronte to Lessing*, Princeton, NJ: Princeton University Press, 1999, xix–xx. Her assessment of Lessing's work did not alter.

13 Toril Moi, *Sexual/Textual Politics: Feminist Literary* Theory, London: Routledge, 1985, 3.

14 *Ibid.*, 9.

15 *Ibid.*, 13.

16 Showalter's use of Woolf and Lessing to frame her book was picked up by Ruth Saxton and Jean Tobin in their edited collection on the two writers. See Ruth Saxton and Jean Tobin (eds), *Woolf and Lessing: Breaking the Mold*, Basingstoke: Macmillan, 1994.

17 Alice Jardine invents the neologism *gynesis* and defines it as 'the putting into discourse of "woman" as that *process* … intrinsic to new and necessary modes of thinking, writing, speaking'. See *Gynesis: Configurations of Woman and Modernity*, Ithaca: Cornell University Press, 1985, 25.

18 Gayle Greene, *Doris Lessing: The Poetics of Change*, Ann Arbor, MI: The University of Michigan Press, 1994, 15.

19 *Ibid.*

20 *Ibid.*, 19.

21 *Ibid.*

22 Doris Lessing, Preface to *The Golden Notebook*, London: Flamingo, 1993, 7–21 (9).

23 *Ibid.*, 13.

24 Rachel Blau DuPlessis refers to her work 'For the Etruscans' this way in an interview with Jeanne Heuving. See Heuving, 'An Interview with Rachel Blau DuPlessis', *Contemporary Literature*, 45, 3, 2004, 397–420 (400).

25 Rachel Blau DuPlessis, 'For the Etruscans', in *The New Feminist Criticism: Essays on Women, Literature and Theory*, ed. Elaine Showalter, London: Virago, 1986, 271–91 (272).

26 Heuving, 413.

27 DuPlessis, 275.

28 *Ibid.*, 279–80.

29 *Ibid.*, 279, 288.

30 Elizabeth Abel, '*The Golden Notebook*, Female Writing and the Great Tradition', in *Critical Essays on Doris Lessing*, eds Claire Sprague and Virginia Tiger, Boston, MA: G. K. Hall, 1986, 101–6 (101).

31 *Ibid.*, 106.

32 *Ibid.*, 103.

33 Molly Hite, *The Other Side of the Story: Structures and Strategies of Contemporary Feminist Narratives*, Ithaca, NY: Cornell University Press, 1989, 2.

34 See Sinead McDermott, 'Notes on the Afterlife of Feminist Criticism', *PMLA*, 121, 5, 2006, 1729–34 and the entire special section of *PMLA*, 121, 5, 2006, entitled 'Feminist Criticism Today' for a discussion of these issues.

35 The journal *Doris Lessing Studies* is the journal of the US-based Doris Lessing Society. The Society is affiliated to the Modern Languages Association (MLA; one of the largest organisations for the study of language and literature in the world) and organises a panel at the annual MLA convention, one of the biggest conferences in the field. The journal publishes short articles on Lessing's work, organises themed special issues on her writing and also on occasion publishes interviews with Lessing. Some interesting and innovative work on Lessing appears here.

36 Josna Rege, 'Editorial: Coming to Age', *Doris Lessing Studies*, 24, 1–2, 2004, 3–7 (3).

37 Diana Wallace, '"Women's Time": Women, Age and Inter-Generational Relations in Doris Lessing's *The Diaries of Jane Somers*', *Studies in the Literary Imagination*, 39, 2, 2006, 43–59 (43).

38 *Ibid.*, 44.

39 *Ibid.*, 47.

40 Phyllis Sternberg Perrakis, *Adventures of the Spirit: The Older Woman in the Works of Doris Lessing, Margaret Atwood, and Other Contemporary Women Writers, Columbus, OH: Ohio State University Press, 2007, 4.*

41 *Ibid.*, 5.

42 See for example the discussion of Homi Bhabha's use of the term 'hybridity' in chapter 2, p. 41.

43 Victoria Rosner, 'Home Fires: Doris Lessing, Colonial Architecture, and the Reproduction of Mothering', *Tulsa Studies in Women's Literature*, 18, 1, 1999, 59–89 (60).

44 *Ibid.*, 59.

45 Louise Yelin, *From the Margins of Empire: Christina Stead, Doris Lessing, Nadine Gordimer*, Ithaca: Cornell University Press, 1998, 6.

46 *Ibid.*

47 Eve Bertelsen (ed.), *Doris Lessing*, Johannesburg: McGraw-Hill, 1985, 25.

48 *Ibid.*

49 Eve Bertelsen, 'Veldtanschauung: Doris Lessing's Savage Africa', *Modern Fiction Studies*, 37, 4, 1991, 647–58 (657).

50 Anthony Chennells, 'Postcolonialism and Doris Lessing's Empires', *Doris Lessing Studies*, 21, 2, 2001, 4–11 (6).

51 *Ibid.*, 7.

52 *Ibid.*, 5.

53 *Ibid.*, 8.

54 *Ibid.*, 10.

55 See Graham Huggan, *The Postcolonial Exotic: Marketing the Margins*, London: Routledge, 2001.

56 This was evident from the range of nationalities of the conference delegates who attended the Second International Doris Lessing Conference at Leeds Metropolitan University in 2007.

57 Nibir K. Ghosh, 'Editorial', *Re-Markings*, 7, 1, 2008, 3–4 (3).

58 Claire Sprague (ed.), *In Pursuit of Doris Lessing: Nine Nations Reading*, Basingstoke: Macmillan, 1990, 13.

59 *Ibid.*, 13–14.

60 Ghosh, 3–4.

61 Greene, 31.

62 Abel, 104.

63 Jeannette King, *Doris Lessing*, London: Edward Arnold, 1989, viii, ix.

64 *Ibid.*, ix.

65 Betsy Draine, *Substance Under Pressure: Artistic Coherence and Evolving Form in the Novels of Doris Lessing*, Madison: Wisconsin University Press, 1983, xii.

66 Claire Sprague, *Rereading Doris Lessing: Narrative Patterns of Doubling and Repetition*, Chapel Hill: University of North Carolina Press, 1987, 4.

67 Sprague, quoted in Greene, 246.

68 Clare Hanson, 'Doris Lessing in Pursuit of the English, or, No Small, Personal Voice', in *In Pursuit of Doris Lessing: Nine Nations Reading*, ed. Claire Sprague, Basingstoke: Macmillan, 1990, 61–73 (68).

69 Hanson's essay first appeared in *PN Review*. See Clare Hanson, 'Doris Lessing In Pursuit of the English; or, No Small, Personal Voice', *PN Review*, 14, 1987, 39–42.

70 Patricia Waugh, *Metafiction: The Theory and Practice of Self-Conscious Fiction*, London: Methuen, 1984, 76.

71 *Ibid.*, 77–8.

72 Magali Cornier Michael, *Feminism and the Postmodern Impulse: Post-World War II Fiction*, Albany: State University of New York Press, 1996, 79, 80.

73 Patricia Waugh, *Feminine Fictions: Revisiting the Postmodern*, London: Routledge, 1989, 197.

74 Virginia Tiger, '"Taking Hands and Dancing in (Dis)unity": Story to Storied in Doris Lessing's "To Room Nineteen" and "A Room"', *Modern Fiction Studies*, 36, 3, 1990, 421–33.

75 Nicole Ward-Jouve, 'Of Mud and Other Matter: *The Children of Violence*', in *Notebooks/Memoirs/Archives: Reading and Re-reading Doris Lessing*, ed. Jenny Taylor, London: Routledge and Kegan Paul, 1982, 75–134 (130).

76 Roberta Rubenstein, *The Novelistic Vision of Doris Lessing: Breaking the Forms of Consciousness*, Urbana: University of Illinois Press, 1979, 7.

77 *Ibid.*, 251.

78 Judith Kegan Gardiner, *Rhys, Stead, Lessing and the Politics of Empathy*, Bloomington: Indiana University Press, 1989, 5.

79 Shadia Fahim, *Doris Lessing: Sufi Equilibrium and the Form of the Novel*, Basingstoke: Macmillan, 1994, 1.

80 *Ibid.*, 235–6.

81 Müge Galin, *Between East and West: Sufism in the Novels of Doris Lessing*, Albany, NY: State University of New York Press, 1997, 21.

82 Phyllis Sternberg Perrakis (ed.), *Spiritual Exploration in the Works of Doris Lessing*, Westport, CT: Greenwood Press, 1999, xi.

83 Jenny Taylor (ed.), *Notebooks/Memoirs/Archives: Reading and Rereading Doris Lessing*, London: Routledge and Kegan Paul, 1982, 15.

84 *Ibid.*, 27.

85 Katherine Fishburn, *The Unexpected Universe of Doris Lessing*, Westport, CT.: Greenwood Press, 1985, 3.

86 *Ibid.*, 4.

87 Lucie Armitt, 'Your Word is My Command: The Structures of Language and Power in Women's Science Fiction', in *Where No Man Has Gone Before: Essays on Women and Science Fiction*, ed. Lucie Armitt, London: Routledge, 1990, 123–38 (124).

88 Eve Bertelsen, 'Interview with Doris Lessing', in *Doris Lessing*, ed. Eve Bertelsen, Johannesburg: McGraw-Hill, 1985, 93–120 (113).

89 Lorna Sage, *Doris Lessing*, London: Methuen, 1983, 11.

90 Bertelsen, 93.

91 *Ibid.*

Bibliography

Abel, Elizabeth, '*The Golden Notebook*, Female Writing and the Great Tradition', in *Critical Essays on Doris Lessing*, eds Claire Sprague and Virginia Tiger, Boston, MA: G. K. Hall, 1986, 101–6.

Adair, Tom, 'Questing Again', *The Scotsman*, 18 June 2005, <http://www.lexisnexis.com> (accessed 27 July 2009).

Agatucci, Cora, 'Breaking from the Cage of Identity: Doris Lessing and *The Diaries of Jane Somers*', in *Redefining Autobiography in Twentieth-Century Women's Fiction: An Essay Collection*, eds Janice Morgan and Colette T. Hall, New York: Garland, 1991, 45–56.

Aldiss, Brian,'My Sort of Fairy Tale', *The Guardian*, 17 April 1999, 8.

Alexander, Marguerite, *Flights from Realism: Themes and Strategies in Postmodernist British and American Fiction*, London: Edward Arnold, 1990.

Allardyce, Lisa, 'Saturday Interview', *The Guardian*, 13 October 2007, 33.

Alter, Robert, 'Doris Lessing in the Visionary Mode', *The New York Times*, 11 January 1981, <http://www.lexisnexis.com/uk> (accessed 19 June 2008).

Anderson, Benedict, *Imagined Communities: Reflections on the Origins and Spread of Nationalism*, London: Verso, 1991.

Anon., <http://nobelprize.org/nobel_prizes/faq.html> (accessed 11 September 2009).

Anon., 'La Guerra y la Memoria No Acaban Nunca', *El Pais*, 21 October 2007, <http://www.elpais.com/articulo/reportajes/guerra/memoria/acaban/elpepusocdmg/20071021elpdmgrep_2/Tes> (accessed 13 September 2009).

Anon., 'Lessing Says 9/11 "Not That Bad"', *BBC News Channel*, 24 October 2007, <http://news.bbc.co.uk/1/hi/entertainment/7057601.stm> (accessed 8 September 2009).

Anon., 'UK's Lessing Wins Nobel Prize in Literature', *Associated Press*, 11 October 2007, <http://www.msnbc.msn.com/id/12784353/> (accessed 11 September 2009).

Appignanesi, Lisa, 'Interview: Doris Lessing', *Bookforum*, Spring 2002, <http://www.bookforum.com/archive/spr_02/interview_lessing.html> (accessed 4 September 2009).

Arias, Rosario, '"All the World's a Stage": Theatricality, Spectacle and the *Flaneuse* in Doris Lessing's Vision of London', *Journal of Gender Studies*, 14, 2005, 3–11.

Armitt, Lucie (ed.), *Where No Man Has Gone Before: Essays on Women and Science Fiction*, London: Routledge, 1990.

Armitt, Lucie, 'Your Word is My Command: The Structures of Language and Power in Women's Science Fiction', in *Where No Man Has Gone Before: Essays on Women and Science Fiction*, ed. Lucie Armitt, London: Routledge, 1990, 123–38.

Ashcroft, Bill, Gareth Griffiths and Helen Tiffin, *Key Concepts in Post-Colonial Studies*, London: Routledge, 1998.

Barnacle, H., 'On Thin Ice', *Sunday Times*, 4 April 1999, 9.

Barthes, Roland, 'The Death of the Author', in *Image-Music-Text*, ed. Stephen Heath, London: Fontana, 1977, 142–8.

Bazin, Victoria, 'Commodifying the Past: Doris Lessing's *The Golden Notebook* as Nostalgic Narrative', *Journal of Commonwealth Literature*, 43, 2, 2008, 117–31.

Becket, Fiona, 'Environmental Fables?: The Eco-politics of Doris Lessing's "Ifrik" Novels', in *Doris Lessing: Border Crossings*, eds Alice Ridout and Susan Watkins, London: Continuum, 2009, 129–42.

Beckett, Andy, *When the Lights Went Out: Britain in the Seventies*, London: Faber, 2009.

Bedell, Geraldine, 'Ancestral Voices: Doris Lessing Evokes a Storytelling Tradition in her Haunting Novel', *The Observer*, 3 July 2005, <http://www.lexisnexis.com> (accessed 27 July 2009).

Bentley, Nick, 'Doris Lessing's *The Golden Notebook*: An Experiment in Critical Fiction', in *Doris Lessing: Border Crossings*, eds Alice Ridout and Susan Watkins, London: Continuum, 2009, 44–60.

Berg, Mari-Ann, 'Toward Creative Understanding: Bahktin and the Study of Old Age In Literature', *Journal of Aging Studies*, 10, 1, 1996, 15–26.

Bertelsen, Eve (ed.), *Doris Lessing*, Johannesburg: McGraw-Hill, 1985.

Bertelsen, Eve, 'Interview with Doris Lessing', in *Doris Lessing*, ed. Eve Bertelsen, Johannesburg: McGraw-Hill, 1985, 93–120.

Bertelsen, Eve, 'Veldtanschauung: Doris Lessing's Savage Africa', *Modern Fiction Studies*, 37, 4, 1991, 647–58.

Bhabha, Homi, *Nation and Narration*, London: Routledge, 1990.

Bhabha, Homi, '"Race", Time and the Revision of Modernity', in *Post-colonial Criticism*, eds B. Moore Gilbert, G. Stanton and W. Maley, Harlow: Addison Wesley Longman, 1997, 166–90.

Bhabha, Homi K., *The Location of Culture*, London: Routledge, 1994.

Black, Shameem, 'Cosmopolitanism at Home: Amitav Ghosh's *The Shadow Lines*', *Journal of Commonwealth Literature*, 41, 3, 2006, 45–65.

Blake, William, 'Auguries of Innocence', in *Songs of Innocence and Experience and Other Works*, ed. R. B. Kennedy, Plymouth: Macdonald and Evans, 1970, 134.

Boehmer, Elleke, 'Postcolonial Writing and Terror', *Wasafiri*, 22, 2, 2007, 4–7.

Bourdieu, Pierre, *Distinction: A Social Critique of the Judgement of Taste*, trans. Richard Nice, London: Routledge and Kegan Paul, 1984.

Bourdieu, Pierre, 'The Field of Cultural Production; or, the Economic World Reversed', in *The Field of Cultural Production: Essays on Art and Literature*, ed. Randal Johnson, Cambridge: Polity Press, 1993, 29–73.

Boym, Svetlana, *The Future of Nostalgia*, New York: Basic Books, 2001.

Brah, Avtar, *Cartographies of Diaspora: Contesting Identities*, London: Routledge, 1996.

Brennan, Timothy, *At Home in the World: Cosmopolitanism Now*, Cambridge, MA: Harvard University Press, 1997.

Brickman, Celia, 'Primitivity, Race, and Religion in Psychoanalysis', *Journal of Religion*, 82, 1, 2002, 53–74.

Burton, Antoinette, 'The Ugly Americans: Gender, Geopolitics and the Career of Postcolonial Cosmopolitanism in the Novels of Santha Rama Rau', *Journal of Commonwealth Literature*, 41, 2, 2006, 5–19.

Butler, Judith, *Gender Trouble: Feminism and the Subversion of Identity*, London: Routledge, 1990.

Butler, Judith, *The Psychic Life of Power: Theories in Subjection*, Stanford, CA: Stanford University Press, 1997.

Byrne, Jennifer, 'Interview with Doris Lessing', *Foreign Correspondent*, 24 October 2001, <http://www.abc.net.au/foreign/stories/s390537.htm> (accessed 11 September 2009).

CAIN (Conflict Archive on the Internet - Conflict and Politics in Northern Ireland (1968 to the Present) <http://cain.ulst.ac.uk/index.html> (accessed 8 September 2009).

Cairnie, Julie, 'Rhodesian Children and the Lessons of White Supremacy', *Journal of Commonwealth Literature*, 43, 2, 2008, 145–56.

Chambers, Claire, 'Postcolonial Science Fiction: Amitav Ghosh's *The Calcutta Chromosome*', *Journal of Commonwealth Literature*, 38, 1, 2003, 57–72.

Chatterjee, Partha, *Nationalist Thought and the Colonial World: A Derivative Discourse*, London: Zed Books, 1986.

Cheah, Pheng and Bruce Robbins (eds), *Cosmopolitics: Thinking and Feeling Beyond the Nation*, Minneapolis: University of Minnesota Press, 1998.

Cheah, Pheng, 'Introduction Part II: The Cosmopolitical Today', in *Cosmopolitics: Thinking and Feeling Beyond the Nation*, eds Pheng Cheah and Bruce Robbins, Minneapolis: University of Minnesota Press, 1998, 20–44.

Cheng, Anne Anlin, *The Melancholy of Race: Psychoanalysis, Assimilation, and Hidden Grief*, Oxford: Oxford University Press, 2001.

Chennells, Anthony, 'Doris Lessing and the Rhodesian Settler Novel', in *Doris Lessing*, ed. Eve Bertelsen, Johannesburg: McGraw-Hill, 1985, 31–43.

Chennells, Anthony, 'From Bildungsroman to Family Saga: *The Sweetest Dream*', *Partisan Review*, 69, 2002, 297–301.

Chennells, Anthony, 'Postcolonialism and Doris Lessing's Empires', *Doris Lessing Studies*, 21, 2, 2001, 4–11.

Chennells, Anthony, 'Reading Doris Lessing's Rhodesian Stories in Zimbabwe', in *In Pursuit of Doris Lessing: Nine Nations Reading*, ed. Claire Sprague, Basingstoke: Macmillan, 1990, 17–40.

Clark, Alex, 'Growing Pains: Alex Clark Finds Lessing's Sequel as Freakish as Its Hero', *The Guardian*, 17 June 2000, <http://books.guardian.co.uk/reviews/generalfiction/0,,332971,00.html> (accessed 8 September 2009).

Clifford, James, 'Traveling Cultures', in *Cultural Studies: Now and in the Future*, eds Larry Grossberg, Cary Nelson and Paula A. Treichler, New York: Routledge, 1992, 96–112.

Collins, J. and R. Wilson, 'The Broken Allegory: Doris Lessing's *The Fifth Child* as Narrative Theodicy', *Analecta Husserliana: The Yearbook of Phenomenological Research*, 41, 1994, 277–91.

Corbeil, Carole, 'The Observer Author's Neo-Con Ideals Spawn a Loser of a Novel', *The Globe and Mail*, 19 December 1985, <http://www.lexisnexis.com/uk> (accessed 3 July 2009).

Cosslett, Tess, Celia Lury and Penny Summerfield (eds), *Feminism and Autobiography: Texts, Theories, Methods*, London: Routledge, 2000.

Crossman, Richard H. (ed.), *The God that Failed*, New York: Columbia University Press, 2001.

Crown, Sarah, 'Doris Lessing Wins Nobel Prize', *The Guardian*, 11 October 2007 <http://www.guardian.co.uk/books/2007/oct/11/nobelprize.awardsandprizes> (accessed 6 September 2009).

Danziger, Marie A., *Text/Countertext: Postmodern Paranoia in Samuel Beckett, Doris Lessing, and Philip Roth*, New York: Peter Lang, 1996.

De Man, Paul, 'Autobiography as De-facement', *Modern Language Notes*, 94, 1979, 919–30.

Dean, Sharon L., 'Lessing's *The Fifth Child*', *Explicator*, 50, 1992, 120–2.

Deleuze, Gilles and Felix Guattari, *Kafka: Toward a Minor Literature*, trans. Dana Polan, fwd. Reda Bensmaia, Minneapolis: University of Minnesota Press, 1986.

Derrida, Jacques, 'Freud and the Scene of Writing', in *Writing and Difference*, trans. Alan Bass, Chicago: University of Chicago Press, 1978, 196–231.

Donoghue, Denis, 'Alice, the Radical Homemaker', *The New York Times*, 22 September 1985, <http://www.lexisnexis.com/uk> (accessed 3 July 2009).

Draine, Betsy, 'Nostalgia and Irony: The Postmodern Order of *The Golden Notebook*', *Modern Fiction Studies*, 26, 1980, 31–48.

Draine, Betsy, *Substance Under Pressure: Artistic Coherence and Evolving Form in the Novels of Doris Lessing*, Madison: Wisconsin University Press, 1983.

DuPlessis, Rachel Blau, 'For the Etruscans', in *The New Feminist Criticism: Essays on Women, Literature and Theory*, ed. Elaine Showalter, London: Virago, 1986, 271–91.

Eagleton, Mary, *Figuring the Woman Author in Contemporary Fiction*, Basingstoke: Palgrave Macmillan, 2005.

Eng, David L. and David Kazanjian (eds), *Loss: The Politics of Mourning*, Berkeley: University of California Press, 2003.

Engel, Marian, 'Lessing Still in Outer Space, But This Time Cataloguing a Myriad of Planets', *The Globe and Mail*, 21 February 1981, <http://www.lexisnexis.com/uk> (accessed 19 June 2008).

Ettler, Justine, 'Drunken Dinner Parties and a Quest for Truth', *The Observer*, 23 September 2001, <http://books.guardian.co.uk/reviews/eneralfiction/0,6121,556330,00.html> (accessed 6 November 2002).

Fahim, Shadia, *Doris Lessing: Sufi Equilibrium and the Form of the Novel*, Basingstoke: Macmillan, 1994.

Faludi, Susan, *Backlash: The Undeclared War Against American Women*, New York: Crown, 1991.

Feng, Pin-Chia, 'Rituals of Rememory: Afro-Caribbean Religions in *Myal* and *It Begins with Tears*', *Melus*, 27, 2002, 149–75.

Fishburn, Katherine, *The Unexpected Universe of Doris Lessing*, Westport, CT: Greenwood Press, 1985.

Foot, Paul, 'The Lessing Legend', *Socialist Review*, 216, February 1998, 26–7, <http://pubs.socialistreviewindex.org.uk/sr216/foot.htm> (accessed 4 September 2009).

Foucault, Michel, *Madness and Civilization: A History of Insanity in the Age of Reason*, trans. Richard Howard, New York: Pantheon, 1965.

Foucault, Michel, 'What is an Author?', in *Modern Criticism and*

Theory: A Reader, ed. David Lodge, London: Longman, 1988, 197–210.

Freud, Sigmund, 'Mourning and Melancholia', in *The Standard Edition of the Complete Psychological Works of Sigmund Freud*, vol. 14, trans. and ed. James Strachey, London: Hogarth Press, 1955, 1–59.

Freud, Sigmund, 'The "Uncanny"', *Standard Edition of the Complete Psychological Works of Sigmund Freud*, vol. 17, trans. James Strachey, London: Hogarth Press, 1955, 217–56.

Galin, Müge, *Between East and West: Sufism in the Novels of Doris Lessing*, Albany, NY: State University of New York Press, 1997.

Gardiner, Judith Kegan, *Rhys, Stead, Lessing, and the Politics of Empathy*, Bloomington: Indiana University Press, 1989.

Garrard, Greg, *Ecocriticism*, Abingdon: Routledge, 2004.

Gasiorek, Andrzej, *Post-War British Fiction: Realism and After*, London: Edward Arnold, 1995.

Gee, Maggie and Lisa Appignanesi, 'The Contemporary Writer: Gender and Genre', in *Writing: A Woman's Business. Women, Writing and the Marketplace*, eds Judy Simons and Kate Fullbrook, Manchester: Manchester University Press, 1998, 172–82.

Ghosh, Nibir K., 'Editorial', *Re-Markings*, 7, 1, 2008, 3–4.

Gibbons, Fiachr, 'Lay off Men, Lessing Tells Feminists', *The Guardian*, 14 August 2001, <http://www.guardian.co.uk/Archive/Article/0,4273,4238674,00.html> (accessed 4 September 2009).

Gillis, Stacey, Gillian Howie and Rebecca Munford (eds), *Third Wave Feminism: A Critical Exploration*, second edition, Basingstoke: Palgrave, 2007.

Gilroy, Paul, *Postcolonial Melancholia*, New York: Columbia University Press, 2005.

Glover, Jayne, 'The Metaphor of the Horse in Doris Lessing's *The Marriages Between Zones Three, Four and Five*: An Ecofeminist Question?', *Current Writing: Text and Reception in Southern Africa*, 18, 1, 2006, 119–33.

Goodman, Walter, 'Books of the Times', *The New York Times*, 17 September 1985, <http://www.lexisnexis.com/uk> (accessed 3 July 2009).

Greene, Gayle, *Doris Lessing: The Poetics of Change*, Ann Arbor, MI: The University of Michigan Press, 1994.

Greene, Gayle, '*The Diaries of Jane Somers*: Doris Lessing, Feminism, and the Mother', in *Narrating Mothers: Theorising Maternal Subjectivities*, eds Brenda O. Daly and Maureen T. Reddy, Knoxville: Tennessee University Press, 1991, 139–56.

Hague, Angela, 'Picaresque Structure and the Angry Young Novel', *Twentieth Century Literature*, 32, 1986, 209–20.

Hanford, Jan, *Doris Lessing: A Retrospective* <http://lessing.redmood.com/between.html> (accessed 26 November 2009).

Hanson, Clare, 'Doris Lessing in Pursuit of the English, or, No Small, Personal Voice', in *In Pursuit of Doris Lessing: Nine Nations Reading*, ed. Claire Sprague, Basingstoke: Macmillan, 1990, 61–73. First published in *P N Review* , 14, 1987, 39–42.

Hanson, Clare, 'Reproduction, Genetics, and Eugenics in the Fiction of Doris Lessing', *Contemporary Women's Writing*, 1, 1–2, 2007, 171–84.

Hardin, Nancy Shields, 'The Sufi Teaching Story and Doris Lessing', *Twentieth-Century Literature*, 23, 3, 1977, 314–26.

Henke, Suzette, 'Doris Lessing's *The Golden Notebook*: A Paradox of Postmodern Play', in *Rereading Modernism: New Directions in Feminist Criticism*, ed. Lisa Rado, New York: Garland, 1994, 157–87.

Henstra, Sandra, 'Nuclear Cassandra: Prophecy in Doris Lessing's *The Golden Notebook*', *Papers on Language and Literature*, 43, 1, 2007, 3–23.

Heuving, Jeanne, 'An Interview with Rachel Blau DuPlessis', *Contemporary Literature*, 45, 3, 2004, 397–420.

Hite, Molly, *The Other Side of the Story: Structures and Strategies of Contemporary Feminist Narratives*, Ithaca, NY: Cornell University Press, 1989.

Hokensen, Jan, 'Intercultural Autobiography', *A/b: Auto/Biography Studies*, 10, 1995, 92–113.

hooks, bell, 'Postmodern Blackness', in *Yearning: Race, Gender and Cultural Politics*, Boston, MA: South End Press, 1990, 23–33.

Huggan, Graham, *The Postcolonial Exotic: Marketing the Margins*, London: Routledge, 2001.

Jagan, Janet, 'Letter in Response to "The Jewel Of Africa"', *New York Review of Books*, 50, 16, 23 October 2003 <http://www.nybooks.com/articles/16693> (accessed 8 September 2009).

Jameson, Fredric, *Archaeologies of the Future: The Desire Called Utopia and Other Science Fiction*, London: Verso, 2005.

Jardine, Alice, *Gynesis: Configurations of Woman and Modernity*, Ithaca: Cornell University Press, 1985.

Jouve, Nicole Ward, 'Of Mud and Other Matter: *The Children of Violence*', in *Notebooks/Memoirs/Archives: Reading and Rereading Doris Lessing*, ed. Jenny Taylor, London: Routledge and Kegan Paul, 1982, 75–134.

Jullien, Dominique, 'In Praise of Mistranslation: The Melancholy Cosmopolitanism of Jorge Luis Borges', *The Romantic Review*, 98, 2–3, 2007, 205–23.

Kakutani, Michiko, 'Books of the Times: A Four-Decade Kitchen-Sink Tale (as in Everything But)', *The New York Times*, 1 February 2002, <http://query.nytimes.com/gst/fullpage.html?res=990CE2DE163DF932A35751C0A9649C8B63> (accessed 16 July 2003).

Kakutani, Michiko, 'Books of the Times; His Weirdness Attracts Types Even More Weird', *The New York Times*, 8 August 2000, <http://query.nytimes.com/gst/fullpage.html?res=9A04E2DB103CF93BA3575BC0A9669C8B63> (accessed 8 September 2009).

Kakutani, Michiko, 'Books of the Times; Where Millenniums are Treated Like Centuries', *The New York Times*, 26 January 1999, <http://query.nytimes.com/gst/fullpage.html?res=9D0DE2DD1539F935A15752C0A96F958260> (accessed 8 September 2009).

Keay, D., 'Aids, Education and the Year 2000', Interview with Margaret Thatcher, *Woman's Own*, 31 October 1987, 8–10.

King, Jeannette, *Doris Lessing*, London: Edward Arnold, 1989.

Koestler, Arthur, *Darkness at Noon*, London: Vintage Classics, 1994.

Krasner, James, 'Accumulated Lives: Metaphor, Materiality, and the Homes of the Elderly', *Literature and Medicine*, 24, 2, 2005, 209–30.

Kristeva, Julia, *Black Sun: Depression and Melancholia*, trans. Leon S. Roudiez, New York: Columbia University Press, 1989.

Kristeva, Julia, *Strangers to Ourselves*, trans. Leon S. Roudiez, Hemel Hempstead: Harvester Wheatsheaf, 1991.

Kynaston, David, *Austerity Britain 1945–1951*, London: Bloomsbury, 2007.

Laing, R. D., *Sanity, Madness and the Family*, London: Tavistock, 1964.

Laing, R. D., *The Divided Self: A Study of Sanity and Madness*, London: Tavistock, 1960.

Laing, R. D., *The Politics of Experience*, Harmondsworth: Penguin, 1967.

Le Guin, Ursula, 'Saved by a Squirt', *The Guardian*, 10 February 2007 <http://www.guardian.co.uk/books/2007/feb/10/fiction.dorislessing> (accessed 8 September 2009).

Lessing, Doris, 'A Hunger for Books', *The Guardian*, 8 December 2007, <http://www.guardian.co.uk/books/2007/dec/08/nobelprize.classics> (accessed 4 September 2009).

Lessing, Doris, *A Proper Marriage*, London: Paladin, 1990.

Lessing, Doris, 'A Reissue of *The Golden Notebook*', in *Time Bites: Views and Reviews*, London: Fourth Estate, 2004, 138–41.

Lessing, Doris, *A Ripple from the Storm*, London: Grafton, 1966.

Lessing, Doris, *A Small, Personal Voice: Essays, Reviews, Interviews*, ed. Paul Schlueter, London: Flamingo, 1994.

Lessing, Doris, *African Laughter: Four Visits to Zimbabwe*, London: Flamingo, 1993.

Lessing, Doris, 'Afterword to *The Story of an African Farm* by Olive Schreiner', in *A Small, Personal Voice: Essays, Reviews, Interviews*, ed. Paul Schlueter, London: Flamingo, 1994, 161–84.

Lessing, Doris, *Alfred and Emily*, London: Fourth Estate, 2008.

Lessing, Doris, *Ben, In the World*, London: Flamingo, 2000.

Lessing, Doris, 'Between the Fax and the Fiction', *The Guardian*, 13 December 1991, <http://lessing.redmood.com/between.html> (accesed 4 September 2009).

Lessing, Doris, *Briefing for a Descent into Hell*, London: Granada, 1972.

Lessing, Doris, *Going Home*, New York: Harper Collins, 1996.

Lessing, Doris, *In Pursuit of the English*, London: Flamingo, 1993.

Lessing, Doris, 'In the World, Not Of It', in *A Small Personal Voice: Essays, Reviews, Interviews*, ed. Paul Schlueter, London: Flamingo, 1994, 193–202.

Lessing, Doris, *Landlocked*, London: Grafton, 1967.

Lessing, Doris, *Love, Again*, London: Flamingo, 1996.

Lessing, Doris, *Mara and Dann*, London: Flamingo, 1999.

Lessing, Doris, *Martha Quest*, London: Paladin, 1990.

Lessing, Doris, 'On Not Winning the Nobel Prize', 7 December 2007, <http://nobelprize.org/nobel_prizes/literature/laureates/2007/lessing-lecture.html> (accessed 4 September 2009).

Lessing, Doris, *Prisons we Choose to Live Inside*, London: Perennial, 1987.

Lessing, Doris, *Retreat to Innocence*, London: Michael Joseph, 1956.

Lessing, Doris, *Shikasta: Re: Colonised Planets*, St Albans: Granada, 1981.

Lessing, Doris, *The Cleft*, London: Fourth Estate, 2007.

Lessing, Doris, *The Diaries of Jane Somers*, Harmondsworth: Penguin, 1985.

Lessing, Doris, *The Fifth Child*, London: Flamingo, 1993.

Lessing, Doris, *The Four-Gated City*, London: Grafton, 1972.

Lessing, Doris, *The Golden Notebook*, London: Flamingo, 1993.

Lessing, Doris, *The Good Terrorist*, London: Paladin, 1990.

Lessing, Doris, *The Grass is Singing*, London: Michael Joseph, 1950.

Lessing, Doris, 'The Jewel of Africa', *New York Review of Books*, 50, 6, 10 April 2003, <http://www.nybooks.com/articles/16170> (accessed 4 September 2009).

Lessing, Doris, *The Making of the Representative for Planet 8*, St Albans: Granada, 1983.

Lessing, Doris, *The Marriages Between Zones Three, Four, and Five*, London: Panther, 1981.

Lessing, Doris, *The Memoirs of a Survivor*, London: Picador, 1976.

Lessing, Doris, *The Sentimental Agents in the Volyen Empire*, London: Grafton, 1985.

Lessing, Doris, *The Sirian Experiments*, London: Grafton, 1982.

Lessing, Doris, 'The Small Personal Voice', in *A Small Personal Voice: Essays, Reviews, Interviews*, ed. Paul Schlueter, London: Flamingo, 1994, 7–26.

Lessing, Doris, *The Story of General Dann and Mara's Daughter, Griot and the Snow Dog*, London: Harper Collins, 2005.

Lessing, Doris, *The Summer Before the Dark*, London: Jonathan Cape, 1973.

Lessing, Doris, *The Sweetest Dream*, London: Flamingo, 2001.

Lessing, Doris, 'The Tragedy of Zimbabwe', in *Time Bites: Views and Reviews*, London: Fourth Estate, 2004, 231–46.

Lessing, Doris, *The Wind Blows Away Our Words and other Documents Relating to the Afghan Resistance*, London: Picador, 1987.

Lessing, Doris, *This Was the Old Chief's Country: Collected African Stories, Volume One*, London: Flamingo, 1994.

Lessing, Doris, *Time Bites: Views and Reviews*, London: Fourth Estate, 2004.

Lessing, Doris, *Under My Skin: Volume One of my Autobiography, to 1949*, London: Harper Collins, 1994.

Lessing, Doris, *Walking in the Shade: Volume Two of my Autobiography, 1949–1962*, London: Flamingo, 1998.

Lessing, Doris, 'What Novel or Novels Prompted Your Own Political Awakening?', *Time Bites: Views and Reviews*, London: Fourth Estate, 2004, 251–2.

Lessing, Doris, 'Writing Autobiography', in *Time Bites: Views and Reviews*, London: Fourth Estate, 2004, 90–103.

Levinson, Deirdre, 'Future Shocked', *The Nation*, 23 November 1985, 557–9.

Lifson, Martha, 'Structural Patterns in *The Golden Notebook*', *Michigan Papers in Women's Studies*, 2, 1978, 95–108.

Louw, Pat, 'Inside and Outside Colonial Spaces: Border Crossings in Doris Lessing's *African Stories*', in *Doris Lessing: Border Crossings*, eds Alice Ridout and Susan Watkins, London: Continuum, 2009, 26–43.

Luckhurst, Roger, 'Cultural Governance, New Labour, and the British SF Boom', *Science Fiction Studies*, 30, 2003, 417–35.

Luckhurst, Roger, 'The Contemporary London Gothic and the Limits of the "Spectral Turn"', *Textual Practice*, 16, 2002, 527–46.

Lukács, Georg, *Theory of the Novel: A Historico-Philosophical Essay on the Forms of Great Epic Literature*, trans. Anna Bostock, London: Merlin Press, 1971.

Maschler, Tom (ed.), *Declaration*, London: MacGibbon and Kee, 1957.

Maslen, Elizabeth, *Doris Lessing*, Plymouth: Northcote House, 1994.

McCallister, John, 'Knowing Native, Going Native: *African Laughter*, Colonial Epistemology, and Post-Colonial Homecoming', *Doris Lessing Studies*, 22, 2001, 12–15.

McCrum, Robert, 'Writing is Something I Have to Do', Review Section, *The Observer*, 14 October 2007, 8.

McDermott, Sinead, 'Notes on the Afterlife of Feminist Criticism', *PMLA*, 121, 5, 2006, 1729–34.

McLeod, John, *Postcolonial London: Rewriting the Metropolis*, London: Routledge, 2004.

Merrill, Stephanie, '*The Sweetest Dream*', *New Statesman*, 130, 4557, 2001, 83.

Messud, Claire, 'Future Imperfect', *New Statesman*, 13 June 2005, <http://www.lexisnexis.com> (accessed 27 July 2009).

Michael, Magali Cornier, *Feminism and the Postmodern Impulse: Post-World War II Fiction*, Albany: State University of New York Press, 1996.

Moi, Toril, *Sexual/Textual Politics: Feminist Literary Theory*, London: Routledge, 1985.

Morrison, Toni, 'Home', in *The House that Race Built*, ed. Wahneema Lubiano, New York: Vintage, 1998, 3–12.

Morrison, Toni, 'The Site of Memory', in *Out There: Marginalisation and Contemporary Cultures*, eds R. Ferguson, M. Gever, T. Minh-ha and C. West, The New Museum of Contemporary Art, New York: Documentary Sources in Contemporary Art Vol. 4, Cambridge, MA: MIT. Press, 1990, 299–305.

Mukherjee, Bharati, 'Waiting for Lefties', *Bookforum*, Spring 2002, <http://www.bookforum.net/mukher.html> (accessed 6 November 2002).

Mulkeen, Anne, 'Twentieth-Century Realism: The "Grid" Structure of *The Golden Notebook*', *Studies in the Novel*, 4, 1972, 262–74.

Mullan, John, *Anonymity: A Secret History of English Literature*, London: Faber and Faber, 2007.

Nolan, Maggie and Carrie Dawson, 'Who's Who: Mapping Hoaxes and Imposture in Australian Literary History', in 'Who's Who? Hoaxes, Imposture and Identity Crises in Australian Literature', eds Maggie Nolan and Carrie Dawson, special issue of *Australian Literary Studies*, 21, 3, 2004, v–xx.

O'Regan, Nadine, 'Grande Dame Can Still Deliver', *The Sunday Business Post Online*, 26 October 2003, <http://archives.tcm.ie/businesspost/2003/10/26/story188365199.asp> (accessed 11 September 2009).

Peel, Robin, *Writing Back: Sylvia Plath and Cold War Politics*, Madison, NJ: Fairleigh Dickinson University Press, 2002.

The Permanent Secretary, 'The Nobel Prize in Literature 2007: Doris Lessing', Press Release, 11 October 2007, <http://nobelprize.org/nobel_prizes/literature/laureates/2007/press.html> (accessed 4 September 2009).

Perrakis, Phyllis Sternberg (ed.), *Adventures of the Spirit: The Older Woman in the Works of Doris Lessing, Margaret Atwood, and Other Contemporary Women Writers*, Columbus, OH: Ohio State University Press, 2007.

Perrakis, Phyllis Sternberg (ed.), *Spiritual Exploration in the Works of Doris Lessing*, Westport, CT: Greenwood Press, 1999.

Perrakis, Phyllis Sternberg, 'Sufism, Jung and the Myth of Kore: Revisionist Politics in Lessing's *Marriages*', in *Doris Lessing*, Bloom's Modern Critical Views, ed. Harold Bloom, Broomall, PA: Chelsea House, 2003, 61–86.

Perrakis, Phyllis Sternberg, 'The Porous Border Between Fact and Fiction: Empathy and Identification in Doris Lessing's *The Cleft*', in *Doris Lessing: Border Crossings*, eds Alice Ridout and Susan Watkins, London: Continuum, 2009, 143–59.

Perrakis, Phyllis, Sandra Singer and Jeanie Warnock (eds), *Doris Lessing Studies*, Ottawa, Doris Lessing Society.

Port, Cynthia, '"None Of It Adds Up": Economies of Aging in *The Diary of a Good Neighbour*', *Doris Lessing Studies*, 24, 1–2, 2004, 30–5.

Porter, Dennis, 'Realism and Failure in *The Golden Notebook*', *Modern Language Quarterly*, 35, 1974, 56–65.

Powell, Enoch, 'Like the Roman, I see the River Tiber Foaming with Much Blood', 20 April 1968, <http://www.sterlingtimes.org/powell_speech.doc> (accessed 8 September 2009).

Pughe, Thomas, 'Reading the Picaresque: Mark Twain's *The Adventures of Huckleberry Finn*, Saul Bellow's *The Adventures of Augie March*, and More Recent Adventures', *English Studies*, 77, 1996, 59–70.

Punter, David, *Gothic Pathologies: The Text, the Body and the Law*, Basingstoke: Macmillan, 1998.

Pye, M., 'The Creature Walks Among Us', *The New York Times*, 6 August 2000, <http://query.nytimes.com/gst/fullpage.html?res=9D06E4DE163DF935A3575BC0A9669C8B63> (accessed 8 September 2009).

Rabinow, Paul, *Essays on the Anthropology of Reason*, Princeton, NJ: Princeton University Press, 1996.

Rege, Josna, 'Editorial: Coming to Age', *Doris Lessing Studies*, 24, 1–2, 2004, 3–7.

Rege, Josna and Ruth Saxton (eds), 'Coming to Age', special issue of *Doris Lessing Studies*, 24, 1–2, 2004.

Reid, Michelle, 'Postcolonial Science Fiction', *The Science Fiction Foundation*, <http://www.sf-foundation.org/publications/academic-track/reid.php> (accessed 6 September 2009).

Rich, Motoko and Sarah Lyall, 'Doris Lessing Wins Nobel Prize in Literature', *The New York Times*, 11 October 2007, <http://www.nytimes.com/2007/10/11/world/11cnd-Nobel.html?_r=4&hp&oref=slogin&oref=slogin&oref=slogin&oref=slogin> (accessed 13 September 2009)

Ridout, Alice, 'Review of *Third Wave Feminism: A Critical Exploration*', *Contemporary Women's Writing*, 1, 1–2, 2007, 208–9.

Robbins, Bruce, 'Introduction Part I: Actually Existing Cosmopolitanism', in *Cosmopolitics: Thinking and Feeling Beyond the Nation*, eds Pheng Cheah and Bruce Robbins, Minneapolis: University of Minnesota Press, 1998, 1–19.

Roberts, Adam, 'Doris Lesfing' [sic.], *The Valve: A Literary Organ*, 12 October 2007, <http://www.thevalve.org/go/valve/article/doris_lessfing/> (accessed 6 September 2009).

Roberts, Adam, *The History of Science Fiction*, Basingstoke: Palgrave Macmillan, 2005.

Roberts, Michele, 'Chilling News from the Frozen Future', *The Independent*, 17 June 2005, <http://www.lexisnexis.com> (accessed 27 July 2009).

Rogers, Jane, 'Saturday Rereadings: Dark Times: Jane Rogers Revisits a Novel She Was First Drawn To When She Was Living In A Squat', *The Guardian*, 3 December 2005, <http://www.lexisnexis.com/uk> (accessed 3 July 2009).

Rosenfeld, Aaron S., 'Re-membering the Future: Doris Lessing's "Experiment in Autobiography"', *Critical Survey*, 17, 1, 2005, 40–55.

Rosner, Victoria, 'Home Fires: Doris Lessing, Colonial Architecture, and the Reproduction of Mothering', *Tulsa Studies in Women's Literature*, 18, 1, 1999, 59–89.

Rowe, Margaret Moan, *Doris Lessing*, Basingstoke: Macmillan, 1994.

Rubenstein, Roberta, 'Briefing on Inner Space: Doris Lessing and R. D. Laing', *The Psychoanalytic Review*, 63, 1976, 83–93.

Rubenstein, Roberta, 'Fixing the Past: Yearning and Nostalgia in Woolf and Lessing', in *Woolf and Lessing: Breaking the Mold*, eds Ruth Saxton and Jean Tobin, New York: St Martin's Press, 1994, 15–38.

Rubenstein, Roberta, *The Novelistic Vision of Doris Lessing: Breaking the Forms of Consciousness*, Urbana: University of Illinois Press, 1979.

Rusk, Lauren, *The Life Writing of Otherness: Woolf, Baldwin, Kingston and Winterson*, London: Routledge, 2002.

Sage, Lorna, *Doris Lessing*, London: Methuen, 1983.

Said, Edward, *Reflections on Exile and Other Literary and Cultural Essays*, London: Granta Books, 2000.

Saxton, Ruth and Jean Tobin (eds), *Woolf and Lessing: Breaking the Mold*, Basingstoke: Macmillan, 1994.

Scanlan, Margaret, 'Language and the Politics of Despair in Doris Lessing's *The Good Terrorist*', *Novel: A Forum on Fiction*, 23, 2, 1990, 182–98.

Scott, Ann, 'The More Recent Writings: Sufism, Mysticism and Politics', in *Notebooks/Memoirs/Archives: Reading and Rereading Doris Lessing*, ed. Jenny Taylor, London: Routledge and Kegan Paul, 1982, 164–90.

Segal, Lynne, 'Formations of Feminism: Political Histories of the Left (II)', *Radical Philosophy* 123, 2004, 8–27.

Shah, Idries, *The Way of the Sufi*, London: Jonathan Cape, 1968.

Showalter, Elaine, *A Literature of Their Own: British Women Novelists from Bronte to Lessing*, London: Virago, 1978. Revised edition, Princeton, NJ: Princeton University Press, 1999.

Simons, Judy and Kate Fullbrook (eds), *Writing: A Woman's Business. Women, Writing and the Marketplace*, Manchester: Manchester University Press, 1998.

Singer, Sandra, 'London and Kabul: Assessing the Politics of Terrorist Violence', in *Doris Lessing: Interrogating the Times*, eds Phyllis Sternberg Perrakis, Debrah Raschke and Sandra Singer, Columbus: Ohio State University Press, forthcoming.

Sizemore, Christine Wick, *A Female Vision of the City: London in the Novels of Five British Women*, Knoxville: The University of Tennessee Press, 1989.

Sizemore, Christine W., '*In Pursuit of the English*: Hybridity and the Local in Doris Lessing's First Urban Text', *Journal of Commonwealth Literature*, 43, 2, 2008, 133–44.

Slemon, Stephen, 'Unsettling the Empire: Resistance Theory for the Second World', *World Literature Written in English*, 30, 2, 1990, 30–41.

Solomon, Barbara Probst, 'The Lady Laureate', *The New York Sun*, 12 October 2007, <http://www.nysun.com/article/64471> (accessed 4 September 2009).

Sprague, Claire (ed.), *In Pursuit of Doris Lessing: Nine Nations Reading*, Basingstoke: Macmillan, 1990.

Sprague, Claire, *Rereading Doris Lessing: Narrative Patterns of Doubling and Repetition*, Chapel Hill: University of North Carolina Press, 1987.

Squires, Claire, *Marketing Literature: The Making of Contemporary Writing in Britain*, Basingstoke: Palgrave Macmillan, 2007.

Steele, Murray, 'Doris Lessing's Rhodesia', in *Doris Lessing*, ed. Eve Bertelsen, Johannesburg: McGraw-Hill, 1985, 44–54.

Stoler, Ann, *Carnal Knowledge and Imperial Power: Race and the Intimate in Colonial Rule*, Berkeley: University of California Press, 2002.

Stoneman, Colin (ed.), *Zimbabwe's Inheritance*, New York: St Martin's Press, 1981.

Svenska Academien, 'The Nobel Prize in Literature 2007: Bio-Bibliography', <http://nobelprize.org/nobel_prizes/literature/laureates/007/bio-bibl.html> (accessed 4 September 2009).

Sylvester, Christine, *Zimbabwe: The Terrain of Contradictory Development*, Boulder: Westview Press, 1991.

Takolander, Maria and David McCooey, 'Fakes, Literary Identity and Public Culture', *Journal of the Association for the Study of Australian Literature*, 3, 2004, 57–66.

Taylor, Jenny (ed.), *Notebooks/Memoirs/Archives: Reading and Rereading Doris Lessing*, London: Routledge and Kegan Paul, 1982.

Taylor, Jenny, 'Situating Reading', in *Notebooks/Memoirs/Archives: Reading and Rereading Doris Lessing*, ed. Jenny Taylor, London: Routledge and Kegan Paul, 1982, 1–42.

Tiffin, Helen, 'The Body in the Library: Identity, Opposition and the Settler-Invader Woman', in *Postcolonial Discourses: An Anthology*, ed. Gregory Castle, Oxford: Blackwell, 2001, 374–88.

Tiger, Virginia, 'Ages of Anxiety: *The Diaries of Jane Somers*', in *Spiritual Exploration in the Works of Doris Lessing*, ed. Phyllis Sternberg Perrakis, Westport, CT: Greenwood Press, 1999, 1–16.

Tiger, Virginia, '"Taking Hands and Dancing in (Dis)unity": Story to Storied in Doris Lessing's "To Room Nineteen" and "A Room"', *Modern Fiction Studies*, 36, 3, 1990, 421–33.

Tiger, Virginia, '"The Words Had Been Right and Necessary": Doris Lessing's Transformations of Utopian and Dystopian Modalities in *The Marriages Between Zones Three, Four, and Five*', *Style*, 27, 1, 1993, 63–80 <http://web.ebscohost.com> (accessed 6 September 2009).

Torrents, Nisa, 'Testimony to Mysticism: Interview with Doris Lessing', in *Putting the Questions Differently: Interviews with Doris Lessing, 1964–1994*, ed. Earl Ingersoll, London: Flamingo, 1996, 64–9.

Upchurch, Michael, 'Back to Ifrik', *The New York Times*, 10 January 1999, <http://query.nytimes.com/gst/fullpage.html?res=9C05E2DD1E3FF933A25752C0A96F958260> (accessed 8 September 2009).

Varsamopoulou, Evy, 'The Idea of Europe and the Ideal of Cosmopolitanism in the Work of Julia Kristeva', *Theory, Culture and Society*, 26, 1, 2009, 24–44.

Vice, Sue, 'Helen Darville, *The Hand that Signed the Paper*: Who is "Helen Demidenko"', in *Scandalous Fictions: The Twentieth-Century Novel in the Public Sphere*, eds Jago Morrison and Susan Watkins, Basingstoke: Palgrave Macmillan, 2006, 172–86.

Visel, Robin, '"Then Spoke the Thunder": *The Grass is Singing* as a Zimbabwean Novel', *Journal of Commonwealth Literature*, 43, 2, 2008, 157–66.

Vlastos, Marion, 'Doris Lessing and R. D. Laing: Psychopolitics and Prophecy', *PMLA*, 91, 2, 1976, 245–58.

Wagner, Erica, 'Good on Science', *The Times*, 25 March, 1999, 42.

Walder, Dennis, '"Alone in a Landscape": Lessing's African Stories Remembered', *Journal of Commonwealth Literature*, 43, 2, 2008, 99–115.

Wallace, Diana, '"Women's Time": Women, Age and Inter-Generational Relations in Doris Lessing's *The Diaries of Jane Somers*', *Studies in the Literary Imagination*, 39, 2, 2006, 43–59.

Ward-Jouve, Nicole, 'Of Mud and Other Matter: *The Children of Violence*', in *Notebooks/Memoirs/Archives: Reading and Re-reading Doris Lessing*, ed. Jenny Taylor, London: Routledge and Kegan Paul, 1982, 75–134.

Waterman, David, 'Who Am I When the Other Disappears?: Identity and Progress in Doris Lessing's *The Sirian Experiments*', *Journal of Evolutionary Psychology*, 29, 1–2, 2006, 74–86.

Watkins, Susan, '"Grande Dame" or "New Woman"?: Doris Lessing and the Palimpsest', *LIT: Literature Interpretation Theory*, 17, 3–4, 2006, 243–62.

Waugh, Patricia, *Feminine Fictions: Revisiting the Postmodern*, London: Routledge, 1989.

Waugh, Patricia, *Metafiction: The Theory and Practice of Self-Conscious Fiction*, London: Methuen, 1984.

Weiss, Ruth, *Zimbabwe and the New Elite*, London: British Academic Press, 1994.

Whelehan, Imelda, *Overloaded: Popular Culture and the Future of Feminism*, London: The Women's Press, 2000.

Whittaker, Ruth, *Doris Lessing*, Basingstoke: Macmillan, 1988.

Williams, Hywel, 'The Dream is Over', *The Guardian*, 22 September 2001, <http://books.guardian.co.uk/reviws/generalfiction/0,6121,555617,00.html> (accessed 6 November 2002).

Williams, Jennifer D., 'Motherless Girls: Melancholy Cosmopolitanism in Andrea Lee's *Sarah Phillips* and Jamaica Kincaid's *Lucy*', conference paper, 'Unsettling Women: Contemporary Women's Writing and Diaspora', University of Leicester, 11–13 July 2008.

Williams, Raymond, *The Long Revolution*, London: Chatto and Windus, 1961.

Winterson, Jeannette, *The Stone Gods*, London: Hamish Hamilton, 2007.

Woolf, Virginia, *Three Guineas*, London: The Hogarth Press, 1947.

Yelin, Louise, *From the Margins of Empire: Christina Stead, Doris Lessing, Nadine Gordimer*, Ithaca: Cornell University Press, 1998.

Young, Robert J. C., *Colonial Desire: Hybridity in Theory, Culture and Race*, London: Routledge, 1995.

Index

Page numbers followed by n and a number (eg. 187n.29) indicate the page where a note can be located and the number of the note.

CPSIA information can be obtained at www.ICGtesting.com
Printed in the USA
BVOW03s1143190515

400333BV00004B/11/P

9 780719 097348